Exchange Rate Regimes in the Modern Era

Exchange Rate Regimes in the Modern Era

Michael W. Klein and Jay C. Shambaugh

The MIT Press
Cambridge, Massachusetts
London, England

For information about special discounts, please email special_sales@mitpress.mit.edu

This book was set in Palatino on 3B2 by Asco Typesetters, Hong Kong.
Printed and bound in the United States of America.

Library of Congress Cataloging-in-Publication Data

Klein, Michael W., 1958–.
Exchange rate regimes in the modern era / Michael W. Klein and Jay C. Shambaugh.
    p.   cm.
Includes bibliographical references and index.
ISBN 978-0-262-01365-9 (hbk. : alk. paper)
1. Foreign exchange rates. 2. Foreign exchange. I. Shambaugh, Jay C. II. Title.
HG3851.K57   2010
332.4′5—dc22   2009014104

10   9   8   7   6   5   4   3   2   1

To Susan, Gabe, and Noah
MWK

To Lisa, Katie, and Jack
JCS

Contents

Acknowledgments

This book represents over a decade of work in thinking, researching, and writing about exchange rate regimes. Along the way, in both producing this book during the last year, and in generating the research that has gone into it over the last decade, many people have helped us. It is a pleasure to acknowledge them, and to thank them for their support.

First and foremost, we would like to thank our fellow scholars, many of whom had a hand in generating the research discussed in this book. Various chapters draw on joint work with Julian di Giovanni, Philip Lane, Nancy Marion, Maurice Obstfeld, and Alan Taylor. We thank them for working with us, and, more broadly, for contributing to our understanding and appreciation of these issues. In addition, the work in this book was presented at numerous seminars and conferences, and we owe a great deal to seminar participants and discussants, as well as to others who offered comments on our research papers and drafts of this book, including Sven Arndt, Christian Broda, Menzie Chinn, Barry Eichengreen, Charles Engel, Jeff Frankel, Allen Isaac, Richard Levich, Paolo Mauro, Volker Nitsch, Andy Rose, Lars Svensson, Linda Tesar, Eric van Wincoop, and John Williamson. Other colleagues and friends also gave advice regarding both presentation and empirical strategies, and we thank Steven Block, Eric Edmonds, James Feyrer, Jeff Frieden, Linda Goldberg, Matt Kahn, Doug Irwin, Chris Meissner, Nina Pavcnik, and Doug Staiger. Of course, in thanking all these people we do not mean to implicate them for any shortcomings in this book.

Jane Macdonald at the MIT Press has been a wonderful guide through the process of getting this book to publication, and we thank her, the marketing staff, and production team for their efforts. In addition five anonymous reviewers gave us very useful feedback on an initial draft of the book.

We thank our teachers at various stages of our own academic careers for their guidance and support in helping us explore our intellectual interests, and for teaching us how to develop our ideas and share them with the world. In particular, we would like to thank Maury Obstfeld. Maury was the dissertation advisor to each of us, albeit at two different times and on two different coasts of the United States. We both greatly value his mentoring and friendship over the years.

Most of all, we thank our families for their encouragement, support, and patience as we crafted this manuscript. Parents, siblings, spouses, and children have all played essential roles in helping us reach the point where we could write this book, and in providing the time and encouragement for us to complete it.

MWK and JCS

If art from the third quarter of the nineteenth century to the last quarter of the twentieth century is an "era," corresponding in some way to the era inaugurated by the Renaissance, then this modern era is one that contains a confusing multiplicity of visual styles.

—David Britt, *Modern Art: From Impressionism to Post-Modernism*, c. 1974

I   Introduction

1 Exchange Rate Regimes in the Modern Era

The dollar's exchange rate against the euro is surely the world's single most important price, with potentially much bigger economic consequences than the price of oil and computer chips, for example.

—"The not so mighty dollar," *The Economist*, December 4, 2003

The dollar–euro exchange rate, perhaps "the world's single most important price," is determined by market forces, and changes day to day, and even minute to minute. In contrast, each of the countries of the European Union that uses the euro as its national currency experiences no exchange rate changes with the other members of the eurozone because they share a common currency. Why is it that the United States allows its currency to float, while Germany, France, and the other members of the eurozone have abandoned their national currencies and, effectively, have set a fixed exchange rate across Europe? Similarly, why does the government of China fix the value of its yuan to the US dollar, while the world foreign exchange market determines the daily value of the Brazilian real? The overarching policy of the government toward the exchange rate—to allow it to float or instead to fix or peg its value to another currency—is called the exchange rate regime. What are the economic and political implications of these different exchange rate regimes for these nations?

Questions of this type are quite important today, in this modern era of exchange rate regimes. The modern era includes a wide variety of exchange rate regime experiences across countries. Furthermore, during the modern era, many countries have switched from one type of exchange rate regime to another and often have flipped back and forth another time or two.

The widespread ability of governments to choose an exchange rate regime distinguishes the modern era from earlier periods.[1] Before 1973 the choice of whether or not to manage the value of a currency was often bound up with the wider choice of participation in the international monetary and trading system. During the classical gold standard period (1880–1914) it was generally the case that access to the world capital market demanded pegging the value of a country's currency to gold, since this peg served as a country's "Good Housekeeping Seal of Approval."[2] There was also a view that participation in the gold standard benefited countries by promoting their trade with other countries that pegged their currency to gold. Some countries only slowly adopted a gold peg and a handful of countries changed their regime, but by and large, countries participating in the world financial and trade system moved toward a gold peg.[3] Decades later, during the Bretton Woods era (1945–1973), the adoption of a fixed exchange rate to the US dollar was one facet of participation in the international monetary system, with other facets including membership in the Bretton Woods institutions—the International Monetary Fund and the International Bank for Reconstruction and Development (the World Bank)—and in the General Agreement on Trade and Tariffs (the GATT). In both of these eras, pegged exchange rates were pervasive across countries and durable among the countries that pegged.

The modern era has lasted longer than both the Bretton Woods and the classic gold standard periods. It differs from these two earlier periods in important ways. Most notably, the modern era is distinguished by its wide variety of exchange rate experiences for industrial, middle income, emerging market, and developing countries.[4] This period has seen everything from the abandonment of a national currency (e.g., Ecuador's use of the US dollar, and the creation of the euro), experience with a currency board (e.g., Hong Kong, Lithuania, and Argentina), fixed exchange rates (e.g., Saudi Arabia, Mexico, and South Korea), exchange rate bands (the European Monetary System which lasted from 1979 to 1999), heavily managed floating exchange rates (Norway), occasional efforts to stem the appreciation (1985) or slide (1995) of the US dollar, and the benign neglect of a floating exchange rate (United States, 1979–1985).

The exchange rate regime experiences of the modern era provide researchers with a colorful palette, one with enough hues to make it possible to address interesting and important questions about the nature and consequences of exchange rate regime choice. In this book we will both characterize the choice of exchange rate regimes in the modern era and present empirical research that demonstrates the effects of this choice on macroeconomic outcomes and international trade. We address some of the long-standing central issues in international finance, including the pattern of exchange rate regime behavior, the interaction between the exchange rate regime and monetary policies (which is known as the policy trilemma), the influence of exchange rate regimes on the volume and pattern of international trade, and the links between exchange rate regimes and general macroeconomic outcomes such as GDP growth and inflation.

One source of inquiry into the implications of exchange rate regime choice was prompted by the fact that exchange rate volatility at the beginning of the modern era was higher than what economists had generally expected. There had not been much actual experience with floating exchange rates among major industrial countries during the Bretton Woods era, save for the Canadian dollar's float in the 1950s. Floating currencies in the modern era are not simply episodes where countries are unable to peg but generally represent a deliberate choice to float. At the start of the modern era, the prevailing theory had suggested that floating exchange rates might not be especially volatile. The monetary approach to exchange rate suggested that the volatility of the bilateral exchange rate linking two currencies would match the volatility of the difference of the two countries' respective money supplies and outputs.[5] Milton Friedman (1953) had already argued forcefully that speculators would stabilize exchange rates. As it turned out, however, exchange rates were much more volatile than fundamentals at a short horizon, and, even at longer horizons, exchange rates of industrial countries seemed to persistently deviate from fundamental values. Partly for these reasons the exchange rate overshooting model of Dornbusch (1976), which showed how exchange rate volatility results from slowly adjusting goods' prices, captured the attention of the economics profession and became the most cited paper in international economics.[6] Analyses of the implications of the choice of a flexible exchange rate regime in the modern era that are presented in this book will reflect the volatility of floating exchange rates.

Experiences with fixed exchange rates during the modern era also led to new analyses. Countries peg to different base currencies for varying periods of time. Many of their key economic partners may not peg, may peg to a different base, or may break the peg at different intervals. The motivations to peg (controlling inflation, stimulating trade, avoiding volatility) have varied as have the reasons for leaving pegs. Overall, however, there have been a large number of spectacular collapses of exchange rate regimes.[7] Some, such as the devaluations of the Italian lira and the British pound during the 1992 European Monetary System crisis, had relatively benign effects. Others, including the 1997 Asian crisis and the collapse of the Argentine convertibility plan in 2001, were accompanied by deep economic hardship. These varied experiences—both within and across pegged and floating regimes—provide an opportunity to explore many important topics.

In this book we focus on these questions of the overarching policy to peg or float and the impact on the economy, as opposed to the determination of the exchange rate or the general effect of the exchange rate itself on the economy. The range of topics we cover can be illustrated by a consideration of the epigraph to this chapter. One reason for the importance of the dollar–euro exchange rate is the large volume of trade between Europe and the United States. There is concern that exchange rate fluctuations, due to a floating exchange rate regime, dampen the volume of international trade (chapter 9). This has implications for exporters, import-competing firms, service providers and the producers of nontraded goods. Differential effects across groups give rise to political pressures surrounding the choice of the exchange rate regime (chapter 5). These pressures also reflect the macroeconomic implications of the exchange rate regime. A fixed exchange rate limits monetary policy independence (chapters 2 and 8). Therefore, because its currency is pegged to the dollar, the Hong Kong Monetary Authority must follow policies of the United States while the United States Federal Reserve has a free hand in determining its monetary policy. This has potential implications for inflation and economic growth in these countries. More generally, the macroeconomic implications of the exchange rate regime figure into the decisions by governments in all countries (chapters 10 and 11). This is true even though many countries have flipped back and forth from one exchange rate regime to another (chapter 4). Despite the prevalence of flipping, however, there are important differences in exchange rate behavior between fixed and flexible exchange rate regimes (chapters 6 and 7).

The results presented in this book, which draw on streams of recent research and also include original results, challenge some of the "stylized facts" that inform economists' views on the choice and consequences of exchange rate regimes. We will discuss the theory of how the exchange rate regime is determined. We also discuss the consequences of the exchange rate regime for the broader economy. Some previous research has suggested that exchange rate regimes have a limited impact on general economic outcomes. We will provide empirical results, however, showing the exchange rate regime often plays an important role in the economy.

In part II we discuss the nature of exchange rate regimes themselves. Chapter 2 reviews overarching frameworks on both the choice and effects of exchange rate regimes. The next chapter of that section focuses on what we mean by the term "exchange rate regime." The discussion in chapter 3 raises issues that arise when considering the classification of exchange rate regimes, and presents four different classification schemes that have been used by researchers. In chapter 4 we present characteristics of exchange rate regimes in the modern era that challenge some of the standard views presented in chapter 2 by showing that the pattern of exchange rate regimes during the past four decades is marked by pervasive "flipping," that is, going off a peg for a short period of time and then reestablishing a new peg. Of course, this means that the short duration of pegged exchange rates is matched by a short duration of periods during which a country has a floating exchange rate. This is an important result because it calls into question any study that dichotomizes the world into a set of countries that have durable pegs and a set of countries that consistently have market-determined flexible exchange rates. We also show, however, that there are important examples of long-lived fixed exchange rate regimes in the modern era, contrary to the impression one would draw from some influential research published in the 1990s that calls fixed exchange rates a "mirage."[8] Part II concludes with a chapter that analyzes the manner in which countries choose an exchange rate regime. There are both political and economic theories on this topic. Empirical results presented in chapter 5 offer support for both sets of theories in explaining countries tendencies toward one type of exchange rate regime or another.

The dichotomy between fixed and floating exchange rates is meaningful only if there is evidence that behavior under these two exchange rate regimes differs significantly. Part III of this book shows that the behavior of nominal and real exchange rates in fact depends on the exchange rate regime in place. At one level, this would seem to be a tautological point; if we define a fixed exchange rate as one that does not change by a certain amount over a specified period, then it must differ from a flexible exchange rate. There are two reasons to examine this issue more closely, however. The first is that the recent "fear of floating" result claims little actual difference in nominal bilateral floating exchange rates from nominal bilateral fixed rates.[9] We examine this claim in chapter 6, and show that there is a significant and economically meaningful difference between fixed and floating exchange rates. Second, an exchange rate is only pegged against one other currency. A peg against a base currency does not ensure stability against other currencies, some of which may be especially important for multilateral trade or investment. We study the multilateral consequences of bilateral pegging in chapter 7.

In part IV we turn from characterizing exchange rate regimes to considering their consequences. One of the central theoretical results in international finance is the policy trilemma, whereby the government of a country can choose a pair from the triplet of exchange rate management, monetary policy autonomy, and international capital mobility. While this is a well-established theoretical result, its empirical validity has recently been called into question. We examine this central debate in empirical international finance in chapter 8, and conclude that the policy trilemma is alive and well.

Another important economic impact of exchange rate regimes is the effect on international trade. Studies dating from the 1970s based on the estimation of import and export equations have failed to find much evidence that a fixed exchange rate regime promotes bilateral trade. More recently, however, an alternative methodology using estimates of gravity equations for trade has presented compelling evidence for the statistically significant and economically meaningful effects of fixed exchange rates on trade. We discuss the evolution of this literature, and present results showing the effect of the exchange rate regime on trade in chapter 9.

Fixing the exchange rate may provide a nominal anchor for the economy by fixing the price of one particular asset to help discipline the central bank from printing too much money. This should reduce inflation. In addition a persistently pegged exchange rate should temper the expectation of inflation, which itself dampens inflation. There is a long-standing literature suggesting that this could work in theory. We review this theory in chapter 10, and also offer new evidence that shows a role for the exchange rate regime in the determination of inflation.

Ultimately, the central concern in economics is living standards. Thus we conclude in part IV with an examination of whether exchange rate regimes affect growth of real GDP. A number of studies lately (Levy-Yeyati and Sturzenegger 2003; Rogoff et al. 2006; etc.) have considered the question but with different classifications, different samples, and different econometric techniques, and consequently, different results. We use common data and techniques to compare results across classifications. We find that the impact of the exchange rate regime on long run GDP growth, controlling for other factors, is relatively weak. This stands in contrast to some influential results in the literature.

In the 2000s answers to questions about the effects of exchange rate regimes on economic performance, and the very nature of exchange rate regimes, have changed with new empirical analyses. Previous skepticism regarding the importance of the exchange rate regime for economic outcomes has been challenged. It is the nature of research that the answers to questions change, even questions that are at the core of a subject. The topics discussed in this book represent classic questions in international finance. Views on these topics have changed as the modern era has progressed, and as new experiences are incorporated into studies. We show in this book that the exchange rate regime can have significant impacts on a variety of aspects of the economy. Our goal is to contribute to our understanding of the modern era and, in so doing, to deepen our knowledge of some of the central empirical issues in international finance.

II The Nature of Exchange Rate Regimes

2   Exchange Rate Regimes in Theory and Practice

So much of barbarism, however, still remains in the transactions of most civilized nations that almost all independent countries choose to assert their nationality by having, to their own inconvenience and that of their neighbors, a peculiar currency of their own.

—John Stuart Mill, *Principles of Political Economy*, 1848

A system of flexible or floating exchange rates [is] . . . absolutely essential for the fulfillment of our basic economic objective: the achievement and maintenance of a free and prosperous world community engaged in unrestricted multilateral trade.

—Milton Friedman, "The case for flexible exchange rates," 1953

More than a full century separates John Stuart Mill's writing of the "barbarism" of countries desiring their own currencies, and Milton Friedman's argument that flexible exchange rates are "absolutely essential" for economic prosperity. If economics progressed like the natural sciences, one might be able to say that Friedman's mid-twentieth-century perspective favoring flexible exchange rates reflected an advance in knowledge over Mill's mid-nineteenth-century view of the desirability of fixed exchange rates backed by precious metals, just as physicists' understanding of electromagnetism today is more subtle than that developed by Michael Faraday, Mill's contemporary. One could even hope that today, at the beginning of the twenty-first century, we might have arrived at a resolution on this central issue of international macroeconomics. But this is not the case. The debate over the relative benefits and costs of different exchange rate regimes remains lively.

Of course, there have been advances in our understanding of the implications of exchange rate regimes in the century-and-a-half since the time of Mill, and in the decades since Friedman wrote his classic article. But some of the issues raised by these great economists remain relevant today.[1] Mill was concerned with instability affecting trade and commerce when national currencies were not anchored to precious metals. These concerns are mirrored in contemporary efforts by central banks to gain credibility by pegging exchange rates to the currencies of countries with a history of relatively low inflation. Friedman, on the other hand, thought that flexible exchange rates could facilitate market adjustment. Debate over the appropriate exchange rate policies of countries like China that run large and persistent trade imbalances while pegging their currencies echo the arguments raised by Friedman more than a half-century ago.

In this chapter we provide a context for much of the rest of the book by introducing standard views on exchange rate regimes and their economic consequences. Exchange rate regimes can be analyzed using various frameworks, and arguments based on these different perspectives motivate much of the empirical work throughout the rest of this book. Section 2.1 considers the constraints imposed on macroeconomic policy by fixed exchange rates, a topic that is the focus of chapter 9. Section 2.2 examines the arguments for fixing the exchange rate in order to stabilize the economy, a topic explored in chapter 11. Section 2.3 presents a theory that offers guidance for whether countries or regions should use a common currency that is based on the balance between macroeconomic flexibility and economic integration, a topic discussed in chapters 10 and 12. Section 2.4 surveys the political economy motives for exchange rate regime choice that, as discussed further in chapter 5, may dominate purely economic considerations when governments make the decision of whether to peg their currency. We draw on these frameworks as we conclude this chapter with a discussion of exchange rate regimes and the international monetary system over the last 150 years. This brief history provides a context for our analysis of the modern era.

The standard textbook exposition of exchange rate regimes places countries into one of two categories: those that fix the price of their currency against that of another currency (or, synonymously, peg their currency), and those that allow their currency to float and be determined by market forces. This categorization is pedagogically convenient, and in this section we will use it to discuss some standard results from international macroeconomics. But we also note up front that as shown in the next two chapters, there are few examples of countries that have persistently maintained either of these two polar stances over the entire modern era. Further there are differences between a currency peg and abandoning a national currency altogether via dollarization (e.g., as in Ecuador) or a currency union (e.g., as in the euro area).[2] Frequently the issues involved in the decision to peg or float are similar to those arising when considering the formation of a currency union, but we will note where the distinction is important. Also, as discussed in the chapter 3, there are a range of intermediate regimes between these extremes of a free float and a stable peg. Nevertheless, there are valuable insights one gains from considering the differences between the textbook versions of fixed and flexible exchange rate regimes even though a complete understanding of exchange rate regimes in the modern era requires us to go well beyond this simple dichotomy.

2.1 The Open Economy Trilemma

The clean division of countries into those that fix and those that float allows for the straightforward illustration of a central result in international macroeconomics, the policy trilemma.[3] The policy trilemma states that the monetary authorities of a country can choose no more than two of three policy options: free capital mobility, fixed exchange rates, and domestic monetary autonomy. This then limits the scope for a country's policy options.

The policy trilemma is sometimes depicted using the diagram in figure 2.1. The corners of this triangle represent three policy options facing a government: free capital mobility, which allows people in a country to transfer funds abroad and people outside a country to purchase its assets; a fixed exchange rate (or peg), which enables a government to fix the bilateral exchange rate with another country; and monetary autonomy, which means that a country's central bank has a free hand in setting monetary policy. The sides of the triangle represent the policy options available to a government. For example, side A in this figure represents the choice of an exchange rate peg and free capital mobility, implying the country has forgone domestic monetary autonomy while side B represents the choice of monetary autonomy and free capital mobility meaning the country does not attempt to manage its exchange rate. The key point of the policy trilemma is that a government can choose a pair of policies corresponding to A, B, or C, but does not have the ability to simultaneously fix the exchange rate, control the

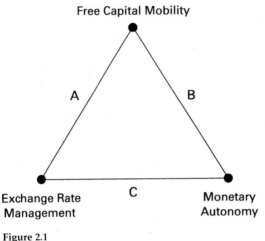

Free Capital Mobility

A   B

Exchange Rate   C   Monetary
Management   Autonomy

Figure 2.1
The policy trilemma.

money supply, and allow for free capital mobility. The theory does not require that a government choose a pure corner solution, embracing two policies and abandoning the other altogether. Rather, there are trade-offs across the three policies. For example, there is an increasingly large sacrifice of monetary autonomy or capital mobility (or both) as a government attempts to have greater control of its exchange rate.

The reason that governments are constrained in a way described by the policy trilemma can be understood using any one of a number of macroeconomic models of an open economy. The fundamental aggregate relationships in these models do not depend on the exchange rate regime in place. Rather, in these models, the choice of exchange rate regime determines which variables are exogenous and determined by authorities, and which are endogenous and the outcome of markets. Under flexible exchange rates the monetary authorities choose an interest rate that suits domestic economic considerations. In this case the value of the exchange rate reflects this choice as well as the value of other exogenous factors, like domestic fiscal policy, exogenous domestic investment demand, or the foreign interest rate. The exchange rate will also depend on expectations of its future value. In contrast, a fixed exchange rate regime requires that monetary policy is directed toward the maintenance of the pegged value of the exchange rate. In this case, monetary policy meets this goal by responding passively to peg the value of the currency in the face of changing economic circumstances, or changing perceptions about the future.[4]

If capital markets are open and the exchange rate is fixed (and is expected to stay pegged at a constant rate), the interest rate on a representative domestic bond must equal the interest rate on a similar bond denominated in the currency of the country to which the exchange rate is pegged. If the interest rate on the domestic bond was lower, investors would clearly favor the foreign bond, and, consequently, domestic investors would purchase foreign exchange in order to buy the higher yielding foreign bond. This would force the domestic central bank to sell its foreign currency in order to short-circuit an excess demand for foreign currency that would cause the domestic currency to weaken and would break the peg if the central bank did not respond. The resulting decrease in the domestic money supply would raise the interest rate on the domestic bond to parity with that of the foreign bond (this illustrates the lack of monetary autonomy with a fixed exchange rate and open capital markets). If, however, the central bank attempted to maintain some monetary autonomy and forestall this interest rate increase, it would eventually run out of foreign exchange; at that point the peg would break and there would be a devaluation of the domestic currency. In this case the trilemma operates through giving up exchange rate management in order to have monetary autonomy.

The policy trilemma thus shows that with capital mobility, monetary policy becomes subordinated to pegging the value of the currency for a country operating with a fixed exchange rate, or for countries in a currency union. A country that pegs its currency to that of another country must follow the monetary policy of that country. Also there is only a single monetary policy for all countries participating in a currency union. There are important implications of this for understanding the relative merits of fixed versus flexible exchange rates. One source of concern with fixed exchange rates in the presence of capital mobility is that governments that peg their currencies lose the use of a potentially important stabilization policy. The cost of foregoing monetary autonomy for a particular country depends on the extent to which the monetary policy of the base country mimics the monetary policy that it would undertake were it to have the latitude to set this policy independently.[5] We explore the empirical relevance of the policy trilemma in chapter 8.

2.2   Fixed Exchange Rates and Stabilization Policy and Adjustment

The loss of monetary policy autonomy may, in certain circumstances, even benefit a country. One example is when the automatic monetary policy response that occurs with a fixed exchange rate serves to stabilize an economy. Such could be the case for a small economy that is open to trade and depends on a particular export for much of its foreign exchange revenues. The small economy's exchange rate whose value is pegged to the price of the main export commodity would then depreciate with a fall in that price, helping to offset contractionary effects, and appreciate with a rise in that price, mitigating the expansion due to the favorable change in the country's terms of trade.[6]

Another example of the advantageous automatic stabilization properties of a fixed exchange rate, in this case for a more diversified economy than the one considered in the previous paragraph, occurs when potential disruptions come from asset markets or unstable money demand, rather than goods markets. In this case the appropriate policy response would be to offset these shocks through monetary policy. In contrast, when the economy is buffeted by events like a collapse in investment demand, or an increase in the price of oil or food, policies to maintain a fixed exchange rate could exacerbate problems. In these cases a flexible exchange rate system may be more desirable, since the exchange rate serves as a shock absorber for the economy.[7] Its depreciation in the face of adverse shocks of this type, and its appreciation when the economy is stimulated due to an expansion in the demand for goods, mitigates the overall movement in national income. In contrast, a fixed exchange rate exacerbates the effects of these shocks on national income. In essence, recognition of this type of stabilization from flexible exchange rates led to the acceptance of widespread floating at the beginning of the modern era while countries were trying to adapt to rapid increases in the price of oil and food.[8]

Another situation where there is an advantage to surrendering monetary policy autonomy to the requirements of a fixed exchange rate occurs when a central bank fails to perform well if left to its own discretion. This is one basis of Mill's argument for fixing the exchange rate to the value of a precious metal. More recently economists have focused on the consequences of the perception of central bank profligacy, and how to anchor people's expectations to improve economic performance. Research on central bank credibility shows that rules that bind the actions of a central bank can result in a better outcome than what would occur without this type of commitment.[9] As shown by the policy trilemma, a fixed exchange rate can serve as this type of rule since, with open capital markets, a central bank that must maintain a peg does not have a free hand to set monetary policy. In fact, because the efficacy of a rule depends, in part, on the ability of people to under-stand the rule and to be able to verify adherence to it, a fixed exchange rate may be a particularly useful commitment device for a monetary authority. The exchange rate is a very public price and is known in the market at all times; thus, actors in the economy are constantly aware of whether the central bank is maintaining its commitment. For this rea-son, a number of countries have centered stabilization plans on an ex-change rate goal, including Argentina, Chile, Uruguay, and Israel.[10] Furthermore European countries that had a history of poor inflation performance, like Italy, saw a monetary union as a way to import anti-inflation credibility and, in so doing, more easily bring down inflation in their own country. Chapter 10 presents an empirical analysis of the effect of fixed exchange rates on inflation.

These efforts to stabilize economies through a fixed exchange rate have often not worked out well, however. Most exchange-rate-based stabilization plans have not succeeded in a sustained reduction in infla-tion (Végh 1992). Also the history of the last four decades is littered with examples of spectacular collapses of fixed exchange rate regimes. These include several episodes in Latin America (including Mexico in 1982 and 1994, and Argentina in 2001–2002), the collapse of the Euro-pean Monetary System in 1992, and the 1997–1998 Asian crises. In some of these cases, like Argentina in 2002 and Thailand in 1997, these initial exchange rate collapses were followed by severe economic hard-ship. In other cases, like the United Kingdom in 1992, the exchange rate devaluation spurred exports and led to economic growth.

Fixed exchange rates can also lead to problems when they help sus-tain differences in relative prices across countries that lead to trade imbalances and painful adjustment through rising unemployment in countries with trade deficits, and unwanted inflationary pressures in countries with trade surpluses.[11] In particular, it is often easier to have a currency depreciation in the face of a trade deficit than to rely on overall price deflation. As mentioned above, Milton Friedman argued in 1950 that flexible exchange rates could facilitate this process, writ-ing, "It is far simpler to allow one price to change, namely, the price of foreign exchange, than to rely upon changes in the multitude of prices that together constitute the internal price structure" (ibid., p. 173).

This view, that flexible exchange rates would smoothly allow for overall trade adjustment, was common then. For example, Sidney Wells begins the chapter entitled "For and Against Fluctuating Ex-change Rates" in his 1968 textbook *International Economics*:

The first and most obvious advantage of a fluctuating exchange rate is ... depreciation or appreciation can be expected automatically to restore equilibrium in a country's balance of payments. There is no need for unemployment to be created or restrictions to be imposed in order to reduce imports and increase exports. (p. 192)

But experiences have shown that flexible exchange rates have not served to maintain balanced trade, nor have they kept countries from suffering unemployment due to competition from other countries. An important reason for this is that exchange rates respond strongly to asset market conditions, and not just trade imbalances. Real exchange rates, that is, exchange rates adjusted for price differentials across countries, move around for reasons unrelated to trade while having a strong impact on exports, imports, and economic activity related to these activities.[12]

2.3 Optimum Currency Areas

The previous section has shown that neither theory nor experience provides support for unambiguously favoring one exchange rate regime over another. While economics often looks for a single optimal solution to a problem, the simple truth is that the appropriate exchange rate regime depends on the particular circumstances of a country.[13] An influential line of research does, however, provide some guidance concerning which exchange rate regime might be appropriate for a particular country. This research began with the 1961 contribution of Robert Mundell, research that was cited when he was awarded the Nobel Memorial Prize in Economics in 1999. In this paper Mundell offers criteria for an optimum currency area (OCA).[14]

As Mill argues, national currencies are inconvenient because they make international exchange of goods and services more difficult by forcing people to trade currencies when they purchase something from another country (or, depending on the way the exchange is structured, when they sell something to another country). While this is true with fixed as well as flexible exchange rates, credibly fixed exchange rates have the virtue of locking in the domestic currency price of a future payment denominated in foreign currency. This could theoretically promote international trade by reducing uncertainty, and as shown in chapter 9, there is empirical support for this argument since trade is higher, all else held equal, between two countries with a fixed exchange rate than between two countries with a flexible exchange rate.

Thus one advantage of a fixed exchange rate regime is that it facilitates trade among its members by removing price risk. There are also thought to be corresponding benefits for investment stemming from the removal of uncertainty regarding exchange rates. But, as the trilemma demonstrates, a disadvantage of pegging is that it ties the hands of monetary authorities who could otherwise attempt to offset shocks to the economy with countercyclical policy. The basic insight of OCA analysis is to weigh these two effects, and to consider the extent to which other factors may substitute for them, in order to determine whether a set of countries should have a common currency.

This consideration of the relative costs and benefits of a common currency can be illustrated by considering two countries. The case for a common currency is bolstered by an extensive amount of trade between these countries, since a fixed exchange rate would lower the cost of a high volume of transactions. But such a policy would prevent the monetary authorities in one country or the other from pursuing an independent policy. This concern would be mitigated if there were little need for conflicting monetary policy in the two countries because, for example, the countries shared a common economic profile and hard times in one country were likely to occur when there were also hard times in the other country. This might be the case if, for example, both countries' economies were dominated by the production of the same set of agricultural products. The concern with foregoing monetary autonomy would also be mitigated if there were other means to offset differential economic performance across the two countries. Fiscal transfers are one such alternative. In this case, the country that is prospering would transfer funds to the country that is lagging to soften the hard times. Another alternative to independent monetary policies is labor mobility. If workers could easily move from a depressed country to one that is thriving, then the need for differential monetary policies is reduced.

Thus the potential benefits of a single currency increase with the level of integration with respect to trade and investment among countries that share that currency. But its potential costs rise with the differences in macroeconomic shocks across its members, and with the absence of shock absorbers like labor mobility or fiscal transfers. A similar set of insights applies for a system of fixed exchange rates.

While these insights from OCA analysis are valuable, they do not provide a metric by which one can judge whether or not a set of countries is, in fact, an optimum currency area. One way to illustrate these concepts, however, is to consider a benchmark case. In recent years, especially in the period leading up to the single currency in Europe, the benchmark used by many researchers is the United States.

The United States is a very large and economically diverse country. One could imagine a situation in which regions of the United States had independent currencies; there could be a New England dollar, a mid-Atlantic dollar, a southern dollar, and so on. This would, of course, complicate trade across regions. The cost of trade would rise, and given the extensive amount of trade that occurs between New York and Texas, or California and Illinois, this would represent a large cost to the United States.

But what about the benefits of regional currencies? Separate currencies that floated against each other would allow regional monetary authorities to respond to local needs. There have been large disparities in economic performance across regions in recent years, such as the waning fortunes of the Midwest in the 1980s when the term "rustbelt" was coined, the downturn in New England in the early 1990s in the wake of changes in the hi-tech sector, and the way in which the fortunes of Texas change with the price of oil. Wouldn't it be advantageous to have policy responses to these local disruptions, even given the increased cost of trade arising from regional currencies?

The generally agreed-upon answer to this question is "no." While acknowledging ongoing regional differences in economic performance, economists also point to mechanisms that serve as a substitute for regional monetary policies. National fiscal policy serves as an automatic stabilizer across regions. A region in recession will pay less federal tax and receive more transfers from Washington. Labor mobility is also an important feature of the United States economy. Workers leave areas that are suffering an economic downturn, moving to more prosperous areas, and this helps mitigate the effects of regional recessions. Overall, then, no one argues that the United States should give up the national currency for regional monies.[15]

There was, of course, a protracted argument on whether European countries should abandon their national currencies for the euro in the 1990s. Economists considered the question of the desirability of a single currency in light of OCA arguments, and some used the United States as a benchmark.[16] In these comparisons Europe did not seem nearly as desirable a currency area as the United States because of the lower amount of intra-European trade as compared to trade within the United States, the paucity of transfers from a central European authority to separate countries as compared to federal transfers in the United States, and the much lower level of labor mobility across European countries (or, as it turns out, even within European countries) as compared to the footloose nature of Americans. But perhaps this was too high a bar. While the United States is inconvertibly an OCA, maybe Europe is as well, even though its case is not as strong.

As discussed in chapter 5, there is empirical support for the view that a country's choice of an exchange rate regime is based on economic considerations raised by OCA theory. But, as shown in that chapter, there is also evidence that other, noneconomic arguments significantly contribute to this choice. The politics behind the choice of an exchange rate regime is a lively area of research in international political economy. We next turn to a discussion of some of the main considerations in this area.

2.4   Political Economy and the Exchange Rate Regime

The choice of an exchange rate regime, like any other economic policy decision, is influenced by political factors as well economic considerations. This is especially true during the modern era as there is not a single dominant exchange rate regime as was the case during the gold standard or the Bretton Woods era.[17] Clearly, there are some countries during the current era whose exchange rate regime choice was influenced by the decisions made by its neighbors, such as countries participating in the various fixed and semi-fixed exchange rate regimes in Europe, and the eight francophone West African countries that use the Franc CFA as their national currency (where CFA stands for *Communauté Financière d'Afrique*). But many other countries have had a wider set of options available to them than in earlier eras. For these countries it may be important to recognize the political dimension of the choice of an exchange rate regime. As noted in a 2001 survey by Broz and Frieden, two prominent political scientists, "[Exchange rate] regime decisions involve trade-offs with domestic distributional and electoral implications: thus, selecting an exchange rate regime is as much a political decision as an economic one" (p. 331). In this section we review some of the political decisions involved in exchange rate regime choice, including the influence of interest groups, partisan politics, and political institutions.

An understanding of interest group politics involved in exchange rate regime choice builds on the economic implications of fixed and floating exchange rates discussed above. An exchange rate successfully pegged to the currency of a base country reduces the riskiness of transactions with that country.[18] Thus those interest groups that would benefit from these transactions, including the management and workers of domestic firms engaged in international trade and cross-border investment, would support a fixed exchange rate. A fixed exchange rate also limits monetary autonomy, and the ability of the central bank to respond to deteriorating economic conditions. Managers and workers at domestic firms that sell nontraded goods and services and do not engage in international transactions, and therefore do not benefit from the lower risk associated with a fixed exchange rate regime, may support currency flexibility.

One of the challenges with verifying this interest group theory is that industries do not divide neatly into the two groups outlined in the previous paragraph. Firm-level survey data shows that owners and managers of firms producing tradable goods more strongly support fixed exchange rates than owners and managers of other firms (Broz, Frieden, and Weymouth 2008). But there is a high degree of heterogeneity within narrowly defined manufacturing industries with respect to exposure to international competition or opportunities abroad (Klein, Schuh, and Triest 2003). Also only a small percentage of firms within any given industry are involved in exporting and importing (Bernard et al. 2007).[19] Thus, even if people associated with particular firms did behave in a way consistent with interest group theory, it might be difficult to find industry-based evidence of this.[20]

It may also be difficult to find evidence of strong partisan effects on exchange rate regime choice, for many of the same reasons it is difficult to demonstrate industry-level interest group effects. One might think that center-right parties, which reflect business interests, tend to support a fixed exchange rate regime both for reasons of lowering the uncertainty associated with trade and because of the discipline it imposes on monetary policy. But empirics are not supportive of this hypothesis, and empirical tests "have produced mixed and often perverse results" (Broz and Frieden 2001, p. 328). This may be due to mitigating factors such as the linkage of exchange rate regime choice to other policies (trade, agricultural policies, etc.) and the independence of the central bank.

An independent central bank can deliver low inflation without the discipline imposed by a fixed exchange rate. In an open society, independent groups can monitor the actions of the central bank. This is not as likely in an autocratic regime. For this reason these regimes may find it difficult to credibly commit to central bank independence. In this case a pegged exchange rate offers an alternative commitment mechanism that is transparent and verifiable. Empirically it has been shown that autocracies are more likely to have a fixed exchange rate regime than democracies (Broz 2002).

The constraints on a central bank due to a fixed exchange rate might be viewed negatively by politicians in a democracy who hope to influence monetary policy in an effort to advance their own opportunities. For example, there is a well-established link between a strong economy and the likelihood that an incumbent is returned to power in an election. An institutional implication of this is that flexible exchange rates (which offers a central bank more influence on the economy, and politicians more opportunity to affect economic outcomes if they can influence the central bank) are more likely in democracies where there is a high political return to influencing the economy. This would be the case where a small change in votes can lead to a large change in political party, for example in countries with a single-party plurality. Bernhard and Leblang (1999) develop these arguments, and test them in a sample of twenty industrial democracies. They find evidence that countries in which the opposition has little political power are more likely to have a flexible exchange rate. They also find significant evidence that countries in which the dates of elections are not controlled by the party in power are more likely to have flexible exchange rates. In this case an incumbent cannot choose the date of an election to coincide with a good economic environment, so the ability to influence the central bank and alter the economy is more valuable.

The political basis for exchange rate regime choice builds on and extends the economic considerations presented in the previous sections. For some today, especially Americans, exchange rate regime policies may seem fairly abstract and unlikely to rate a debate question between presidential candidates. But currently, and in the recent past, the appropriate exchange rate regime has been a large political issue in a great many countries (Argentina, Brazil, Denmark, etc.) and it was also an important issue in the United States at many times over the last 150 years. We conclude this chapter with a brief discussion of the timeline of the international monetary system.

2.5 A Brief History of the International Monetary System

The trilemma is a useful lens through which to view the history of the world's monetary system. As noted in the introduction, the ability to

choose one's own exchange rate regime is a relatively recent phenomenon. Prior to that, there was more often a coherent "system" of which
countries were a part. The system itself, though, varied greatly over
time as the system moved from one solution to the trilemma to
another.[21]

From 1880 to 1914, most countries that chose to take part in the international economy adhered to the gold standard. Each country pegged
the value of its currency to gold, and hence all currencies were pegged
to one another. Countries also had open capital markets leading to
large scale capital flows, and as we learn from the policy trilemma,
this led to a lack of monetary autonomy.[22] Peripheral countries in the
world economy did not join the gold standard immediately, and there
were some countries that floated or controlled the capital account as a
prelude to joining the gold standard, but the agreed-upon solution to
the trilemma—pegs with open capital markets and no monetary autonomy—was not in dispute.[23]

The gold standard became unstable when World War I led to deficit
spending in Europe and when countries refused to allow shipments of
gold. After the hostilities ceased, efforts to return to the gold standard
at pre-war parities either failed or led to deflation. This era, generally
known as the interwar years, saw a variety of solutions to the trilemma
not by choice as much as necessity. Countries tried to rejoin the gold
standard but often lacked the reserves or the discipline to maintain the
agreed pegs.[24] Those countries that were forced to allow their currencies to float were often economically (and politically) chaotic, and
at times suffered hyperinflations. Other countries instituted exchange
controls or raised interest rates higher than what was best from a
purely domestic perspective in order to keep a peg to gold. The constraints imposed by pegging were never more apparent than when
countries clung to the gold standard despite a clear need for relaxing
monetary policy in the face of the Great Depression. In fact those that
remained on the gold standard longest typically faced the most severe
economic contraction in the 1930s.[25]

Mindful of the mistakes of the interwar years, representatives from
44 Allied nations met at Bretton Woods, New Hampshire, in 1944 to
establish a postwar international monetary regime. The Bretton Woods
system established an asymmetric system of fixed exchange rates, with
the United States at its center. Initially, the system was intended to
solve both of the perceived concerns with the interwar years—the
chaos of floating rates and the lack of monetary autonomy of the gold

standard. All countries pegged to the US dollar and the dollar was pegged to gold. At the same time capital controls were kept in place, and changes in pegs were intended to allow any necessary adjustment to long run imbalances while IMF lending could cushion short term imbalances. Thus this system aimed for the peg with monetary autonomy side of the trilemma, openly sacrificing the free flow of capital.

However, increasing world trade in both goods and capital led, over time, to a shift in the trilemma from pegs with monetary autonomy to pegs with limited autonomy and some capital mobility. Countries were compelled to set their monetary policy in line with that of the United States, which, as the center country in this asymmetric system, retained latitude in setting its own monetary policy. Monetary expansion in the United States, and the pressures that put on the maintenance of the gold standard, led to the de-linking of the dollar from gold in 1971 and the full collapse of the Bretton Woods system in 1973.

When the Bretton Woods era ended, there was an initial intention to quickly return to a system of newly pegged currencies. In fact the end of the Bretton Woods era marked the end of a single coherent international monetary system in which nearly all countries followed one choice within the trilemma. The subsequent era, which we call the modern era and is the focus of this book, is distinguished by a variety of solutions to the trilemma as opposed to a single system with one dominant set of policies. It is also distinct from the chaotic interwar years when countries failed to establish any sustained and stable position in the trilemma. Instead, as chapter 4 shows, a variety of choices exist in the modern era, both across countries and, in many cases, across time as many countries change from one solution to the trilemma to another, sometimes due to a crisis and at other times by their own choice.

The modern era first saw worldwide inflation and subsequently a moderation of inflation, a sustained growth in international trade, and steady opening of capital markets, but throughout, the exchange rate regimes have varied across countries and over time. As Bretton Woods ended, most developing countries tried to retain a peg, either to the United States or to a former colonial power. Further many European countries pegged to one another, but by and large, major industrial countries floated against one another. Over time, arrangements changed for many countries. In the 1970s and 1980s, many Latin American countries pegged or had crawling pegs, but rarely consistently. Countries in the European Union kept a pegged system, the European

Monetary System (EMS), but many broke or realigned pegs and others stayed out of the system except for brief stints. Some countries have consistently maintained a peg (e.g., Saudi Arabia) while others, such as Argentina, have created a "harder" peg that mandates the peg by law and requires adequate international reserve backing through a currency board. Some countries have even dispatched with their own currency (e.g., Ecuador). Sets of other countries have joined in an arrangement with a cross-national currency and single central bank, as is the case with the initially eleven, but currently (at the time of this writing) sixteen eurozone countries. Many countries have both pegged and floated over the modern era. And pegging one bilateral rate does not ensure overall exchange rate stability. Countries peg to a variety of base currencies, so two countries that both peg, but to different bases, might have an unstable bilateral exchange rate.

As we will see, nearly all countries have chosen to peg at some point, and nearly all have chosen to float at some point. The characterization of these exchange rate regimes, their dynamics, and the motivations behind a government's choice of its exchange rate regime are the focus of the next three chapters of this book.

3   Exchange Rate Regime Classifications

Everything should be made as simple as possible, but not simpler.

—Albert Einstein

Exchange rates are precisely measured. Exchange rate regimes are not. The first challenge facing those who want to understand the characteristics and consequences of exchange rate regimes is the identification and implementation of a classification scheme. This scheme must define the categories that constitute an exchange rate regime and provide a set of criteria that classifies a country's experience in a particular time period into one of those categories. These are far from trivial tasks, and as Frankel has noted, "placing actual countries into those categories is more difficult than one who has never tried it would guess."[1]

Exchange rate regime classification schemes vary along several dimensions. A central dichotomy is between regimes declared by the government, typically to the IMF (a *de jure* classification) and those based on actual data (a *de facto* classification). These data will include exchange rates, but may also include other variables, such as interest rates or central bank reserves. Another distinction is the number of categories. Classification schemes may include only two broad categories (e.g., "pegged" and "nonpegged"), or a larger set of more narrowly defined ones (e.g., "managed floating" and "limited flexibility"). A third consideration is the time period that constitutes one observation for a country. Many schemes are based on behavior over a calendar year, but one well-known system uses longer-run rolling averages. This feature of a classification scheme will affect how frequently one can observe switches from one category to another. The frequency of switching is also determined by other rules used to categorize observations. For example, a one-time discrete devaluation could count as a break in a pegged exchange rate, or it could be categorized as a continuation of a fixed rate, albeit at a different peg before and after the devaluation.

The range of issues that a classifications scheme must address suggests that there is no one "correct" way to categorize exchange rate regimes. Rather, those studying the characteristics or the consequences of exchange rate regimes need to consider which classification scheme is most appropriate for the question at hand. For example, a study of the monetary constraints imposed by a fixed exchange rate, that is the empirical relevance of the policy trilemma, would be best served by a *de facto* classification that categorized exchange rates as fixed or floating, and did not count a one-time discrete devaluation as a break in a fixed exchange rate episode. A study of the length of peg episodes, however, may be based on a system in which a break in a peg counts as a floating exchange rate for that one year. Another type of study, one that focuses on longer-lived regime behavior, may use categories based on annual moving averages rather than yearly observations. Finally, one may want to consider data on reserves as well as that on exchange rates, and allow for a multiplicity of categories beyond "fixed" and "floating" in an analysis of the macroeconomic behavior of countries that intervene extensively but operate in an environment where exchange rates are typically very volatile.

This chapter begins, in section 3.1, with a discussion of exchange rate regimes reported by the IMF in its *Annual Report on Exchange Arrangements and Exchange Restrictions* (*EAER*). This is considered the standard *de jure* classification scheme, since the data were initially based on self-reporting by governments. But, as discussed in section 3.1, these data became a hybrid between a *de jure* and a *de facto* classification scheme, beginning with the 1999 volume of *EAER* when the IMF began to augment government self-reported exchange rate arrangements with their own staff's evaluations. This was a response to the view that "the authorities own descriptions of exchange rate regimes in the *EAER* is patently inaccurate for some countries" (Fischer 2001, p. 4, n. 2). We also show, in this section, the evolution in the categories used to classify exchange rate regimes in the *EAER*. This reflects the change in exchange rate arrangements during the modern era. It also highlights some difficulties in comparing exchange rate regime categorization at the time of the collapse of Bretton Woods in the early 1970s to subsequent experience.

Scholars outside of the IMF have undertaken their own efforts to characterize exchange rate regimes, and we discuss a number of these *de facto* classification schemes in section 3.2. These classifications have been used to investigate a range of issues in international macroeconomics, and partly for that reason, the methods and data used across them vary widely. The discussion in this section highlights this variety and, in so doing, raises issues like the appropriate number of categories in a classification scheme and the data required to establish membership in a particular category. Of course, there is no one correct answer concerning the number of categories or the data employed. Instead, the focus of the research influences the characteristics of the classification scheme.

The fact that the exchange rate classification schemes presented in sections 3.1 and 3.2 differ does not mean that there are no overarching results about exchange rate regimes in the modern era. Classification schemes vary, and the extent of measured variation depends partly on choices made in attempting to compare schemes with different numbers of categories. The practical question, however, is the extent of differences, and similarities, across these classification schemes. We address this question in section 3.3 by comparing and contrasting the data from the various exchange rate regime classifications. This comparison will prove important as we consider the characterization of exchange rate regime behavior in the next chapter, and the consequences of exchange rate regimes for economic performance in subsequent chapters.

3.1   IMF Reporting of Exchange Rate Regimes

One way to determine a country's exchange rate regime is simply to ask its government what type of exchange rate system it has in place. The International Monetary Fund does this in an ongoing manner. Annual reports that presented data from country surveys on exchange rate arrangements and exchange restrictions have been published by the IMF since 1950. These reports, titled *Annual Report on Exchange Arrangements and Exchange Restrictions*, include narratives on member states' exchange rate systems (and exchange restrictions) as well as tables that summarize this information.[2]

Table 3.1 shows the evolution of the exchange rate categories presented in the summary tables in volumes of the *Annual Report on Exchange Arrangements and Exchange Restrictions* from the 1973 volume (reflecting exchange rate arrangements in 1972) until the 2006 volume. As shown in this table, the 1973 volume, reflecting the arrangements in

Table 3.1
AREAR classifications over time

1973 Volume	1974–1987 Volumes	1988–1996 Volumes
Par value or central rate exists	Exchange rate maintained within relatively narrow margins in terms of	Exchange Rate determined on basis of peg to
Par value or central rate applied	—US dollar (1974–87)	—US dollar (1988–1996)
Effective rate other than par value or central rate applicable to all or most transactions	—Sterling (1974–1987)	—Pound sterling (1988–1995)
(a) fixed rate	—French franc (1974–1987)	—French franc (1988–1996)
(b) fluctuating rate	—Group of currencies (1974)	—Other currencies (1988–1996)
(c) pegged rate	—Average of exchange rates of main trading partners (1974)	—Composite of currencies (1988–1996)
Special rate(s) for some or all capital transactions and/or some or all invisibles	—Group of currencies under mutual intervention arrangements (1975–1986)	Limited flexibility with respect to
Import rate(s) different from export rate(s)	—Composite of currencies (1975–87)	—single currency
More than one rate for imports	—Australian dollar, S. African rand, Spanish peseta (1977–1982)	—cooperative arrangement
More than one rate for exports	—Set of indicators (1979–1982)	More flexible arrangements
	Exchange rate not maintained within relatively narrow margins as above	—adjusted according to set of indicators
	Special exchange rate regime for some or all capital transactions, invisibles	—other managed float
	Import rate(s) differ from export rate(s)	—independently floating
	More than one rate for imports	Special rate(s) for some or all capital transactions and/or some or all invisibles
	More than one rate for exports	Import rate(s) different from export rate(s)
		More than one rate for imports
		More than one rate for exports

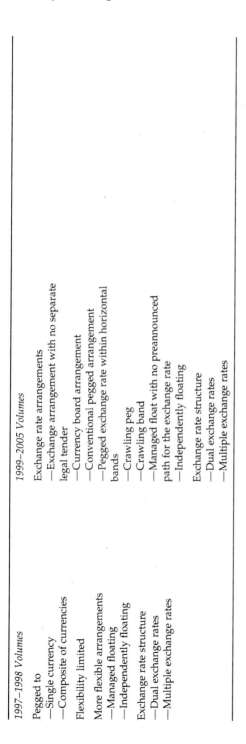

1997–1998 Volumes

Pegged to
—Single currency
—Composite of currencies
Flexibility limited
More flexible arrangements
—Managed floating
—Independently floating
Exchange rate structure
—Dual exchange rates
—Multiple exchange rates

1999–2005 Volumes

Exchange rate arrangements
—Exchange arrangement with no separate legal tender
—Currency board arrangement
—Conventional pegged arrangement
—Pegged exchange rate within horizontal bands
—Crawling peg
—Crawling band
—Managed float with no preannounced path for the exchange rate
—Independently floating
Exchange rate structure
—Dual exchange rates
—Multiple exchange rates

the final full year of the Bretton Woods era, includes the two exchange arrangement categories, "Agreed par value exists" and "Par value applied." Par values were official exchange rates, usually in terms of US dollars, that countries agreed upon with the IMF and had committed to attempt to preserve. The countries that did not have a par value for their currency were included in the category "Unitary effective rate, not par value" (which had the subcategories "fixed rate," "freely fluctuating rate," and "pegged rate"), or in one of the four categories for multiple exchange rates ("Special rate(s) for some or all capital transactions and/or some or all invisibles," "Import rate(s) different from export rate(s)," "More than one rate for imports," and "More than one rate for exports").

The changes in the summary table categories between the 1973 and the 1974 volumes reflect the end of the Bretton Woods era. With the final collapse of the Bretton Woods system in March 1973, the term "par value" disappeared from these tables, and the "unitary effective rate" category was dropped. The 1974 volume of the *Annual Report on Exchange Restrictions* included two categories, "Exchange rate maintained within relatively narrow margins" and "Exchange rate not maintained within relatively narrow margins." This former category was divided up into subcategories of the base currency or currencies, including the US dollar, the British pound sterling, the French franc, a group of other currencies, and an average of exchange rates of main trading partners. These subcategories changed over time. The second column of table 3.1 includes the list of bases and the years in which they appeared in the summary tables.

While the end of the Bretton Woods system is widely viewed as heralding in the period of floating exchange rates, the view at the time, at least as reflected in contemporary *Annual Reports on Exchange Restrictions*, gives a different perspective. An appendix to the 1974 volume entitled "Central Rates and Wider Margins: A Temporary Regime— Revised Decision" reflects the way in which the IMF, and many member states, wrestled with the collapse of the Bretton Woods system. That appendix states that the Fund called on members "to maintain a satisfactory structure of exchange rates within appropriate margins ... during the temporary period preceding the resumption of effective par values" (p. 19). An appendix to the 1975 volume of *Annual Report on Exchange Restrictions* entitled "Guidelines for the Management of Floating Exchange Rates" recommends that countries intervene in foreign exchange markets "to moderate movements in the exchange value of its currency" (p. 21). These sentiments of concern about the market determination of exchange rates are relevant when attempting to compare experiences classified as floating in the early 1970s (which would reflect countries included in the category "Exchange rate not maintained within relatively narrow margin") to those classified as floating in the twenty-first century (which, depending on the way categories are aggregated, might include only those countries classified as "Independently floating").

The new format of the summary exchange rate regime table that appeared in the 1988 volume of the *Annual Report on Exchange Arrangements and Exchange Restrictions* represents a first recognition by that publication of the heterogeneity of exchange rate regimes in the modern era. As shown in table 3.1, the exchange rate categories were altered from the long-standing "maintained within relatively narrow margins" and "not maintained within relatively narrow margins" to the three categories "Peg" (94 countries in the 1988 volume), "Limited flexibility" (12 countries in the 1988 volume), and "More flexible arrangements" (44 countries in the 1988 volume). The peg category included the five subcategories, depending on whether the peg was to the US dollar, the British pound sterling, the French franc, other currencies, or a composite of currencies. The limited flexibility category included two subcategories depending on whether flexibility was limited with respect to a single currency or in a cooperative arrangement. The three subcategories included in the "More flexible arrangements" category included "Adjusted according to a set of indicators," "Other managed floating," and "Independently floating." The four categories for multiple exchange rate regimes remained unchanged.

There was a consolidation of subcategories in summary tables of the 1997 and 1998 volumes of the *Annual Report on Exchange Arrangements and Exchange Restrictions*. The pegged category only included the subcategories "Single currency" and "Composite of currencies" rather than the identification of the particular base currency as in earlier years. The more flexible arrangements category only included "Managed floating" and "Independently floating" rather than the three categories included in previous volumes. Subcategories were no longer included for the category "Flexibility limited." The four multiple exchange rate categories now appeared under the heading "Exchange rate structure" with the two categories "Dual exchange rates" and "Multiple exchange rates."

The most significant changes in the IMF reporting of exchange rate arrangements since the collapse of Bretton Woods began with the 1999 volume of *Annual Report on Exchange Arrangements and Exchange Restrictions*. First, and perhaps most important, reported exchange rate arrangements were based on a database established by the IMF that reflected its staff's assessments of countries' exchange rate policies rather than just relying on the reports of governments. Second, the "Exchange rate arrangements" categories were completely revamped. As shown in table 3.1, the eight new categories included "Exchange rate arrangement with no separate legal tender," "Currency board arrangement," "Conventional pegged arrangement," "Pegged exchange rate within horizontal bands," "Crawling peg," "Crawling band," "Managed float with no pre-announced path for the exchange rate," and "Independently floating." This structure of the summary table continues to the time of this writing.

The expansion of categories, from the two used from 1974 until 1987 that distinguished whether or not the exchange rate was "maintained within relatively narrow margins" to the currently used eight categories, reflects the increasing heterogeneity of exchange rate arrangements. This evolution of categories should bolster concerns about the comparability of the IMF exchange rate regime statistics over time that were raised above in the discussion on the early published views of the desirability of floating exchange rates. Concerns about the comparability of IMF exchange rate regime classification across time may also arise because of the switch from a purely *de jure* system before 1999 to a hybrid *de jure* and *de facto* system subsequently.

Despite these concerns, almost all research using exchange rate regime classifications up until the mid-1990s were based on IMF reporting. Recently, however, this has changed with the development of a number of *de facto* classification schemes. We next turn to a description of these.

3.2   *De facto* Exchange Rate Regime Classifications

The decision by the IMF to verify governments' stated exchange rate regimes, beginning with the 1999 volume of the *Annual Report on Exchange Arrangements and Exchange Restrictions*, reflects the fact that actual exchange rate behavior does not always matched proclaimed intentions. For two decades after the collapse of Bretton Woods, though, the *de jure* classification was the primary method researchers used to classify exchange rate behavior. This changed with the 1995 article "The Mirage of Fixed Exchange Rates" by Obstfeld and Rogoff. In this article the authors argue that a consideration of actual exchange rate behavior shows that few countries pegged for extended periods of time. Calvo and Reinhart (2002) challenged *de jure* coding from the opposite perspective. Their article, "Fear of Floating," used data on exchange rates, interest rates, and reserves to show that very few countries that declared that their currencies floated actually allowed for unfettered market determination of their exchange rates.

These articles highlight the need to examine *de facto* outcomes as opposed to *de jure* claims. Neither, however, provides a systematic classification of all potential country/year observations. In this section we first consider some issues that arise when developing a *de facto* exchange rate classification scheme. We then discuss three well-known exchange rate classification schemes.

3.2.1 *De facto* Classifications' Characteristics

There are a few fundamental characteristics of any *de facto* exchange rate classification scheme. One is the number of categories employed, a consideration that also occurs with a *de jure* scheme. Other characteristics, however, distinguish the construction of *de facto* schemes from that of *de jure* schemes. These include the rules used to assign observations to one or another category, and the data employed to implement these rules. In this section we address some issues on the characteristics of *de facto* exchange rate classification schemes.

The central issue that characterizes any *de facto* exchange rate classification scheme, or for that matter any *de jure* classification scheme, is the number of categories employed. Comparisons of classification schemes must address the comparability of these categories across schemes. And, as we have seen, this issue is even raised when considering results from a single classification scheme if it changes over time. The discussion in the previous section shows how the IMF *de jure* scheme evolved from the early use of essentially two categories (maintained or not maintained within narrow margins) to the more recent use of eight different categories. The wider range of categories allows for finer gradations, but it is not clear that there is a straightforward mapping that cleanly aggregates these newer categories into the smaller set of earlier categories.[3] This problem of comparability is even more acute when attempting to compare results across classification schemes.

The assignment of each country/time period observation to a particular category in a *de facto* exchange rate classification scheme presents another set of challenges, as noted in the quote by Jeffrey Frankel presented at the beginning of this chapter. The rules for assigning an observation to one category or another are not readily apparent when there are a wide number of categories. For example, what are the practical, measurable, data-based differences that would place a country in the category of "managed float" rather than "independently floating"? Even a seemingly straightforward bivariate classification scheme presents challenges when one attempts to assign observations to the two exhaustive categories, "pegged" and "not pegged." Can a pegged exchange rate move at all? Typically the answer is yes, and all of the classification schemes discussed below allow for some exchange rate movement in the "pegged" category. But how much can a pegged exchange rate move? In this case, history offers some guidance. Countries that kept their exchange rate within roughly ± 2 percent bands have been considered pegged, whether this range was for gold points during the gold standard, for dollar exchange rates during the Bretton Woods era, or for exchange rate bands around the central parity during the EMS.

While the ± 2 percent rule seems to be clear, its implementation raises the question of *which* exchange rate should be considered. Most countries peg to a single base; in those cases the base country may be determined through historical relationships or economic linkages. But basket pegs—where a country pegs to an index of other currencies—present a unique challenge. In most cases the weights in the basket are not declared, making verification nearly impossible.[4] Even when weights are declared, or the IMF's SDR (itself a basket) is the base, many declared basket pegs are really direct pegs to an individual currency (see chapter 7 for more discussion of this point). Thus many *de facto* classifications use an individual base regardless of whether the declared base is a basket.[5] Another consideration is the official exchange rate or, in countries with an important parallel exchange rate market, the black market rate. Once again, the role of the use of the classification scheme comes into play. The official rate may be the appropriate choice if one wants to ask whether a government that said it would peg its exchange rate actually kept its word. On the other hand, one might consider the behavior of the black market rate if that is more relevant for most transactions, and the focus of the analysis is the economic impact of exchange rate stability.

The data used to construct *de facto* exchange rate regime classification schemes need not be limited to exchange rates. Some authors (e.g., Levy-Yeyati and Sturzenegger 2003; Ghosh, Gulde, and Wolf 2002) argue that considering exchange rate data alone can lead to improper regime classification, since the exchange rate reflects both actions of the government and the underlying economic environment. Thus some classification schemes use data on interest rates and reserves to confirm that policy has had a hand in generating exchange rate stability. This is meant to ensure that the observation of limited exchange rate movement reflects a policy of a peg rather than merely a quiescent environment that has not put any pressure on the exchange rate to move. A problem with this approach, however, is that a perfectly credible exchange rate peg that is never challenged by the market may not require any government intervention, and therefore no reserve or interest rate responses. At the same time reserves and interest rates can move for many reasons, and their volatility may not reflect an effort to peg the exchange rate to the exclusion of other policy goals.

How important is the concern that spurious exchange rate stability leads to misclassifying regimes as pegs when in fact they just happen to look that way? One answer to this question draws on some results presented in Calvo and Reinhart (2002). They note that the probability that the bilateral exchange rate had a monthly change of less than 2.5 percent was roughly 60 to 70 percent during classic floats like the US dollar/DM rate, the US dollar/yen rate or the US dollar/Australia dollar rate. In these cases the probability of twelve straight months of changes smaller than 2.5 percent (in either direction) is between 0 and 1 percent. In addition, if a classification requires the tighter restriction of staying within the same ± 2 percent bands at all times during the year, the odds of a spuriously coded peg drop further. These statistics suggest that reserve or interest rate data are not vital in order to ensure against spuriously coding quiescent periods as a pegs.

A final consideration concerns moments of transition from one pegged rate to another. For example, suppose there is a one-time discrete devaluation of a currency. The exchange rate is pegged both before and after the devaluation. It is not really accurate to say that the exchange rate "floated" at the moment of the devaluation. On the other hand, the devaluation does mark a change from one exchange rate to another. As in other cases discussed above, the proper coding of this episode depends on the question addressed. One may want to count the year in which the devaluation occurs as a continuation of the peg if the exchange rate classification scheme is being used to address the link between the exchange rate and monetary autonomy. A study of the effects of a pegged exchange rate on trade, however, might find it more useful to distinguish the year in which a devaluation takes place from other years in which the exchange rate is pegged. In any event, the importance of this issue means that we will highlight how this feature of exchange rate behavior is coded in the classifications discussed below.

3.2.2   A Taxonomy of *De facto* Classifications

In this section we provide details on three influential and widely used *de facto* exchange rate classification schemes; those developed by Levy-Yeyati and Sturzenegger (2003), Reinhart and Rogoff (2004), and Shambaugh (2004). Each of these schemes was first used in an article published in a major scholarly journal, and each has been subsequently used extensively by other researchers.[6] The research question posed by each article differs and, partly for this reason, the resulting classification schemes also differ from each other in terms of the number and definition of categories and the assignment rules. The discussion below provides some context for the classification schemes by referring to the focus of the research that it was developed to address. This discussion highlights a point raised above, that choices made about particular attributes of an exchange rate regime classification scheme reflect its intended use.

Levy-Yeyati–Sturzenegger   One of the first attempts to generate a *de facto* classification in recent years is due to the work of Eduardo Levy-Yeyati and Federico Sturzenegger in their article "To Float or Fix: Evidence of the Effects of Exchange Rate Regimes on Growth," which was published in the September 2003 issue of the *American Economic Review*. The motive for their development of a *de facto* exchange rate classification scheme is that "the *de jure* classification based on the regime the governments *claim* to have in place ... ignores the fact that many alleged floats intervene in the exchange market to reduce exchange rate volatility, while some fixers devalue periodically to accommodate independent monetary policies" (p. 1175, emphasis in original).

While the title of this article suggests a bivariate classification, the Levy-Yeyati–Sturzenegger (hereafter LYS) scheme includes three categories; pegged, intermediate, and float. Assignment into these categories is based on cluster analysis using data on the change in the exchange rate, the volatility of the change in the exchange rate, and the change of reserves relative to a monetary aggregate. A year in which a country has low exchange rate volatility but large reserve volatility is categorized as pegged observation. A country that has a year in which there is a relatively constant (though nonzero) rate of change in the exchange rate and a high rate of change in reserves is categorized as an intermediate observation, as is a country with moderate volatility across all variables. A year in which a country has a high level of exchange rate volatility but a low level of reserve volatility is scored as a year of floating. A fourth category in the LYS scheme is called "inconclusive." Country–year observations are considered inconclusive in the cluster analysis when there is a constant exchange rate with low reserve volatility. Observations in this category are subsequently reclassified as pegged if there is no change in the exchange rate or, when there is a declared peg, the exchange rate moves by only a small amount.

The appeal of the LYS strategy is its emphasis on actual behavior over declared intentions. In addition, by analyzing the rate of change of the exchange rate and the reserves volatility, the LYS scheme separates countries that have crawling pegs or heavily managed exchange rates from other nonpegged countries. LYS do not view the exchange rate as sufficient information to separate pegs and floats, but instead combine exchange rate behavior with evidence of deliberate intervention. LYS, though, require intervention to take the form of changes in foreign reserves and draw no distinction between sterilized and unsterilized intervention. A country can maintain a pegged exchange rate without ever changing its reserves if it is willing to change its money supply or interest rates, and a country that changes reserves dramatically may not really be showing concrete commitment to its exchange rate peg if all intervention is sterilized. In addition highly unstable M2 may make the reserve ratio volatile even if there is little or no intervention. LYS state that theory suggests highly variable reserves for a country that is truly pegged, but if a country maintains its exchange rate by constantly changing its interest rate as, for example, Bahrain does, there will be no change in reserves. One could argue that such a country is exhibiting a much stronger commitment to its exchange rate than a country that continually exercises sterilized intervention—changing reserves but unwilling to allow its domestic money supply to be changed in defense of the exchange rate.

This problem becomes clear when one examines the countries that are originally listed as inconclusive by the cluster analysis. Countries such as Bahrain, the Bahamas, or Hong Kong, that have very strong fixed exchange rates against the dollar are not listed as pegged in the first round or even the second round of their exercises. This is because their reserves are not highly volatile; they simply adjust their money supply at all times to avoid the need for intervention, or they are so trusted in their regime that they are rarely challenged. The subsequent decision to code zero percent change countries picks up many of those left out but omits some undeclared *de facto* pegs. On the other hand, countries that intervene dramatically but break their peg, such as Ireland in the EMS crisis, or float but have sufficient reserves volatility, such as New Zealand, are listed as fixed. The LYS coding does not, however, include most years with a discrete devaluation from one fixed rate to another as a peg year because the change in the exchange rate relative to the change in reserves volatility is gauged as being too large to be a peg in those cases.

This system of classification was a large advance over simply relying on the *de jure* codes and has a number of appealing features. It tries to address intent as well as exchange rate behavior, and it tries to separate countries into three groups. This methodology can be quite useful for trying to separate countries that are dirty floats or that are heavily managed. On the other hand, it is not entirely transparent in that it does not yield a clear picture of what it means to be a peg or a float. There is no clear dividing line, but instead a combination of factors contributes to the decision. Furthermore the categorization of some observations as pegs after the cluster analysis classification rounds shows that the statistical methodology cannot itself pick up all the pegged countries. The methodology also codes significantly more pegs than other classifications (59 percent of observations are coded as pegs compared to a maximum of 46 percent in the other classifications). Finally, the data burden (requiring reserves as well as exchange rate data) makes the classification unavailable for many country/year observations.

Reinhart–Rogoff   Carmen Reinhart and Kenneth Rogoff created an exhaustive coding of exchange rate regimes that is largely based on the behavior of parallel, market-determined exchange rates. They present this classification scheme in "The Modern History of Exchange Rate Arrangements: A Reinterpretation" that was published in the February

2004 issue of the *Quarterly Journal of Economics*. They use this coding to reconsider experience with exchange rate regimes in the post–World War II period. For example, they argue that "Very frequently—roughly half the time for official pegs—we find that dual/parallel rates have been used as a form of 'backdoor' floating, albeit one usually accompanied by exchange controls" (p. 2). Thus they contend that *de facto* floating was very common during the Bretton Woods period. They also argue that after pegs, crawling pegs were the most common exchange rate arrangement during the modern period.

The "fine grid" version of the classification scheme includes fourteen categories, and the "coarse grid" aggregates these into five categories.[7] Of particular note is the inclusion of the separate coarse grid "Freely falling" category. This represents instances where depreciation is rapid and sustained and where inflation is high. Roughly 10 percent of all observations are included in this category (roughly 15 percent of all nonpegged observations). Reinhart and Rogoff argue that the inclusion of the "Freely floating" episodes in a broader floating category muddies efforts to discern differences in economic performance across categories.

Observations are assigned to categories based on the odds of the parallel (not official) exchange rate being outside a band over a five-year rolling window. The authors argue that the parallel rate best demonstrates the true stance of the government and that any classification system that fails to distinguish between a unified rate system and one with parallel rates is "fundamentally flawed." They also state that parallel and dual exchange rates were widely prevalent and "enormously important not only in developing countries but in virtually all the European countries up until the late 1950s, and sometimes well beyond" (p. 2).

The five-year rolling window represents an effort to avoid spurious switches in exchange rate regimes due to devaluations or brief periods of volatility (or brief periods of quiescence). This strategy makes it difficult to directly compare this classification scheme with those based on annual data, since the Reinhart–Rogoff classification for a country in a particular year may not match the behavior of that country in that year if it changes regimes frequently. This strategy also implies that a country that pegs sporadically may be classified as a crawling peg throughout the sample when, in truth, it pegs in some years and floats in others. Such behavior might be one source of the prevalence of crawling pegs in this classification system. A third implication of the use of a rolling window is that it allows for far fewer switches in regimes, and consequently lengthier peg and float spells because it smoothes over some transitions.

In some ways the Reinhart–Rogoff classification merges information on capital controls and exchange rate regimes (a point alluded to in their *QJE* article and one also discussed in Shambaugh 2004). A country that has a constant official exchange rate but a volatile black market rate is likely one that has stabilized its official rate via controls on trading or other capital control mechanisms. Such a country may have a plausibly fixed official exchange rate, but will not be coded as such in Reinhart–Rogoff because the parallel rate is not constant.

The Reinhart–Rogoff classification scheme is best suited for analyses that focus on transactions, especially if those transactions tended to take place at the black market rate, which, they argue, "is often the most economically meaningful rate" (p. 2). On the other hand, this classification scheme may be less well suited for studies of central bank commitments made, since countries make no attempt to stabilize the black market rate. When Malaysia institutes capital controls to defend its peg (and presumably the black market rate moves away from the peg), a researcher would have to determine whether this still represents a peg, since the country claims to have maintained its fixed exchange rate and in fact the official rate has not budged, or whether the capital controls represent a deviation from pegging.

Shambaugh   Jay Shambaugh created an exchange rate regime classification scheme in the spirit of that presented by Obstfeld and Rogoff (1995) to consider the empirical relevance of the policy trilemma. The first work using this classification scheme was his article "The Effect of Fixed Exchange Rates on Monetary Policy" published in the same February 2004 issue of the *Quarterly Journal of Economics* as the Reinhart–Rogoff article. The results in the article show that the monetary policies of countries with pegged exchange rates were significantly linked to the monetary policies of the base country to which they pegged, while there was no significant link between the monetary policies of countries that did not peg and the monetary policies of the respective large countries that would be the most likely base country in a pegged system.

Unlike the other two exchange rate regime classification schemes described above, the Shambaugh classification is bivariate and assigns annual country/year observations into either a peg or a nonpeg category. The assignment is based on whether the official exchange rate stays within a ± 2 percent band against the base currency. The base country is the currency to which a country pegs or would peg if it were pegging.[8] This means that a truly multilateral basket peg, one that is not merely a veil for a *de facto* single currency peg, may not be categorized as a peg if it has no true base.[9] Like Reinhart–Rogoff, this classification relies only on the exchange rate to code observations. Unlike Reinhart–Rogoff, it is the official exchange rate, not a parallel rate that is used, because government policies affect the official rate. While it only used the exchange rate volatility to code observations, the classification required two years of staying within a ± 2 percent band to ensure that no observations that randomly lacked volatility were spuriously coded as pegs.

One benefit of this classification scheme is that it allows for relatively straightforward modification in order to best address particular research questions. For example, Obstfeld, Shambaugh, and Taylor (2008) add a third category, soft pegs, which are exclusive from hard pegs. Soft pegs represent observations where the exchange rate stays within ± 5 percent bands, but not within ± 2 percent bands. Importantly, under this classification scheme, classic floats, such as the US dollar against the yen or the deutsche mark, are never classified as soft pegs, which should reduce concerns that countries that allow a fair bit of flexibility are accidentally classified as soft pegs rather than nonpegs.

The original Shambaugh classification scheme does not record a one-time realignment as a break in a peg. This is consistent with his research question, since theory suggests that the exchange rate regime continues to restrict monetary policy when there is a one-time discrete devaluation to a new peg. In practical terms, the rule that was used was that any exchange rate that had a percentage change of zero in eleven out of twelve months is considered fixed.[10] In a modified version of this classification scheme developed to consider the characteristics of fixed and floating exchange rate spells, Klein and Shambaugh (2008) do not count an observation with a discrete devaluations as a peg since this would artificially raise the persistence of pegs (see chapter 4).

Single-year pegs were dropped in the original Shambaugh (2004) classification scheme to ensure that an observation of a stable exchange rate reflects government policy rather than just a quiescent environment. But, in another example of modifying the classification scheme to make it appropriate for the research question, Klein and Shambaugh (2008) include single-year pegs in order to gauge more accurately the length of spells of pegged exchange rates. The original Shambaugh (2004) scheme that eliminates single-year pegs automatically limits the minimum length of pegs to two years. As discussed in the next chapter, there is fairly good evidence that nearly all single-year pegs are in fact legitimate pegs and do not reflect a spurious lack of volatility.

The original Shambaugh coding scheme, as well as its modified versions, is fairly straightforward. It also has the virtue of matching our basic intuition of the properties of a fixed exchange rate since a country is categorized as pegged if its exchange rate stays relatively stable. The use of official exchange rate data allows for wider coverage and easier updating than a classification system requiring parallel rates, or data on interest rates and central bank reserves. Of course, the trade-off here is that this classification system may not be the most appropriate for countries for which the official exchange rate is not the most economically relevant. But, for those countries where the official exchange rate is economically relevant, this system also has the advantage of an annual frequency which matches up well with variables typically used in studies that investigate the effect of exchange rate regimes on trade, monetary policy, and so forth.

3.3   Correlation of Different Exchange Rate Regime Classifications

The previous two sections present four exchange rate classification schemes with different sets of categories and widely different methods for assigning observations to these categories. As discussed, one reason that there is such variety in these classification schemes is that each was developed to address different questions. Still it is reasonable to expect a fair amount of agreement across these schemes, since at their core they all represent efforts to capture the same behavior. In this section we investigate whether in fact this agreement exists.

A comparison of these exchange rate regime classifications requires a mapping of categories across schemes. The common denominator, so to speak, is the distinction between pegged and nonpegged exchange rate regimes, since the Shambaugh classification includes only these two categories. Thus we will compare the results across classification schemes by compressing the categories in the IMF coding, the LYS scheme, and the Reinhart–Rogoff classification system into this binary set. We define the categories of pegs, limited flexibility, and coopera-

Table 3.2
Percentage agreement of various pegged and nonpegged coding methodologies

	IMF	LYS	RR	Shambaugh
IMF	100%			
LYS	74%	100%		
RR	81%	73%	100%	
Shambaugh	86%	80%	82%	100%
Pegged	41%	58%	33%	45%

Note: Shown are percentages of observations where different codings yield the same result as one another. All coding is collapsed to a binary peg and nonpeg coding. The last row shows the share of observations which are coded as peg by each classification. Years: 1973–2004.

tive arrangements in the IMF coding as pegged regimes, and the other categories constitute the nonpegged category. The Levy-Yeyati-Sturzenegger scheme includes a pegged and a floating category, and we include the intermediate category in the set of observations coded as nonpegged for the purposes of this comparison. The set of pegged exchange rates for the Reinhart–Rogoff classification system is the first coarse grid category,[11] which consists of the four fine grid categories "No separate legal tender," "Preannounced peg or currency board arrangement," "Preannounced horizontal band that is narrower than or equal to ±2 percent," and "De facto peg."

Table 3.2 presents the percentage of observations for which binary versions of each classification scheme agree with one another.[12] The statistics in this table show that the results from the four classification schemes are broadly similar. The degree of agreement varies between 73 and 86 percent. This is clearly better than random (where the expected degree of agreement is 50 percent), but there is still a fair amount of disagreement. The biggest distinctions are between the LYS scheme and both the IMF and the Reinhart–Rogoff classifications. Also, as shown in the bottom row of the table, the LYS scheme codes observations as pegs far more often than the other three schemes, while the Reinhart–Rogoff codes observations as pegs far less often. As discussed in the previous section, the LYS scheme generates more peg observations, since reserve volatility can lead to an observation being recorded as a peg even if the exchange rate moves considerably. Alternatively, in most cases large discrete devaluations or revaluations will be considered floats in LYS as the exchange rate volatility will dominate the reserves volatility, but these observations are often

Table 3.3
Percentage agreement of various pegged, intermediate, and float coding methodologies

	IMF	LYS	RR	Shambaugh
IMF	100%			
LYS	59%	100%		
RR	59%	55%	100%	
Shambaugh	68%	65%	65%	100%
Intermediate	18%	19%	38%	22%

Note: Shown are percentages of observations where different codings yield the same result as one another. All coding is collapsed to three categories: pegged, intermediate, and float. The last row shows the share of observations which are coded as intermediate by each classification. Years: 1973–2004.

considered pegs in the Reinhart–Rogoff, Shambaugh, and *de jure* codings. The Reinhart–Rogoff classification codes proportionally more observations as nonpegs than the other three schemes in large part because of their use of the parallel rate exchange rate. Thus, if the official rate is stable, LYS, Shambaugh, and the *de jure* codings may all show a peg that Reinhart–Rogoff designate a float.

Alternatively, we can look at agreement for more finely split categories. Here we can use the three-way classification of peg, intermediate, and float. We will use the soft peg category to augment the Shambaugh classification to make an intermediate category. In this case the expected agreement is lower, and random allocation would now only generate agreements 33 percent of the time. Table 3.3 shows that, while agreement is certainly higher than 33 percent, there is a fair bit of disagreement across the classifications (68 percent is the highest rate of agreement). The table also shows the percentage of observations that are coded as intermediate. Reinhart–Rogoff show almost twice as many intermediate observations as others.[13] This contributes considerably to their disagreement with some other classifications. The more finely the bins are split, the more difficult it is for the classifications to match. In particular, the line between intermediate and float has no clear division, making it difficult to find agreement there. Thus an advantage of using a binary coding is we may more clearly know what we mean by peg and nonpeg, and different codings would more frequently agree. Alternatively, we lose some information by condensing intermediates and floats into one category.

The lack of agreement between *de jure* and *de facto* codings raises the question of why countries declare inaccurately. Certainly one can attribute some miscoding to aspirational declarations. A country may want to peg and even very briefly try, but not seriously commit to it, leading to a *de jure* peg but *de facto* float. However, there are many disagreements that persist, including many long-run pegs that are not declared. Alesina and Wagner (2006) investigate why some countries behave more restrictively than they declare, or vice versa, and find that countries with weak institutions tend to declare pegs but fail to maintain them while those with strong institution frequently have tighter *de facto* regimes than they declare. Genberg and Swoboda (2005) discuss reasons why a government may peg an exchange rate without declaring that as its goal, which suggests that *de jure* declared regimes may not really represent the true goals or actual intent of a government. Thus a country that fixes despite declaring a float is not necessarily breaking a commitment, but trying to send a particular signal.

The lack of agreement across *de facto* exchange rate classification schemes may be viewed as an indication of an inability of these schemes to accurately code country behavior.[14] As this discussion shows, however, disagreements often stem from efforts to address different questions. Thus these differences are not simply a difference in measuring pegs, but a difference in defining them.[15] The Klein–Shambaugh classification measures direct peg spells to consider the length of peg spells and float spells. Shambaugh (2004) measures annual coding of exchange rate behavior based on well-established band criteria as well as allowing discrete devaluations so as to prevent artificially breaking up a consistent regime in an effort to test the monetary policy implications of pegging. Reinhart–Rogoff's classification both smoothes over time to determine regimes as opposed to spells and uses the black market rate—hence merging both exchange rate choices and capital control choices in an effort to consider the implications of policy regime choices broader than that of the choice of peg or float alone. Levy-Yeyati and Sturzenegger use reserves behavior in addition to exchange rate behavior to better distinguish intermediate spells from float spells, while possibly allowing somewhat volatile but heavily managed exchange rates to be considered pegs. Thus the classification scheme one may choose depends on the question posed; those interested in whether a country is pegged and stable in a given year may use the Shambaugh classification scheme, those interested in absolute stability of the peg may choose the Klein–Shambaugh coding, those interested in overarching policy regimes smoothed over time could choose to refer to the Reinhart–Rogoff coding, and those exploring intermediates versus floats or intervention behavior may refer to LYS.

3.4   Conclusion

Exchange rate classification is neither a simple nor a trivial task. Cataloging behavior that runs across a broad spectrum into discrete categories requires some sort of rule and will invariably occasionally divide countries that behave somewhat similarly into different bins. At the same time, any tests that compare outcomes across regimes will inherently depend on categorizing the observations properly. Different techniques provide different insights into the exchange rate regime behavior of countries, and their disagreements should not simply be viewed as one being right or wrong. We will typically use the Shambaugh classification (or one of its modifications, depending on the research question) as our core classification. An advantage of such a procedure, as opposed to looking at relative volatility benchmarks is that this definition of a peg (within a 2 percent band) is clear, invariant over time, and matches the historical definitions of pegs such as the gold points in the gold standard, the bands in Bretton Woods and the EMS. The coding is also available for nearly all years due to its lesser data requirements. Other classifications may be useful, though, depending on the research question.

4 The Dynamics of Exchange Rate Regimes

Because things are the way they are, things will not stay the way they are.
—Bertolt Brecht

The economic consequences of the choice of an exchange rate regime, as outlined in chapter 2, represent one of the classic lines of inquiry in international finance. As discussed in chapter 3, with the advent of the modern era, a wide set of experiences with exchange rate regimes emerged. These experiences over a four-decade time period offer a rich tableau for investigating the effects of exchange rate regimes on trade, growth, stability, and other economic outcomes. But these inquiries are partially predicated on the durability of countries' exchange rate regimes.[1] For example, it is difficult to imagine fixed exchange rates having an impact by anchoring expectations if they break so frequently that people do not take them seriously, or if they are so fleeting that they have no consequences for more persistent variables like inflation or trade flows.

In this chapter we investigate the dynamic behavior of exchange rate regimes. We present data on the duration of both fixed exchange rate regimes and flexible exchange rate regimes. We also go beyond this static analysis and discuss the prevalence of flipping from a fixed exchange rate regime to a flexible exchange rate regime, and then back to a fixed exchange rate regime. This dynamic analysis is important for a complete characterization of exchange rate regimes in the modern era.

The analysis presented in this chapter challenges the simple view that a country is either a "fixer" or a "floater." This was a reasonable characterization of most countries during the gold standard period, and even in the Bretton Woods period. The modern era has, however, included much more switching than in these earlier periods. For example, almost half of the fixed exchange rate episodes that appear in the main data set used in this chapter do not last more than two years. In a similar fashion there are also a large number of short-lived floating exchange rate episodes. The prevalence of these short-lived fixed and floating episodes means that switching is common.

This is not to say, however, that the modern era is an anarchic period where the terms "fixed" and "floating" have ceased to be relevant. A central result presented in this chapter is that the expected duration of a peg increases dramatically if it survives past two years. Consequently, at any one time the set of countries that are pegged includes a large proportion of those with a peg lasting for a relatively long duration. Similarly, the set of floating exchange rate episodes includes a large number of short-lived episodes and a smaller number of countries with persistently floating exchange rates.

The existence of a significant number of stable, meaningful exchange rate regimes runs counter to some recent influential research. The title of the article by Obstfeld and Rogoff, "The Mirage of Fixed Exchange Rates" (1995), reflects their conclusion that long-lived currency pegs are rare and only found among small countries. They write "literally only a handful of countries in the world today have continuously maintained tightly fixed exchange rates against any currency for five years or more" (p. 87).[2] On the other side of the ledger, Calvo and Reinhart (2002) argue that many countries whose governments claim that they allow their currencies to be determined by market forces actually intervene in currency markets to manage exchange rates, a behavior that gives the title to their article "Fear of Floating."

One reason that the "mirage" of fixed exchange rates and governments' "fear of floating" resonated with the research community is that these results seem to accord with strands of earlier research that found little role for exchange rate regimes in determining major macroeconomic and aggregate outcomes beyond the real exchange rate.[3] An important initial contribution in one line of research is the work of Baxter and Stockman (1989). They show that there is no significant distinction in terms of consumption variability or the variability of GDP growth between the experience of countries that had fixed exchange rate regimes and those that had floating exchange rate regimes when using *de jure* codes to mark different exchange rate regimes. Another strand of research failed to uncover a strong effect of exchange rate variability (and, implicitly, of exchange rate regimes) on bilateral international trade flows.[4] The Obstfeld–Rogoff and Calvo–Reinhart results were viewed as consistent with these results; why would the exchange rate regime matter for macroeconomic outcomes, or even for the direction and size of trade flows, if pegs are but a "mirage" and if flexible regimes are not really characterized by floating exchange rates? Thus the message from these two lines of research, one that considers the exchange rate experience with exchange rate regimes and the other that examines the effects of exchange rate regimes on economic performance, is that exchange rate regimes are largely inconsequential.

Much of the rest of this book takes issue with these points of view. Recent research, discussed in later chapters, has found a large number of economic outcomes that vary across exchange rate regime. In this chapter we lay some of the groundwork for this subsequent discussion by analyzing the dynamic behavior of exchange rate regimes. We begin in the next section by defining an exchange rate spell and presenting the distributions of fixed exchange rate spells and floating exchange rate spells. We show that these distributions are similar, with both having a large number of short-lived spells and a smaller number of long-lived spells. An important implication is the flipping of pegged rates, that is, the end of a peg is often followed by the reformation of a new peg. Section 4.2 then presents a statistical analysis of the duration of flexible and fixed exchange rate spells that considers the likelihood of the continuation of a spell for another year, conditional on its survival up to that point. This characterization of the dynamics of exchange rate regimes in the modern era offers a different picture than either the classic stability that marked earlier eras or what one would expect from the results claiming that fixed exchange rates are merely a "mirage."

4.1   Fixed, Floating, and Flipping Exchange Rate Regimes

The basic unit of observation for the analysis of the dynamics of exchange rate regimes in this chapter is a spell. We consider two types of spells, a fixed spell and a floating spell. A fixed spell represents one or more consecutive years during which the exchange rate stays within a narrow range in each year (± 2 percent from one month to the next, as well as ± 2 percent over the course of a year). A floating spell represents one or more consecutive years during which the exchange rate does not stay within that narrow range in any of the years of the spell. Both fixed exchange rate spells and floating exchange rate spells are characterized by the number of years they last. The distributions of the durations of fixed and floating exchange rate spells represent the number of spells of each level of annual duration, from one year up through the full span of thirty-two years, since the data set covers the years 1973 to 2004.

This ±2 percent rule recalls the *de facto* Shambaugh classification scheme described in the previous chapter. The main classification scheme used in this chapter is, in fact, a modified version of that classification scheme, one used in Klein and Shambaugh (2008). In this scheme, as in the Shambaugh scheme, a country is classified as having a pegged exchange rate in a particular year if its official exchange rate against the appropriate base country stays within a ±2 percent band both from one month to the next as well as over the entire year. The two differences between the Klein–Shambaugh scheme and the Shambaugh scheme described in chapter 3 are that the former allows for one-year pegs, and it also counts a one-time realignment as a break in a peg. We include single-year pegs to avoid artificially increasing the durability of pegs. Had we only classified pegs as observations that had limited exchange rate movements for two or more years, we would have pegs look strikingly more persistent.[5] Similarly, we view realignments as breaks in a peg to prevent falsely inflating the durability of pegs.

Table 4.1 presents some basic statistics for the exchange rate regime data based on the Klein–Shambaugh classification scheme.[6] This data set represents the experience of 125 countries over the period 1973 to 2004.[7] We classify the 21 countries that were members of the OECD in 1973 as the subset of industrial countries. Of the 3,924 country–year observations in this data set, 48 percent are pegs.[8] Pegs are more prevalent among developing countries than among industrial countries, with 49 percent of the developing country–year observations representing pegs but only 39 percent of the industrial country–year observations representing pegs. There are 793 exchange rate spells, with 395 floating spells and 398 peg spells. The mean duration of peg spells is 4.7 years, and the mean duration of float spells is 5.2 years. These means are greater than the respective median durations, which are 2 years for both peg spells and float spells.

The fact that the means of the duration of both peg spells and float spells are much larger than their respective medians suggests that both distributions are skewed to the right. The histograms of these distributions, presented in figures 4.1 and 4.2, confirm this. These histograms

Table 4.1
Basic statistics on fixed spells and float spells

	Number of annual observations	Number of countries	Percentage of annual fixed observations	Number of peg spells	Median duration of peg spells	Mean of peg spells	Number of float spells	Median duration of float spells	Mean of float spells
Full sample	3,924	125	48	398	2	4.7	395	2	5.2
Industrial countries	671	21	39	56	2	4.6	61	3	6.7
Developing countries	3,253	104	49	342	2	4.7	334	2	5.0

Note: Durations expressed in years. Sample includes countries with populations >400,000. United States is not in the sample; industrial countries are those with IFS code <200 but not Turkey nor South Africa; developing countries are those with IFS code >200 plus Turkey and South Africa. Currency unions are not included in sample. Years: 1973–2004.

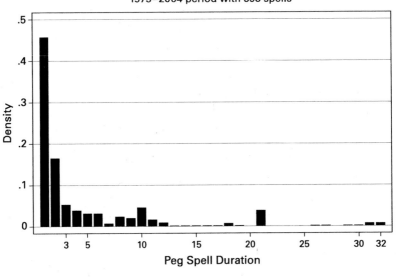

Figure 4.1
Distribution of peg durations, 1973 to 2004, with 398 spells.

of pegged exchange rate spells (figure 4.1) and floating exchange rate spells (figure 4.2) show a remarkable similarity. Both types of spells are characterized by a high proportion of short spells, with one-year spells making up a little under half of fixed spells and more than a third of floating spells. The visual impressions one gets from these figures are confirmed by the statistics in table 4.2. These statistics show that 56 percent of the peg spells and 64 percent of the float spells survive for at least two years; of course, this means that 44 percent of the peg spells and 36 percent of the float spells last for only one year. But not all spells are fleeting. Somewhat less than a third of the peg spells (30 percent), and a little more than a third of the float spells (34 percent), last for at least five years.

The view that pegs frequently break is not uncommon, and has been known for some time.[9] The result that floats are as equally fleeting as pegs is more novel. For example, the fourth column of table 4.2 shows that only 48 percent of float spells last three years. The implication is the prevalence of "flipping." Flipping occurs in both directions; a country that experiences the end of a fixed exchange rate spell begins a new fixed spell after a short experience with a floating exchange rate, and,

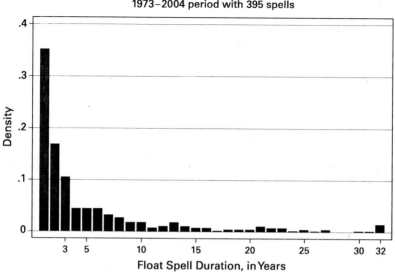

Figure 4.2
Distribution of float durations, 1973 to 2004, with 395 spells.

Table 4.2
Fixed spell and float spell survival statistics, by spell

	Peg spells			Float spells		
	All countries	Industrial	Devel-oping	All countries	Industrial	Devel-oping
At least 2 years	56%	56%	56%	64%	73%	63%
At least 3 years	40%	33%	42%	48%	54%	47%
At least 4 years	35%	33%	35%	38%	42%	38%
At least 5 years	30%	33%	30%	34%	37%	33%
>5 years	28%	33%	27%	30%	32%	30%
Total spells	365	55	310	365	59	306

Note: Sample includes countries with populations >400,000. United States is not in the sample; industrial countries are those with IFS code <200 but not Turkey nor South Africa; developing countries are those with IFS code >200 plus Turkey and South Africa. Currency unions are not included in sample. Years: 1973–2004.

Table 4.3
Longest fixed and float episodes (by country)

Length	Pegs		Length	Floats	
0	7	6%	0	3	2%
1	8	6%	1	22	18%
2	19	15%	2	5	4%
3	6	5%	3	7	6%
4	7	6%	4	0	0%
5+	78	62%	5+	88	70%

This table shows the distribution of the longest peg and float episodes by country. There are 125 countries included. For example, 7 countries never peg, 6 have a longest peg of 3 years, and 78 have one of 5 years or more; 3 never float, and 88 float for 5 or more consecutive years at some point in the sample. Years: 1973–2004.

in a similar fashion, a country may have a short experience with a fixed exchange rate between two floating exchange rate spells. This view, that many countries flip back and forth in their exchange rate arrangements, differs from the conventional view that most countries are characterized as being "fixers" or "floaters." It also importantly contrasts with crisis models which describe the end of a pegged exchange rate, but not what follows that collapse. Our results suggest that crises are simply part of the evolution of the exchange rate regime, and that a re-peg following a crisis is quite likely.

A country might flip from a peg to a float and back to a peg again because of an inability to maintain a consistent exchange rate regime. But if this inability to maintain a consistent policy was pervasive, we would expect to find relatively few instances of long-lived spells. The statistics presented in table 4.3, which presents the longest peg duration and the longest float duration for each of the 125 countries in the sample, shows that this is not the case. As shown in that table, a large number of countries maintain at least one fairly long-lived peg and at least one fairly long-lived float episode in the modern era. Almost 70 percent of the countries in the sample have peg spells of four or more years, and 70 percent have float spells of five or more years. Of course, we cannot know the intentions of the 12 percent of countries that either never peg or have no peg spells that last more than one year, or those of the 20 percent of countries that either never float or have no float spell that lasts for more than one year. It seems unlikely, however, that Israel could not peg for more than one year (its maximum peg is one year) or that Syria could not float for more than one year (its maximum float is one year). Rather, these outcomes seem to reflect policy choices. Similarly, Canada never pegged for more than two years at a time, but certainly other large industrial countries (e.g., France, which has stayed within its EMS bands every year since 1987) have been able to do so.

The result reported in table 4.3, that 78 countries (out of 125) had a peg of at least five years, seems to be at odds with the view that pegs are, in the words of Obstfeld–Rogoff (1995), a "mirage." And while some of the statistics presented in table 4.2 support the notion that pegs are short lived, for example the fact that over 70 percent of fixed spells in the modern era have not lasted for more than five years, this statistic also means that a substantial proportion do last for an extended period. This contrasts with the "remarkably small" (p. 87) number of durable pegs identified by Obstfeld–Rogoff, who list only six "Major Economies with Open Capital Markets" that successfully maintained a peg for at least five years at the time they wrote their article in June 1995 (these countries are Austria, Hong Kong, Luxembourg, the Netherlands, Saudi Arabia, and Thailand).[10]

How is it that over a quarter of our sample of 365 fixed rate spells, including almost a third of the sample of 55 fixed rate spells from industrial countries, have a duration of more than five years while Obstfeld–Rogoff (1995) present only a "handful" of spells with this duration? One reason is a difference in samples, since we include some countries omitted by Obstfeld–Rogoff who considered them too small, in terms of population, to include in their analysis. The more important reason, however, concerns the timing of their study. Their statistics on the duration of fixed exchange rates are based on a snapshot of experience of the duration of fixed exchange rates at one particular date, June 1, 1995. This was a distinctive moment since many long-standing pegs had ended within the previous few years in the wake of the 1992 EMS crisis, the 1994 Tequila crisis, and the 1994 devaluation of the CFA countries against the franc. In fact their article was partly motivated by these events.

After 1995, many of the countries that saw their pegged exchange rates break reestablished new fixed rates. As a result there were just as many long-lived pegs in 2000 as there were in 1990. Thus the time when Obstfeld–Rogoff conducted their analysis was a low point for long-lived fixed exchange rates. This is demonstrated in figure 4.3. This figure shows that 1994 to 1998 was the low point of long-lived pegs with only an average 17 in those years (out of roughly 125 countries in the sample)[11] as compared to 36 long-lived pegs in 2000 and an

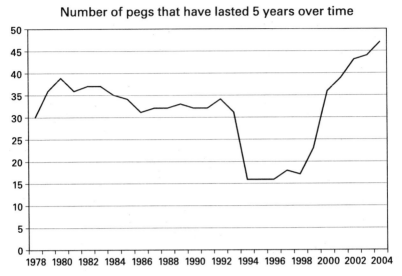

Figure 4.3
Figure shows the number of countries in a peg that has lasted for five or more years at that moment. The panel is roughly balanced with between 122 and 125 countries in the sample. Currency unions are eliminated from the sample with the exception of spells that began as pegs and converted to currency unions (which include some EMU observations).

average of 32 long-lived pegs in the modern era.[12] Thus a focus on exchange rate pegging since 1973, rather than the situation in 1995, and on peg spells, rather than countries, alters the impression one has of the durability of exchange rate pegs.

The results reported so far are based on the Klein–Shambaugh *de facto* exchange rate regime classification scheme. We close this section by offering some results that are based on the other classification schemes. As we will see, differences in spell statistics across classification schemes reflect differences in the way these classification schemes are constructed, as discussed in detail in the previous chapter.

Table 4.4 presents statistics of exchange rate spells that are created through the use of the Reinhart–Rogoff, Shambaugh, and IMF classification schemes discussed in chapter 3.[13] Spells for the Reinhart–Rogoff and IMF schemes are constructed by mapping the respective multiple categories into a bivariate fixed/float classification.[14] This table also reproduces the spell statistics based on the Klein–Shambaugh classification scheme that are presented in table 4.1 to facilitate comparisons across all four schemes.

Table 4.4
Statistics on fixed spells and float spells across classifications

		Annual observations	Countries in sample	Peg observations (%)	Peg spells	Peg median	Peg mean	Float spells	Float median	Float mean
Full sample	RR	3,202	104	34.01	91	8	11.82	107	20	20.31
	JS	3,924	125	46.02	199	5	9.16	191	7	11.09
	DJ	3,924	125	42.03	167	5	9.69	148	14.5	15.17
	KS	3,924	125	47.53	398	2	4.67	395	2	5.21
Industrial countries	RR	671	21	31.74	16	10.5	13.00	20	25	24.00
	JS	671	21	35.62	31	6	7.55	36	5.5	12.00
	DJ	671	21	41.23	21	8	12.52	20	23	20.10
	KS	671	21	39.34	56	2	4.63	61	3	6.67
Developing countries	RR	2,531	83	34.61	75	8	11.57	87	20	19.46
	JS	3,253	104	48.17	168	5	9.46	155	8	10.88
	DJ	3,253	104	42.19	146	5	9.28	128	14	14.40
	KS	3,253	104	49.22	342	2	4.68	334	2	4.95

Note: RR = Reinhart–Rogoff coding; JS = Shambaugh coding; DJ = IMF *de jure* coding; KS = Klein–Shambaugh coding, reproducing statistics from table 4.1. Years: 1973–2004.

Table 4.4 shows that all four classifications have comparable numbers of country–year observations. There is a big distinction, however, in the number of spells identified. The fewest number of spells are generated by the Reinhart–Rogoff coding, and the most by the Klein–Shambaugh coding. The relatively small number of spells based on the Reinhart–Rogoff coding is a consequence of their use of a five-year rolling window, rather than purely annual observations, as discussed in chapter 3. An implication of this is that spells based on the Reinhart–Rogoff classification scheme have much longer duration than those based on the other three schemes, with the median durations of eight years for peg spells and twenty years for float spells. The IMF exchange rate regime classification scheme results in the next fewest number of spells, and the next longest average durations. This reflects an aspect of the *de jure* classification; countries often do not change the declaration of their exchange rate regime, even if pegs break and reform, or if pegs are intermittent. The median durations of fixed and float spells based on the Shambaugh classification scheme are also longer than those based on the Klein–Shambaugh classification scheme, since it does not count the switch from one parity to another as a break in a fixed exchange rate spell, and it also requires that pegs last for more than one year.

This is an important example where the fact that different classifications may generate different results does not mean the results are not robust. Instead, it emphasizes the importance of picking a classification that is appropriate to the question being studied. For example, trying to analyze the switching in and out of exchange rate regimes with the Reinhart–Rogoff classification would not make sense as they are deliberately trying to smooth over switches to look at longer run episodes rather than spells.

4.2   Survival of Fixed and Floating Exchange Rate Spells

Tables 4.1 and 4.2 report the mean and median durations of fixed and floating exchange rate spells, and the proportions of spells that last for at least a certain number of years. These statistics provide an overview of the characteristics of spells. They do not, however, offer the most useful information for people who want to know the likely permanence of a fixed exchange rate over a time horizon that may be relevant for many economic decisions. For example, if someone in a country with a dollar peg has signed a contract for purchasing goods from the

United States, and the contracted price is in dollars, that person would want to know the likelihood that the specific dollar peg still holds at the time in the future when the goods are delivered and payment is made. While the median and mean lengths of fixed exchange rate spells offer some guidance along these lines, a better gauge of the likelihood of the continuation of that peg takes into account other information, including the number of years that the peg has already been in effect and, perhaps, features of the peg relationship (e.g., the base country) and characteristics of the pegging country itself (e.g., whether it is an industrial country).

The previous section provided us with simple odds that did not utilize all the information an economic agent would have. Those are unconditional probabilities. The common thread running through all three sets of results in this section is the conditioning of probabilities of the continuation of a fixed or floating exchange rate spell. These conditional probabilities offer views of peg and float spells that more closely reflects how economic agents who must make decisions at a particular moment view the likely permanence of a peg, or the continuation of a policy of allowing the exchange rate to float.

We begin by presenting statistics on the likelihood of switching from a peg to a float, or vice versa, at different time horizons. These statistics offer a different perspective on the duration of pegs and floats than that afforded by the results presented in the previous section. We then discuss the likelihood that an existing fixed exchange rate peg lasts for one more year, and the chance that a country that has been allowing its currency to float will continue to do so for another year. We show that these probabilities change with the number of years already spent in a fixed or floating exchange rate spell, respectively, through the use of duration analysis. Duration analysis provides estimates of the conditional likelihood of the continuation of a spell as a function of the number of years the spell has already run.[15]

4.2.1 Rates of Switching

We first consider the likelihood of an economy being in a fixed spell or a floating spell at a particular moment, conditional on whether it had a pegged or a floating exchange rate at different times prior to that moment. Table 4.5 reports that the probability of a country having a fixed exchange rate in year t, if it had a fixed exchange rate in the previous year, is 82 percent. (Of course, this implies that the chance a peg breaks, or of having a floating exchange rate conditional on having a

Table 4.5
Probability of switching spell state next year, and of remaining in same spell 1, 3, or 5 years in future, annual data

Years[a]	All countries	Industrial	Developing	Years[a]	All countries	Industrial	Developing
Float(t)|Peg($t-1$)	18%	17%	19%	Peg(t)|Float($t-1$)	17%	13%	18%
Peg(t)|Peg($t-1$)	82%	83%	81%	Float(t)|Float($t-1$)	83%	87%	82%
Peg(t)|Peg($t-3$)	66%	71%	65%	Float(t)|Float($t-3$)	65%	70%	64%
Peg(t)|Peg($t-5$)	55%	62%	54%	Float(t)|Float($t-5$)	54%	61%	52%

Note: Sample includes countries with populations >400,000. The U.S. is not in the sample; industrial countries are those with IFS code <200 but exclude Turkey and South Africa; developing countries are those with IFS code >200 plus Turkey and South Africa. Currency unions are not included in the sample. Samples begin in 1973 and are up through 2003 for the next year's conditional probabilities, up through 2001 for 3 years' included in the sample. Samples begin in 1973 and are up through 2003 for the next year's conditional probabilities, up through 2001 for 3 years' hence conditional probabilities, and 1999 for 5 years' hence conditional probabilities. Countries must remain in same state continuously; that is, Peg(t)\|Peg($t-3$) signifies staying pegged in ($t-3$), ($t-2$), ($t-1$) and (t). Countries that flip in and out of a state are considered to have broken the state.

a. Years in peg spell or in float spells.

fixed exchange rate in the prior year is 100 percent − 82 percent = 18 percent.) The comparable probability of having a floating exchange rate in a given year, conditional on having a float in the prior year, is 83 percent. This suggests both fixed and floating exchange rate regimes are fairly durable. This persistence is also evident if we consider the probabilities of having a fixed exchange rate given that there was a fixed exchange rate three or five years before (and no switching in between), since these probabilities are 66 percent and 55 percent, respectively. The comparable probabilities for floating exchange rates are almost the same, at 65 percent and 54 percent. While these probabilities are somewhat higher for industrial countries than for developing countries in all cases, the differences are not pronounced.[16]

At first, one might be surprised by the high levels of persistence of a state of pegging or floating, given the unconditional probabilities presented in the previous section that show that nearly half of the peg spells and more than a third of float spells end after their first year. The difference across these two sets of statistics reflects the fact that the conditional statistics in table 4.5 are based on annual cross sections rather than spells. Long-lived spells are given a bigger weight when calculating these annual cross sections than when calculating spell-based statistics. This insight is especially important when considering analyses of exchange rate regimes' effects on growth or other variables. Such studies typically involve annual observations, and therefore they will draw more observations from a single long peg spell than from a number of shorter duration spells. Indeed, even though the results in table 4.2 show that flipping back and forth between fixed spells and floating spells is common, the statistics in table 4.3 suggest that countries do stay in longer duration spells with some regularity, giving rise to the results in table 4.5 that show that there is substantial continuity in the persistence of exchange rate regimes from one year to the next, or even from one year to three or five years hence. Thus, rather than looking at how long a newly started peg will last (looking at spells), we are asking that if we randomly took any pegged country right now, what are the odds the peg lasts one year more (or three or five).

4.2.2 Conditional Survival Rates

The continuity in exchange rate spells evident from table 4.5 is based on statistics on the likelihood that a country maintains a fixed or floating spell conditional on being in that respective type of spell in a previous year. People have more information than this, however. In

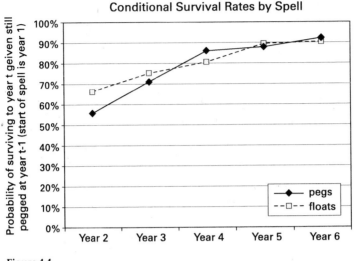

Figure 4.4
Conditional survival rates of peg and float spells.

particular, they know how long a peg spell or a float spell has been in effect. They can use this information to gain a more precise estimate of the likelihood of the continuation of a spell for one more year, given its survival up to that moment.

The conditional survival rate of a spell represents the probability that a spell that has survived through year $(t − 1)$ still is in effect at the end of year t. Figure 4.4 presents these survival rates for fixed exchange rate spells and for floating exchange rate spells at the horizons of two through six years (since, by definition, all spells last for at least one year). The statistics in this table show that 56 percent of the fixed exchange rate spells last for at least two years. This, of course, matches the statistic in presented in table 4.2. Of the 56 percent of the fixed exchange rate spells that last for at least two years, 71 percent last for a third year, and of the 40 percent (= 56 percent × 71 percent) of spells that last for at least three years, 86 percent last for at least a fourth year. These conditional survival rates are somewhat higher for floating exchange rate spells.

The pattern of conditional survival rates for both fixed and floating exchange rate spells is similar in that both are increasing with the number of years already spent in the spell. This represents *positive duration dependence* (which is also called a *decreasing hazard rate*, as discussed below). The longer a peg has been in place, the greater is the likelihood that it will survive for one more year. If these conditional survival rates decreased with the number of years already spent in a spell, this would represent *negative duration dependence* (or an *increasing hazard rate*). As it is, the statistics in figure 4.4 show that people should increase their estimates that a peg will survive for one more year as its duration increases. Even though almost half of all pegs do not survive to a second year, once a peg has been in existence for three years there is a very strong chance (greater than 85 percent) that it will last for a fourth year. The result is similar for floating exchange rate spells. Thus, once a fixed or a floating exchange rate regime has even a small bit of history, as little as three years, it is quite likely to last through any single given subsequent year.

4.2.3 Hazard Functions

The discussion of conditional survival rates shows that spells may be more durable depending how long they have been in existence. That is, they exhibit duration dependence. A way to estimate the duration dependence of a set of spells, and to see how duration dependence shifts with variables other than the time spent on a peg, is through the use of a hazard function. In this context a hazard function, $h(t)$, represents the likelihood that a fixed exchange rate spell that has lasted up until year $t - 1$ ends in year t when the currency begins to float, or alternatively, the likelihood that a floating exchange rate that has lasted up until year $t - 1$ switches to a peg in year t. A decreasing hazard, $h'(t) < 0$, represents positive duration dependence, an increasing hazard, $h'(t) > 0$, represents negative duration dependence, and a constant hazard, $h'(t) = 0$, represents constant duration dependence.[17]

The duration dependence of a set of spells based on the estimate of a hazard function compliments the conditional survival rates discussed above. In addition one can estimate the role of *covariates*—that is, variables other than time spent in a spell—on duration dependence. In this case the arguments of the hazard function include the vector of covariates, $\mathbf{x}$, as well as the time spent in the spell, t.

A commonly used function in duration analysis is the *Weibull hazard function*. This function takes the form

$$h(t, \mathbf{x}; \lambda, \beta) = \lambda t^{(\lambda-1)} \exp(\mathbf{x}\beta) \tag{4.1}$$

where t is the time in the spell, and $\mathbf{x}$ is vector of covariates that shift the hazard function. The parameter λ in the baseline Weibull hazard function $\lambda t^{(\lambda-1)}$ and the vector of coefficients associated with the covariates, $\boldsymbol{\beta}$, are estimated by a maximum likelihood method.

The baseline hazard function $\lambda t^{(\lambda-1)}$ is decreasing in t if $\lambda < 1$ and, in this case, exhibits positive duration dependence. Conversely, it exhibits negative duration dependence if $\lambda > 1$. The baseline hazard is invariate to the time already spent in the spell, and exhibits constant duration dependence, if $\lambda = 1$.

Covariates shift the baseline Weibull hazard function without altering its duration dependence. A positive coefficient β_i means that larger values of its associated covariate x_i increases the hazard function; that is, larger values of x_i makes it more likely that a spell will end in period t, given its survival to period $(t - 1)$.

We investigate the effect of several covariates. One covariate is a dummy variable identifying which fixed exchange rate spells and which floating exchange rate spells are those of industrial countries. Another covariate, used only for fixed exchange rate spells, is whether the base country is the United States. A third covariate, for both fixed exchange rate spells and floating exchange rate spells, is the length of the immediately preceding spell.[18] A positive value of the coefficient associated with the length of the immediately preceding float spell in an estimate of the peg spell hazard function implies that a shorter previous float is associated with a lower subsequent peg spell hazard; that is, peg spells tend to last longer if the immediately preceding float spells are shorter (as we have seen, a high proportion of float spells last for only one year). Also, a positive value of the coefficient associated with the length of the immediately preceding peg spell in an estimate of the float spell hazard function implies that longer peg spells are associated with shorter subsequent float spells.

Results of estimating the Weibull hazard function for fixed exchange rate spells, and also estimating it for floating exchange rate spells, are presented in table 4.6. The estimated value of λ is 0.84 for fixed exchange rate spells, and this estimate is significantly less than 1.00 at the 95 percent level of confidence. Likewise the estimated value of λ is 0.91 for floating exchange rate spells and is significantly less than 1.00 at the 95 percent level of confidence. This confirms the statistical robustness of the conditional survival functions presented above that show that both fixed exchange rate spells and floating exchange rate spells become more durable over time—they exhibit positive duration dependence.[19]

Table 4.6
Estimates of Weibull conditional hazard functions

	Peg spells		Float spells	
	Coefficient	Standard error	Coefficient	Standard error
Previous spell	0.033**	(0.011)	0.047**	(0.014)
Industrial country	0.256	(0.190)	0.211	(0.175)
US base dummy	0.650**	(0.135)		
λ	0.844**	(0.034)	0.912*	(0.041)
Number of spells	397		332	

Note: *significant at 95% level of confidence, **at the 99% level for null hypothesis of $\beta = 0$ for covariates and null hypothesis of $\lambda = 1$ for baseline hazard function parameter.

The estimates presented in table 4.6 show that the coefficient on the previous float spell is positive and significant for peg spells, and the coefficient on the previous peg spell is positive and significant for float spells. This suggests that short float spells are associated with longer subsequent peg spells (since the hazard is lower) and that long peg spells are associated with shorter subsequent float spells. Thus a long peg that breaks tends to flip back to pegging relatively quickly. Finally the results in this table also show that pegs to the US dollar have a higher hazard rate, *ceteris paribus*, than pegs to other bases.[20]

4.3   Re-forming Pegs

We emphasize the re-formation of pegs, but a highly relevant question is "at what exchange rate?" That is, do pegs simply loosen and then re-tighten around the same central band, or are they re-formed at a new level? Table 4.7 examines this question. There are 398 peg spells in table 4.1, and we use the same sample (1973–2004, 125 countries) described there. Sixty-four peg spells are still in existence in 2004, which leaves us with 334 peg breaks to examine. Of these, 210 have re-formed into a new peg within five years.[21] The table shows the exchange rate change from the pegged year to the following year after the break for these 210 observations. We use the annual average exchange rate, so we do not look at the exchange rate in the year of the break, since exchange rate pegs that broke toward the end of the year will appear to have no associated change in the level of the exchange rate. We see that the average exchange rate has moved considerably

Table 4.7
Exchange rate behavior after a peg ends until it reforms

	Spells	Change in the exchange rate from pegged year to year after the peg breaks			
		Average change	25th percentile	Median	75th percentile
Peg breaks	334	87%	1%	13%	49%

	Spells	Change in the exchange rate by time peg is reformed						
Reform after		Average change	25th percentile	Median	75th percentile	Bands overlap	Bands depreciate	Bands appreciate
1 year	103	50%	0%	14%	60%	14%	71%	16%
Immediate	38	69%	18%	86%	100%	0%	89%	11%
Other 1 year	65	38%	0%	6%	17%	22%	60%	18%
2 years	54	53%	-1%	15%	47%	9%	70%	20%
3 years	29	135%	12%	32%	46%	7%	7%	17%
4 years	12	61%	2%	18%	102%	17%	67%	17%
5 years	12	133%	29%	72%	200%	8%	92%	0%

Note: The first row shows the exchange rate behavior after a peg ends. Subsequent rows show the exchange rate change by the time a peg has reformed as well as where the new bands lie with respect to the old exchange rate bands when the peg reforms. Three extreme outliers are excluded from the averages.

(87 percent) after the break of a peg.[22] The median country has depreciated by 13 percent, with a quarter of countries not having depreciated at all the year after the peg breaks, and another quarter having depreciated by a full 50 percent or more.

Subsequent rows show the number of peg spells that have re-formed after a given amount of time, the change in the exchange rate by that time, and, in the last three columns, whether the new bands overlap the old ones or are more depreciated or more appreciated than the original peg bands. There are 103 peg spells that re-form after just one year. Thirty-eight of these are immediate realignments where there is a change in the exchange rate outside the ± 2 percent bands in only the month of the realignment itself.[23] Eighty-nine percent of these 38 discrete realignments are to a new, substantially depreciated exchange rate; the median depreciation is 86 percent. For the other 65 pegs that re-form with only a year break, the median depreciation is only 6 percent, and 22 percent of the spells have re-formed at bands that overlap the old ones. Thus, a fair number of peg breaks are outside their 2 percent bands for only a year and the new peg is reasonably close to the old one.

Pegs that re-form at longer horizons tend to do so at a significantly depreciated exchange rate. The 75th percentile change in the exchange rate by the time the peg has re-formed is near a 50 percent depreciation for pegs that re-form after two or three years, and is above 100 percent for pegs that re-form after four or five years. The average depreciations are also in the range of 50 percent to more than 100 percent at these horizons, even when we exclude two outliers when calculating these statistics.

The results in table 4.7 show that the restoration of a peg can occur with a very large change in the exchange rate. Thus, in some cases, a new peg restores stability, but people who had made long-run decisions based on the old pegged rate now face a substantially more depreciated one. Still, nearly 10 percent of the pegs that re-form within five years do so at a rate close to the old bands, and around 20 percent of these re-peg at a more appreciated rate.

In the end, analyzing the end of peg spells without considering that they re-form is incomplete, but, at the same time, just because a peg re-forms does not mean that it does so at a rate close to its old value. Even though stability returns with a new peg (at least for a short time, anyway), in at least half the cases there is a fairly substantial depreciation, and in about a quarter of the cases there is a very substantial depreciation.

4.4 Conclusion

In chapters 8 through 11 we will discuss recent research that shows substantial effects of the exchange rate regime on trade and a variety of macroeconomic outcomes. These results seem inconsistent with the perception that pegs do not really peg and floats do not really float, that is, that exchange rate regimes do not matter for the exchange rate, let alone other outcomes. In this chapter we find that, despite the fact that many peg spells break soon after they begin, a fair number last beyond five years. These longer spells are overrepresented in an annual cross section, as compared to short spells. In addition, once a peg lasts longer that a year or two, the probability that it will continue for one more year, conditional on lasting up until that year, rises dramatically. The implication is that the length of a particular peg is more important than the less specific knowledge of average peg duration for agents considering actions that are affected by the maintenance of the peg. We also show that float spells have properties similar to those of peg spells, especially with respect to the prevalence of many short duration spells. This shows that many countries re-form pegs quickly after experiencing the end of a peg spell.

A second issue, however, is whether there are significant and important quantitative differences in exchange rate volatility across exchange rate regimes. The mere classification of annual observations into those categorized as "pegs" and those categorized as "floats" (or, more accurately, nonpegs) would not matter if the "fear of floating" truly limited exchange rate flexibility when countries do not peg. As discussed in the chapters 6 and 7, the existence of these differences has been subject to some debate. But we will show that the magnitude of bilateral exchange rate volatility between a country that has a pegged rate and its base country is quite distinct from bilateral volatility when a country does not peg.[24] Countries that peg have lower multilateral volatility as well, mainly because these countries tend to avoid extreme bilateral volatility outcomes.[25]

5   The Empirics of Exchange Rate Regime Choice

To peg or not to peg, that is the question.

—Heard somewhere in Denmark

Governments make a wide range of decisions on economic policy. Some of these decisions represent a set of institutional choices that are made infrequently, such as the development or modification of statutes governing the operation of a central bank. Other choices are made more often, as a response to immediate concerns; for example, the passage of a short-run fiscal stimulus package to counter an economic downturn. In both cases it is also important to recognize that decisions are typically not made by the "benevolent social planner" of economic theory, rather economic choices often reflect political struggles among several competing interest groups.

One of the key economic decisions facing any government is its choice of exchange rate regime. But is this a choice based on deep structural economic and political features that tend to not change much over time? And, if so, which of these factors are most important? Or, instead, does the choice of the exchange rate regime in a particular year mainly reflect current economic and political conditions? These questions are the focus of this chapter.

The nature of the question of exchange rate regime choice is different in the modern era than in earlier times. The choice of whether to participate in the gold standard was bound up with the choice of whether to be engaged in the broader international monetary system. This had implications for international trade, since participation in the gold standard was viewed as a way to foster trade, an advantage that increased with a widening participation in the gold standard system (Flandreau 1996; Meissner 2005). It also had implications for international borrowing, since membership in the gold standard was a way to ensure international investors of creditworthiness (Bordo and Kydland 1996). For these reasons, and also because of limited enfranchisement and a view that governments were not fully responsible for economic conditions, once governments pegged to gold, they had a tendency to consistently maintain this policy, through good times and bad times, up until World War I. After World War II the Bretton Woods system of fixed exchange rates was also relatively stable, with only a few cases of governments opting out of the system and allowing their currencies to float. Unlike the earlier gold standard period, exchange rate regime stability in the Bretton Woods era was supported by restrictions on international capital mobility which, as we learned in chapter 2, afforded countries some scope for setting monetary policy despite participation in a fixed exchange rate system.

As we have seen, the hallmark of the modern era has been a wide heterogeneity in exchange rate experiences, even among countries at similar levels of economic development. So the question of exchange rate regime choice has become more interesting than during the gold standard or Bretton Woods periods, since it is not bound up with the broader question of whether to be engaged in the global economy.

We saw in chapter 4, however, that relatively few countries have demonstrated an unwavering commitment to either a fixed exchange rate or market-determined floating rates during the modern era. Almost all countries have had some experience with floating exchange rates, and some experience with an exchange rate peg, during these times. Few countries can be characterized as pure "peggers" or pure "floaters."

Still, countries do exhibit broad tendencies toward pegging the exchange rate or allowing it to float. One relevant question about exchange rate regime choice then becomes one of linking country characteristics to the tendency to peg or float. In this chapter we examine which of these characteristics are associated with the tendency to have an exchange rate peg rather than a floating exchange rate. The analysis will be guided by the theories discussed in chapter 2 that show the implications of having a fixed or a flexible exchange rate. These theories provides a framework for considering the economic and political reasons behind the exchange rate regime decision, as demonstrated by the discussion that begins the next section and the subsequent review of selected literature. We will show that there are several country characteristics that are associated with the tendency to favor a pegged exchange rate or a floating exchange rate, and that these tend to support some of the predictions of the theories of the relative benefits and costs of different exchange rate regimes. Our analysis will focus on an individual country's choice of regime as part of our view that in the modern era governments have the freedom to make these choices independently. These choices may be made in concert with other countries in the case of a currency union (e.g., the euro area) or a cooperative peg (e.g., the EMS). On the other hand, even in these circumstances, a country still decides whether or not to join; for example, the United Kingdom deferred joining the exchange rate mechanism of the EMS until a decade after it began, and it has decided not to join the euro area.[1]

Another question is if there are other, temporal factors that determine whether a country has a pegged exchange rate or a floating exchange rate in a particular year. Based on the statistics presented in chapter 4 that show that countries often flip from a peg to a float, or from a float to a peg, one might suspect that it may be more difficult to link the exchange rate regime in a particular year to specific variables. We show that this is indeed the case. The dominant characteristics in determining exchange rate regime choice generally do not vary much across time for a particular country. Therefore we can identify whether a particular country tends to have a pegged exchange rate or a floating exchange rate, but for the most part, we cannot link most time-varying country characteristics to the exchange rate regime in a particular year.[2]

The next section of this chapter briefly revisits the theories discussed in chapter 2 in order to develop a list of variables that can be expected to affect exchange rate regime choice. Section 5.2 then shows how these predictions have held up in previous research on this topic. We offer some new results on the links between country characteristics and exchange rate regimes in section 5.3. The chapter concludes with a discussion of the importance of these results for subsequent analysis in the book that examines the effects of exchange rate regimes on trade and macroeconomic performance.

5.1   Theoretical Determinants of Exchange Rate Regime Choice

The basic assumption behind an empirical analysis of the determinants of a country's choice of its exchange rate regime is that this decision reflects the informed decision of either the government as a whole or a sufficiently powerful subset of political interests in a country. The

impact of the exchange rate regime choice can be understood by referring to optimum currency area theory, theories of economic performance under fixed and flexible exchange rates, and theories that focus
on the implications of the exchange rate regime for interest groups
within a country. Thus these theories suggest which variables should
be included in an empirical investigation of exchange rate regime
choice and the qualitative relationship between these variables and the
choice of a fixed or a floating exchange rate. We begin this chapter by
revisiting these theories and discussing the relevant variables used in
an empirical analysis. An important point is that while some of the
concepts presented in these theories easily lend themselves to variables
that can serve as empirical counterparts, others do not correspond to
actual variables one could readily employ in an empirical specification.

A central framework for considering the relative benefits and costs
of a fixed exchange rate versus a flexible exchange rate is optimum currency area (OCA) theory, originally formulated by Mundell (1961).
Strictly speaking, this theory focuses on the choice of a country to participate in a currency union, but its insights can be used to consider the
relative desirability of a fixed exchange rate as opposed to a floating
exchange rate since the relevance of its main precepts do not differ if
one considers a currency union or, instead, a fixed exchange rate.[3] The
central message of OCA theory is that a country should weigh the
microeconomic benefits of membership in a currency union (or a fixed
exchange rate) against its macroeconomic costs. The microeconomic
benefit is the reduction in exchange rate uncertainty for trade with
other members of the currency union (or alternatively, with the base
country and with other countries that peg to the same base). The
macroeconomic cost is forgoing monetary policy independence, which
could otherwise be used to stabilize business cycles. This cost is mitigated if the country has other means to deal with downturns, such as
a high degree of labor mobility or fiscal transfers from the other members of the currency union. The cost of forgoing monetary policy for a
particular country is also smaller if there is a high "natural" correlation
in business cycles between that country and the country in the currency union whose central bank has a free hand in setting monetary
policy.[4]

One implication of OCA theory for the choice of a fixed exchange
rate versus a flexible exchange rate is that two countries benefit more
from having a fixed exchange rate if they trade more, or if there is a
higher potential for trade between them. Thus the level of trade with

the base country (or the potential base country; see the discussion in chapter 3) should be positively correlated with the choice of a fixed exchange rate. One could also justify a multilateral trade indicator, since it is typically the case that the currencies of many countries are tied to that of a single-base country, and pegging a currency to the base country currency creates a web of fixed exchange rates.

One difficulty with using the actual level of trade with the base country in a regression that attempts to determine the tendency for a country to peg its currency is that the level of trade itself may itself be a function of the exchange rate regime.[5] For this reason it may be preferable for an empirical specification to include country-specific variables that can be reasonably expected to affect potential for the level of trade with the base but are themselves not a function of the exchange rate regime. A good example of this is the distance between the country and the base country (or for a country with a flexible exchange rate, its potential base country). It is well established in empirical work that all else equal, two countries are more likely to trade with each other if they are closer because transportation costs are lower over shorter distances. Other factors that affect the potential for trade between a country and its base, such as whether they share a common border or a common language, are also candidates for inclusion in a regression explaining the tendency for a country to peg or float. We would expect to find distance to be negatively associated with the tendency to peg, and a shared border or a common language to be positively associated with a tendency to peg.

Other variables linked to the potential for trade are specific to the country itself rather than the relationship between a country and its base country. A country with a bigger population may have less tendency to peg its currency because there is less need for trade; that is, all else equal, residents in a more populous country will have less reason to turn abroad to buy or sell goods as compared to residents in a more sparsely populated country. Likewise the geographic size of a country could be negatively associated with the tendency to peg its currency. This is because transportation costs make it more difficult to trade from the interior of larger countries but also because larger countries may have more scope for intranational trade than smaller countries. Further, to the extent that richer countries tend to produce a more diverse set of goods than poorer countries, there may be a negative relationship between an indicator such as income per capita and the tendency to peg.[6] This could be offset, however, by the demand for a wider set of goods, including those imported from abroad, for citizens of richer countries as compared to citizens of poorer countries. Thus, unlike distance, a common border, and a common language, it is difficult to predict the sign that income per capita would have in a regression testing the determinants of exchange rate regime choice.

Counter to the microeconomic benefits identified by OCA theory are the macroeconomic costs of pegging a currency. OCA theory focuses on economic features that could mitigate the cost of business cycle fluctuations, such as fiscal transfers and labor mobility. It is likely, however, that these two features are not especially relevant for many countries. Countercyclical transfers across national borders tend to be quite small, with a few exceptions (e.g., transfers from France to former colonies that used the CFA franc). Immigration restrictions in many countries have, over the past four decades, tended to limit countercyclical movements of workers. This is not to say that these factors are not important in exchange rate regime choice or maintenance. It may be the case that the single currency in Europe, for example, is importantly supported by the relative ease with which citizens of countries that are members of the European Union to work in other member countries. Rather, the point is that in a cross-country analysis it may be difficult to identify variables that are useful proxies for those things identified by Mundell that make membership in a currency union more attractive by mitigating the adverse consequences of foregoing an independent monetary policy.

OCA theory also points out that forgoing monetary autonomy is less of a problem when there is a natural coherence in business cycles among members of a currency union. It may be the case that two countries that are physically more proximate, or that share a common border, have a higher degree of natural coherence in their business cycles. If this is true, it would augment the relationship identified in the discussion above on the effect of distance and a common border on regime choice through their effects on the natural levels of trade between two countries. So, for example, there may be a tendency for two contiguous countries to have a pegged exchange rate both because there is a potential for a large volume of trade between them and because their business cycles may be aligned due to common climate or endowments.

The second theoretical framework discussed in chapter 2 that informs our understanding of the choice of an exchange rate regime also focuses on macroeconomic considerations. The policy trilemma was a central concept in that discussion, and it pointed out the fact that, in the presence of international capital mobility, a fixed exchange rate ties the hands of monetary authorities. Therefore we might expect to see a greater tendency for a country to have a fixed exchange rate when it has controls on international capital flows, since this would allow some level of monetary autonomy, even when there is a fixed exchange rate. The discussion in chapter 2 also pointed out that output is relatively more stable with a fixed exchange rate rather than a flexible exchange rate if the shocks hitting an economy are dominated by asset market disruptions rather than disruptions in the goods market. This insight, however, is more difficult to translate into an empirical specification than some of the other concepts discussed above, since it is not obvious how to measure the average level of asset market shocks relative to goods market shocks facing an economy. A somewhat related point, also discussed in chapter 2, is that an economy dependent on a single export that is denominated in dollars in the world market may benefit from pegging its currency to the dollar. For example, one would expect to find a higher tendency to peg among oil exporters.[7]

The third set of theories that contribute to our understanding of the relative preference for a pegged exchange rate or a floating exchange rate concerns political factors and an analysis of competing interests in an economy. As discussed in chapter 2, flexible exchange rates are more likely in democracies, where there is a high political return to influencing the economy, since fixed exchange rates limit the scope for influencing the macroeconomy. Indicators of the level of democracy should, according to this view, be associated with a tendency toward a flexible exchange rate. Another political factor, the competence of a country's bureaucracy and its level of corruption, can also influence the exchange rate regime choice. A fixed exchange rate may provide a country with an easily monitored commitment mechanism that can partially offset, in the minds of international investors, risks associated with a poorly functioning or corrupt bureaucracy. As discussed in the next section, there are cross-country measures of the relative quality of the bureaucracy and the level of corruption, and one would expect to find that a country with a less well-functioning bureaucracy or a higher level of corruption may be more likely to opt for a fixed exchange rate. More pessimistically, more corrupt countries may also opt for a fixed exchange rate because it provides scope for gain among influential members of the society who can take advantage of illegal opportunities.

Before turning from this analysis of the lessons from theory to a review of previous research, it is useful to note that many of the variables we have identified as potential determinants of the choice of an exchange rate regime, like distance to the base country, do not vary over time for a particular country.[8] The cross-country rankings of other variables, such as population, bureaucratic quality, the level of democracy, and even income per capita, are also largely time invariant. This suggests that an investigation of the determinants of exchange rate regime choice is likely to be more successful across countries than, for a particular country, across time. In the next section we show that most studies have in fact focused on a cross-sectional analysis while in section 5.3 we confirm that time-varying factors contribute little to our understanding of what exchange rate regime a country chooses in a particular year.

Time-varying factors are important, however, in determining the timing of the transition from a peg to a float. For example, Klein and Marion (1997) show that a peg is significantly more likely to end in the face of an overvalued real exchange rate, or in the wake of a transfer of government power (especially if that transfer is "irregular"), conditional on the time already spent in the peg. There is, in fact, a large theoretical and empirical literature on the determinants of the collapse of a fixed exchange rate.[9] But the collapse of a peg, and more broadly, regime transition, are topics that are distinct from regime choice. Regime transition considers the inconsistency between an exchange rate policy and other policies, or the manner in which expectations, political factors, or a changing macroeconomic landscape forces a government to abandon a peg. In this chapter we instead focus on the economic and political factors that influence the choice of an exchange rate regime. This topic is more in keeping with the overall scope of this book, with its focus on the determinants and consequences of exchange rate regimes rather than the factors that affect the value of the exchange rate at any moment, or the effect of exchange rate movements on macroeconomic variables.

5.2   Empirical Analyses of Exchange Rate Regime Choice

Optimum currency area theory was developed in the 1960s, but an empirical investigation of its predictions for the post–World War II world, as well as those of the other theories of exchange rate regime choice, had to wait until there was enough variation in countries' experiences with exchange rate regimes to merit cross-country analysis.[10] A theme of this book is that the modern era provides a wide range of exchange rate experiences and, within a few years of the end of the Bretton Woods system, economists began to test OCA theory using cross-country data. As economic theory progressed to consider a range of other implications of different exchange rate regimes, the scope of variables used in empirical analyses broadened to include other macroeconomic and political indicators. In this section we review the literature on this topic, tying it in to the discussion of the previous section and prefacing our own empirical analysis to be presented in section 5.3.

Three of the earliest empirical research papers on the choice of the exchange rate regime in the modern era were published in the final two years of the 1970s: Heller (1978), Dreyer (1978), and Holden, Holden, and Suss (1979). Each of these three studies analyzes the role of variables suggested by OCA theory in exchange rate regime choice. Heller finds GNP, imports relative to GNP, and trade concentration playing the biggest role in determining the exchange rate regime. Dreyer reports a higher degree of openness and a greater diversification of trade with respect to both geography and industry concentration are associated with the tendency for greater fixity in the exchange rate. Paul Holden, Merle Holden, and Esther Suss (HHS) also find a similar effect of openness. These three studies effectively provided some basis for an early view that OCA theory served as an appropriate conceptual framework for understanding exchange rate regime choice at the outset of the modern era.

Three later studies, by Collins (1996), Rizzo (1998), and Bayoumi and Eichengreen (1998), offer support for some of the predictions of OCA theory over a longer span. These three papers are distinguished from the three earlier ones by their use of a time dimension as well as a cross-sectional dimension. Rizzo estimates a separate model for each of five subperiods between 1977 and 1995. He finds significantly greater exchange rate flexibility associated with greater size (measured by GDP), greater economic development (measured by GDP per capita), greater openness (measured as the ratio of exports to GDP), higher inflation, and less geographic diversification (measured as the percentage share of the largest three export destinations).[11] Collins analyzes annual data for 24 Latin American and Caribbean countries over the 1978 to 1992 period. She finds significantly greater exchange rate flexibility associated with higher GDP, greater openness, higher inflation, larger current accounts relative to GDP, and participation in an IMF stabilization program. Eichengreen and Bayoumi find that exchange rate volatility is large when GDP shocks are more different and that intervention to stop that volatility is higher when geographic factors encouraging trade are higher. In a related vein, Meissner and Oomes (2009) find that the volume of trade between countries, a key OCA criterion, is an important determinant of the choice of a base country for countries that peg their currency. But Poirson (2001) finds standard OCA variables, including GDP per capita, the geographic concentration of trade, and trade openness are not significant in her analysis of the exchange rate regime in place in 1999 in 93 industrial and developing countries.

Optimum currency area theory is one of several frameworks available for understanding exchange rate regime choice. Another branch of theory emphasizes differences in short-run macroeconomic performance across exchange rate regimes. As discussed in chapter 2, a fixed exchange rate tends to do a better job of insulating an economy from domestic asset market shocks while a flexible exchange rate serves better in the face of goods market shocks, or shocks in foreign prices. Melvin (1985) finds, as predicted by theory, a negative relationship between domestic money market shocks and greater exchange rate flexibility, and a positive relationship between foreign price shocks and greater exchange rate flexibility, even when the OCA variables of openness, trade concentration, inflation differential, and GNP were included in the logit regression. Savvides (1990) also finds greater real exchange rate variability and lower domestic monetary variability are significantly associated with greater exchange rate flexibility, and that greater exchange rate flexibility is associated with higher GDP per capita, and lower levels of capital mobility and trade concentration.

The discussion in chapter 2 raises another potential role of the exchange rate regime in macroeconomic stability. A fixed exchange rate can serve as a commitment mechanism by a government to conduct monetary policy in a measured way. This has clearly been an important motivation for pegging a currency in some instances, for example, the Tablita plans of Argentina, Chile, and Uruguay in the late 1970s and early 1980s, and the Argentine convertibility plan of the 1990s (see Végh 1992). Does this motive arise more systematically across countries and across time? Carmignani, Colombo, and Tirelli (2008) argue that it does not. They find that a stable and efficient political system is associated with a *de facto* peg and, if a country has a *de facto* peg, it is more likely to announce it (i.e., have a *de jure* peg as well) if it is less prone to social and political risk, and if it has a less fragmented political system. But the commitment device is more important, and the announcement of an actual peg would be more likely, for an unstable, fragmented country. Thus the authors interpret their results as not supportive of the view that the exchange rate regime systematically serves as a commitment device.[12]

A third strand of research on the determinants of exchange rate regime choice focuses on the role of political factors. An early study in this area, by Edwards (1996), considers the effects of an indicator of political instability and an indicator of the strength of the government, while controlling for variables associated with OCA theory. His results suggest that more unstable countries have a significantly lower probability of selecting a pegged exchange rate, and also that there is a marginally significant association between a country having a stronger government and it having a pegged exchange rate. Edwards attributes this to the political cost of a devaluation which is less easily borne in a more politically unstable country or by a weaker government.

It is possible, however, that both instability and government strength are a function of economic conditions which may, in turn, be linked to efforts to peg the currency. Thus, other research has focused on political institutions of a country since these affect political incentives and are relatively stable over time. Bernhard and Leblang (1999) argue that, in industrial countries, a majoritarian system tends to produce a single-party government that does not favor the constraints placed on policy by a fixed exchange rate. In contrast, a proportional representation system favors the constraints placed on the majority by a fixed exchange rate, and a fixed exchange rate offers one type of constraint. For a similar reason, rules that allow for a stronger opposition, in either a majoritarian or a proportional representation system, might be associated with a fixed exchange rate, since this is a constraint that the opposition can impose on the ruling party. Their empirical results support this hypothesis. Proportional–strong opposition systems were most strongly associated with fixed exchange rates and majoritarian–weak opposition systems were most strongly associated with flexible exchange rates, and these differences were statistically significant.

Bernhard and Leblang also considered whether predetermined election timing (e.g., the first Tuesday in November in every fourth year) affects exchange rate regime choice since an implication of political business cycle theory is that an incumbent party will try to stimulate the economy in advance of an election to maximize its chance of retaining office. If this is the case, the ruling party would favor a flexible exchange rate, since this gives it more latitude in efforts to stimulate the economy in advance of election day. The political advantage of a flexible exchange rate is smaller, however, when a government can call an election at its discretion and pick a date in a period when the economy happens to be strong. Bernhard and Leblang report a significant effect of the expected sign for the coefficient on this electoral timing dummy variable.[13]

The political structure of developing countries differs from that of industrial countries. Consequently, variables used in a study of the political determinants of exchange rate regime choice in developing countries may differ from those used in an industrial country study. This is evident in the Leblang (1999) study of the exchange rate regime choices of developing countries over the 1974 to 1994 period in which the indicator used is the degree of democracy in a country, a variable that exhibits far more variation in developing countries than in industrial democracies. Leblang presents results showing that the likelihood of a floating exchange significantly increases with an increase in the democracy indicator. The explanation he offers is that a less democratic regime is better able to weather its citizens' dissatisfaction with a poor economic performance that may arise due to the constraints imposed by a fixed exchange rate system.[14]

A comparison of the Bernhard and Leblang (1999) and Leblang (1999) studies also shows that the expected effect of the same variable may differ depending on the sample. Leblang argues that in the developing world a proportional representative system is associated with greater political fragmentation, which can in turn lead to more intense competition among parties for political support.[15] One implication of this is that a proportional representative system may be associated with a floating exchange rate, since this allows for greater scope for stimulative policies. Of course, this result contrasts with the predictions, as well as results concerning majoritarian as opposed to proportional representative governments made in Bernhard and Leblang (1999). Still it would not be surprising if these two types of effects, which work in opposite directions, were found to have different relative importance in industrial and developing countries. Already, the empirical results in Leblang (1999) show that the proportional representation dummy variable is significantly associated with a higher likelihood of floating for the developing country sample.

Von Hagen and Zhou (2007) consider the effects of political variables, as well as those suggested by OCA theory, macroeconomic stabilization considerations, and the determinants of currency crises. One point of emphasis in their work is the source of regime persistence. Exchange rate regimes may be persistent because their determinants, such as variables associated with OCA theory, are persistent (which von Hagen and Zhou call spurious persistence), or they may exhibit persistence even conditional on the persistence of these variables (which they call true persistence). Von Hagen and Zhou argue that the persistence they observe in their data is best explained by true persistence. This conclusion, of course, depends on the proper specification of the model and, in particular, that there are not omitted variables that are persistent.

The issue of regime persistence can be broadened to consider the challenges of identifying the determinants of exchange rate regime choice in light of the discussion in chapter 4. That chapter shows that there is extreme exchange rate regime persistence for a few countries, but a good deal of flipping back and forth between pegs and floats for many other countries. An analysis based on data from one moment in time (e.g., each of the three earliest studies, Heller, Dreyer, and HHS), or from a cross section in which the dependent variable, the exchange rate regime, represents a value at the end of the period and the independent variables are period averages (e.g., Rizzo or Poirson), may not be robust since a country's exchange rate regime in a particular year is somewhat random. Exchange rate regime flipping also means that it may be difficult to link structural characteristics, like those identified by OCA theory, to the annual exchange rate regime choice in a time-series cross section, like those of Collins or Bernhard and Leblang.

Juhn and Mauro (2002) highlight the potential difficulties in finding a relationship between the exchange rate regime in place at a particular moment and both long-lived country characteristics and long-term averages of time-varying variables. They estimate the determinants of *de facto* (using the LYS classification) and *de jure* exchange rate regimes in place in 1990, the *de facto* (LYS) regimes in place in 1999, and the *de jure* regimes in place in 2000. The independent variables they use include the average of the respective prior decades' values of variables suggested by OCA theory, macroeconomic variables, and indicators of the capital account openness, as well as time-invariant historical and institutional variables. They report that almost no variables are individually significant in most regressions, and none are consistently significant across different time periods and classification schemes. This result holds for a more parsimonious specification as well. Remarkably this is even true when the sample is restricted to countries that had the same exchange rate regime in 1990, 1995, and 2000 (they do not say, however, if these countries continually had the same exchange rate regime during this decade).

In our own empirical analysis presented in the next section, we attempt to address this point by using the proportion of years a country is in a *de facto* peg as a dependent variable. We next turn to this analysis.

5.3 Exchange Rate Regime Choice in the Presence of Flipping

The discussion to this point offers a number of perspectives for considering the choice of the exchange rate regime. Optimum currency area analysis weighs the microeconomic benefits of a peg, through its fostering trade, against the costs it imposes by limiting monetary autonomy. The policy trilemma suggests that these limits on monetary policy are more severe if a country has open capital markets. The political economy literature highlights noneconomic considerations, and predicts that democracies are more apt to float while the likelihood to have a peg increases with the level of corruption, or the general tendency for a government to intervene.

In this section we estimate the likelihood of a country to peg. We use a panel (time-series cross-sectional) data set that includes *de facto* exchange rate regimes over the last quarter century. Estimation is by a linear probability model (i.e., OLS), taking care to estimate the standard errors properly.[16] This technique allows us to seamlessly work across panel, time-series, and cross-sectional data, and it also offers a more direct interpretation of the regression coefficients than nonlinear alternatives like logit.[17]

The regressors we use are suggested by the discussion presented above. Optimum currency area suggests that countries with more potential to trade are more likely to have a pegged exchange rate. We expect potential trade to be negatively associated with distance from the base country, whether a country is landlocked, and the population of a country. Therefore we expect these variables to be negatively associated with the likelihood to peg. In contrast, potential trade is higher if a country shares a border with the base country or if it is a former colony, and we expect that these variables to be positively associated with the likelihood to peg. Former colonies may also have other economic ties with the base country, such as foreign aid that is countercyclical. These transfers may act as shock absorbers, mitigating the costs of the loss of monetary autonomy, and further bolstering the likelihood of a peg.

A variable associated with a higher likelihood to float, one suggested by the policy trilemma, is an indicator of the openness of a country's financial account since the monetary constraints of pegging are more binding in this case. The analysis of the optimal response to shocks suggests that pegging may cushion the effects of asset-market disturbances. A well-developed financial sector (often approximated in empirical work by the size of a broad monetary aggregate like M2 relative to GDP) may also serve to cushion an economy from these shocks, however, and in the presence of this there may be less of an urgency to peg. Another issue related to macroeconomic stability is the diversity of production in an economy. For this reason, non-oil-exporting richer countries, which tend to be more diversified, may have less incentive to peg while oil exporters may want to peg to stabilize the dollar value of their exchange rate.

Finally there are a set of variables suggested by the political economy literature. These include whether a country is a democracy and the level of corruption. Both are associated with a higher likelihood to peg (our first results do not include these variables since they limit the size of the sample). We do not include macroeconomic variables that are quite likely outcomes as much as determinants of exchange rate regime choice, such as the volatility of the real exchange rate, inflation, or levels of reserves.

Table 5.1 presents the first set of results. The sample is 155 countries from 1973 to 2002 (the sample years are based on data availability for some covariates).[18] The dependent variable in this regression is a dummy variable where 1 indicates a country is pegged and a 0 indicates it is not pegged.[19] The standard errors in this regression are clustered at the country level to control for serial correlation and for heteroskedasticity across countries.[20]

Column 1 shows the basic panel result. Countries likely to trade more with the base (because they share a border, or were former colonies) are significantly more likely to peg, and those that are less likely to trade with the base (because they have large populations) are less likely to peg. As expected, rich countries are less likely to peg and fuel

Table 5.1
Basic panel estimation

Sample	1 Full	2 Pol sample[a]	3 Pol sample[a]
ln(distance)	−0.026	0.029	0
	(0.041)	(0.043)	(0.040)
Contiguous	0.238*	0.286*	0.286*
	(0.110)	(0.137)	(0.134)
Colony	0.252**	0.326**	0.316**
	(0.075)	(0.103)	(0.099)
Fuel exporter	0.003*	0.003**	0.002+
	(0.001)	(0.001)	(0.001)
ln(GDP/capita)	−0.050*	−0.036	0.004
	(0.021)	(0.023)	(0.023)
ln(M2/GDP)	0.045	0.101*	0.103*
	(0.036)	(0.047)	(0.044)
Financially open	0.064	0.177	0.219+
	(0.111)	(0.119)	(0.114)
Trade/GDP	0.030	0.072	0.071
	(0.068)	(0.076)	(0.066)
Landlocked	−0.022	−0.022	−0.026
	(0.066)	(0.083)	(0.081)
ln(population)	−0.069**	−0.039+	−0.028
	(0.018)	(0.022)	(0.021)
Govt/GDP	−0.002	0.004	0.005
	(0.003)	(0.004)	(0.004)
Democracy			−0.067**
			(0.017)
Corruption			−0.030
			(0.020)
Constant	1.858**	0.332	0.412
	(0.466)	(0.502)	(0.425)
Observations	3,570	1,920	1,920
R^2	0.154	0.160	0.197

OLS estimation.
Note: The dependent variable is peg status. Sample is 155 countries from 1973–2002.
Standard errors are clustered at the country level and are reported below coefficients;
+ significant at 10%; *significant at 5%; **significant at 1%.
a. The "pol" sample is the sample where political variables are available (eliminates
small countries and starts in 1984).

exporters more likely to peg. The coefficient on distance is not significantly different from zero if the contiguous dummy variable is included as a regressor, although it is significant when this variable is omitted. Financial depth and financial openness are not significant. The overall level of trade openness is also not significantly different from zero, but some of the other variables in the regression, such as population, may be serving as a proxy for this variable.

Column 2 limits the sample to those countries for which political data are available. This eliminates many small, poor countries that have capital controls and also have a tendency to peg.[21] The results that do not include these smaller countries have a smaller coefficient on population, an insignificant coefficient on the income level, and a significant positive coefficient on M2/GDP, the indicator of financial development. Also, in this sample, pegging is positively associated with proximity to the base, with countries having a former colonial relationship with the base, and with countries that are small or oil exporters. The results presented in column 3 show that democracies are significantly less likely to peg while there is no independent effect of the level of corruption on the likelihood to peg. Adding these variables has little impact on other coefficients (although there is a slight drop in the propensity of fuel exporters to peg as they tend to both peg and not be democracies).

Quantitatively, countries that share a border with their base are roughly 30 percent more likely to peg than those that do not, and those that were once a colony of their base are likewise roughly 30 percent more likely to peg.[22] Other impacts are a bit smaller. A one standard deviation move in the democracy variable leads to a 10 percent decrease in the likelihood of pegging. A country moving from full financial autarky to full openness (moving from 0 to 1 in the index) would see a 22 percent increase in the chances of being pegged, but more realistically, a change of one standard deviation generates a 6 percent change in the odds of being pegged.[23]

These results offer some support for the basic premises of OCA theory and the political economy rationales of exchange rate regime choice, although the results for financial openness and financial depth have a somewhat less straightforward interpretation. All this analysis, however, mixes both understanding the changes in a particular country's peg status with reasons a particular country may be more likely to peg. Many of these variables are very slow moving. Borders do not typically change. Colonial history is unvarying. Democracy and

Table 5.2
Country fixed effects estimation (within country identification)

	1 Full CFE	2 Pol sample CFE	3 Pol sample CFE	4 Pol sample CFE, YFE
Fuel exporter	0.001	0.002	0.002	0.002
	(0.001)	(0.001)	(0.001)	(0.001)
ln(GDP/capita)	0.208**	0.268*	0.272*	0.308*
	(0.075)	(0.116)	(0.115)	(0.125)
ln(M2/GDP)	0.014	0.013	0.014	0.009
	(0.021)	(0.034)	(0.034)	(0.033)
Financially open	0.015	−0.104	−0.095	−0.060
	(0.070)	(0.086)	(0.087)	(0.091)
Trade/GDP	−0.082	−0.070	−0.066	−0.048
	(0.060)	(0.094)	(0.095)	(0.096)
ln(population)	−0.335**	0.141	0.140	0.281
	(0.089)	(0.134)	(0.135)	(0.310)
Govt/GDP	0.005*	0.006+	0.006+	0.006+
	(0.002)	(0.003)	(0.003)	(0.003)
Democracy			−0.007	−0.007
			(0.017)	(0.017)
Corruption			−0.003	0.001
			(0.017)	(0.019)
Constant	4.031**	−4.016*	−3.997*	−6.568
	(1.333)	(1.961)	(1.937)	(5.399)
Observations	3,600	1,939	1,939	1,939
R^2	0.509	0.53	0.53	0.534

Country fixed effects estimation
a. The "pol" sample is the sample where political variables are available (eliminates small countries and starts in 1984).
Note: Standard errors clustered at the country level below coefficients; + significant at 10%; * significant at 5%; ** significant at 1%.
Sample period: 1973–2002.

corruption may change over time, but they tend to evolve slowly. Financial openness and depth can change, and may even do so rapidly, but the norm is a slower evolution.

These results suggest that most of our ability to understand exchange rate regime choice comes down to generally knowing which countries are more likely to peg rather than when a particular country is more likely to peg. We explore this in the next table. Table 5.2 adds country fixed effects to the regressions. This means that the estimates indicate a likelihood to peg due to a change in a country's characteristics, rather than due to differences across countries, since the latter effect is absorbed by the country dummy variables. Thus these estimates cannot indicate the effect of unvarying country-specific variables like distance to the base, sharing a border with the base, or being land-locked. The remaining variables tend not to enter the regression significantly. Coefficients on oil revenues, financial openness, financial depth, and political variables are not significant. There is a weak tendency for countries to peg more often with a higher government share of GDP and income per capita.

This point is important for the interpretation of results presented in later chapters. The choice to peg is largely related to variables that only change slowly, if at all.[24] This diminishes concerns of endogeneity, whereby variables of interest, like inflation or economic growth, are both determined by the peg and determine the likelihood to peg. Rather, controlling for the level of development, political variables, and the relationship with the base country—or simply using country or country-pair fixed effects—seems to address adequately concerns with endogeneity.

This result implies that the true dimension of interest is the cross section, not the time series. A full panel may therefore present unwarranted significance levels, even when adjusting the standard errors by clustering. For this reason we also examine cross-sectional results with specifications that are similar to those in table 5.1. We find almost identical results as those found in that table, bolstering our contention that the cross section is sufficient for understanding the choice of the exchange rate regime (results not shown due to similarity with table 5.1).

Our last three tables examine some of the insights presented in chapter 4. First, we have noted that some countries peg for long periods of time, but many pegs are short lived and countries flip back and forth. Thus we will try to see if the determinants of being in a "long peg" look any different than that of being in a peg in general. As in chapter 4 we define a long peg as one that lasts at least five years. This does not mean that an observation is coded as a long peg only after it has lasted five years. The idea is that any pegged observation that is part of a peg spell that lasts for at least five years is considered a long peg and pegged observations that are part of a spell that breaks before five years are considered a short peg. Likewise any float observation that is part of a float spell that lasts at least five years is considered a long float, and any observation that is a float that does not last that long is a short float.[25] We also merge the short pegs and short floats to create a "short spell." Thus countries that flip frequently are continually marked as being in a short spell.

We take the same set of covariates to see if there are different determinants of being in a long peg, a short peg, or a short spell. The first question, addressed in table 5.3, is to see if long pegs are driven by a different set of economic variables than short pegs. The next question, addressed in tables 5.4 and 5.5, asks if there is something different about the countries that flip across exchange rate regimes.

Comparing the first column of table 5.3 to the first column of table 5.1, we see almost no difference between the determinants of long pegs and the determinants of all pegs.[26] This also generally holds when including political variables, as shown by comparing columns 2 and 3 in these two tables (in each, the second column limits the sample to observations for which political variables are available and the third column augments the regression specification in the first column with the democracy and corruption indicators). The only difference in the determinant of long pegs versus all pegs is that the former are more likely to arise in the presence of an open financial market.

The determinants of short pegs are investigated in the next three columns of table 5.3, which compare short pegs to floats. The results in these columns show that there is no tendency for short pegs to be contiguous with the base, nor to have been a former colony. Also, countries in a short peg are no more likely to be oil exporters nor are they any more likely to be democracies. This distinguishes these results from those for long pegs. The only common significant determinant of short pegs and long pegs relative to floats is that both are slightly more likely to be found when financial depth is greater. There is a marked difference in the overall goodness of fit of the short peg and long peg regressions. The R^2 statistics are between 0.20 and 0.30 in the long peg regressions, but are basically zero in the short peg regressions. The overall message, then, is that none of the variables that successfully explain why a country pegs in general can tell us why a country engages in a short peg.

Table 5.4 considers a different question inspired by chapter 4; is there something different about countries that flip? The dependent variable is a dummy for being in a "short spell," which is defined as either a short peg or short float. Countries that are flippers, that is, that have short spells, are less likely to have been a colony than countries that peg or float, and they are less likely to be far from the base. These results are logical in that short-spell countries are more apt to be close to the base country than long-term floaters, and less likely to have been colonies of the base country than long-term peggers. The results

Table 5.3
Long pegs and short pegs in panel estimation

Dependent variable Against	1 Long peg All	2 Long peg All	3 Long peg All	4 Short peg Floats	5 Short peg Floats	6 Short peg Floats
ln(distance)	−0.017 (0.046)	0.063 (0.047)	0.036 (0.045)	−0.016 (0.016)	−0.033+ (0.019)	−0.035+ (0.019)
Contiguous	0.225+ (0.133)	0.343* (0.152)	0.340* (0.151)	0.084+ (0.046)	0.006 (0.053)	0.014 (0.051)
Colony	0.312** (0.088)	0.403** (0.118)	0.394** (0.114)	−0.005 (0.043)	−0.041 (0.050)	−0.039 (0.044)
Fuel exporter	0.003* (0.001)	0.003** (0.001)	0.002* (0.001)	0.001 (0.001)	0.000 (0.001)	0.000 (0.001)
ln(GDP/capita)	−0.037+ (0.022)	−0.022 (0.025)	0.015 (0.025)	−0.026* (0.011)	−0.022+ (0.013)	−0.010 (0.015)
ln(M2/GDP)	0.036 (0.041)	0.079 (0.048)	0.081+ (0.046)	0.019 (0.015)	0.045+ (0.023)	0.048* (0.023)
Financially open	0.132 (0.117)	0.271* (0.121)	0.316** (0.115)	−0.071 (0.049)	−0.077 (0.052)	−0.062 (0.052)
Trade/GDP	0.043 (0.074)	0.055 (0.083)	0.057 (0.071)	−0.012 (0.042)	0.047 (0.048)	0.041 (0.050)
Landlocked	0.016 (0.074)	0.008 (0.090)	0.002 (0.089)	−0.051+ (0.027)	−0.039 (0.033)	−0.042 (0.031)
ln(population)	−0.076** (0.020)	−0.043+ (0.022)	−0.031 (0.021)	−0.012 (0.010)	0.000 (0.015)	−0.001 (0.015)
Govt/GDP	−0.003 (0.004)	0.005 (0.004)	0.006 (0.004)	0.000 (0.002)	−0.001 (0.002)	0.000 (0.002)
Democracy			−0.074** (0.020)			−0.008 (0.014)
Corruption			−0.014 (0.019)			−0.021 (0.014)
Constant	1.657** (0.520)	−0.120 (0.546)	−0.062 (0.441)	0.669** (0.251)	0.474+ (0.281)	0.484+ (0.290)
Observations	3,570	1,920	1,920	2,289	1,381	1,381
R^2	0.205	0.235	0.277	0.016	0.019	0.024

Note: Standard errors clustered at the country level shown below the coefficients; + significant at 10%; *significant at 5%; **significant at 1%.
Long pegs are those that last at least 5 years. Eliminating the short pegs from the first 3 columns (and hence testing long pegs vs. floats) makes no difference in the results.
Sample period: 1973–2002. Columns 2, 3, 5, and 6 use sample period of 1984–2002 for which political variables are available.

Table 5.4
Determinants of short spells

Dependent variable	1 Short spell	2 Short spell	3 Short spell
ln(distance)	−0.040 (0.027)	−0.067* (0.028)	−0.070* (0.030)
Contiguous	−0.010 (0.080)	−0.061 (0.093)	−0.058 (0.092)
Colony	−0.119* (0.047)	−0.142* (0.059)	−0.142* (0.058)
Fuel exporter	0.000 (0.001)	0.000 (0.001)	0.000 (0.001)
ln(GDP/capita)	−0.024 (0.015)	−0.030 (0.022)	−0.025 (0.023)
ln(M2/GDP)	0.025 (0.024)	0.063+ (0.036)	0.064+ (0.036)
Financially open	−0.146* (0.070)	−0.234* (0.094)	−0.239* (0.096)
Trade/GDP	−0.003 (0.049)	0.006 (0.062)	0.003 (0.061)
Landlocked	−0.042 (0.044)	−0.065 (0.059)	−0.064 (0.058)
ln(population)	0.019 (0.013)	0.006 (0.022)	0.005 (0.022)
Govt/GDP	0.002 (0.003)	−0.002 (0.004)	−0.002 (0.003)
Democracy			0.009 (0.016)
Corruption			−0.021 (0.019)
Constant	0.445 (0.353)	0.900+ (0.480)	0.927+ (0.484)
Observations	3,570	1,920	1,920
R^2	0.028	0.047	0.050

Note: Standard errors are clustered at the country level and are shown below the coefficients; + significant at 10%; * significant at 5%; ** significant at 1%.
The dependant variable is being in a short spell, either a short lived peg or float.
Sample period: 1973–2002. Columns 2 and 3 use sample period of 1984–2002 for which political variables are available.

in this table also show that flippers are more likely to have closed financial markets than other countries.

Table 5.5 lets us more carefully isolate characteristics of countries that flip a great deal as opposed to looking at all observations where a country is in a short spell. The estimates in this table are based on a data set of country means, using the sample that includes political variables. Thus there are 120 observations, representing the average values for countries from 1984 to 2002, with one observation per country. We group countries into three types: long peggers, long floaters, and flippers. Long floaters are in a long float for at least ten years, long peggers are in a long peg for at least ten years, and flippers fall into neither of these categories.[27] The results in column 1 show long peggers are apt to be contiguous to the base and to have been a colony, but they are less likely to be democratic. Fuel-exporting status does not show up as a significant variable in this specification, and while there is a tendency toward financial openness, its statistical significance is weak. When compared to all countries, long floaters are less likely to have been colonies, but nothing else is statistically significant. Similarly few things mark flipping countries when they are compared to both long pegs and long floats (column 4). They are less likely to be financially open and more likely to have financial depth, but nothing else stands out.

In summary, some variables that are consistent with basic theory about exchange rate regime choice can tell us which countries are likely to engage in long pegs. However, there is little that can contribute to our understanding of when a country pegs rather than floats, nor is there a set of variables which significantly predict which countries are likely to flip back and forth across pegging and floating as opposed to staying in a long-term float. Crisis models, and the level of the exchange rate, can help predict the timing of the end of a peg, but not the duration of a float nor why some countries float and others flip. Further, once the very small, very poor, long-term peggers are dropped from the sample, some fairly basic, time-invariant variables (proximity to the base and colonial relationship) seem to be dominant rather than aspects about a country's economy (e.g., GDP per capita and usually not financial depth or population). Thus some fairly basic controls concerning the relationship to the base (and certainly country fixed effects) may be able to offset many of the concerns related to endogeneity that one may have about the choice to peg when studying the effects of pegging.

Table 5.5
Regression of country types on country characteristics

	1 Long pegger[a]	2 Long floater[b]	3 Flipper[c]
ln(distance)	0.026	0.046	−0.066
	(0.054)	(0.070)	(0.055)
Contiguous	0.327+	−0.179	−0.112
	(0.175)	(0.209)	(0.199)
Colony	0.492**	−0.370**	−0.098
	(0.131)	(0.132)	(0.091)
Fuel exporter	0.001	0.000	−0.001
	(0.001)	(0.002)	(0.001)
ln(GDP/capita)	0.046	−0.076	0.018
	(0.042)	(0.050)	(0.038)
ln(M2/GDP)	0.058	−0.121	0.112+
	(0.086)	(0.099)	(0.065)
Financially open	0.509+	0.019	−0.499+
	(0.276)	(0.344)	(0.279)
Trade/GDP	0.026	−0.142	0.039
	(0.135)	(0.138)	(0.116)
Landlocked	−0.033	0.043	−0.063
	(0.108)	(0.127)	(0.078)
ln(population)	−0.048	0.012	0.027
	(0.031)	(0.041)	(0.039)
Govt/GDP	0.009	−0.004	−0.005
	(0.007)	(0.008)	(0.006)
Democracy	−0.089*	0.060	0.019
	(0.042)	(0.055)	(0.038)
Corruption	−0.046	0.098	−0.039
	(0.045)	(0.061)	(0.049)
Constant	0.173	0.655	0.227
	(0.641)	(0.910)	(0.763)
Observations	123	123	123
R^2	0.337	0.203	0.114

Note: Robust standard errors shown below the coefficients; + significant at 10%; *significant at 5%; **significant at 1%.
a. Long pegger is in a long peg at least 50% of the time.
b. Long floater is in a long float at least 50% of the time.
c. Flipper is neither (spends most of their time in a short spell).
Regressions run on country means over the 1984–2002 sample where political variables are available.

5.4 Conclusion

This chapter differs from others in the book in that it considers the determinants of the exchange rate regime rather than its consequences or its attributes. A central result is that country-specific variables that are largely time invariant do a better job of explaining exchange rate regime choice than time-varying variables.

There is an important implication of the result that constant country characteristics are a central determinant of exchange rate regime choice for the analysis presented in later chapters. In those chapters, we examine the consequences of exchange rate regime choice for international trade, growth, and macroeconomic stability. The results presented in this chapter suggest that endogeneity is not likely to be a problem for those regressions as long as proper controls are considered, a result confirmed in those chapters.

III Exchange Rate Consequences of Exchange Rate Regimes

6 Exchange Rate Regimes and Bilateral Exchange Rates

Let deeds match words.

—Titus Maccius Plautus, ancient playwright

Saying doesn't make it so. Or, in the case of exchange rate regimes, a government that declares that it has a floating exchange rate might not in fact allow its currency to freely fluctuate. For the exchange rate regime to matter to economic outcomes, it seems a prerequisite that the regime makes a difference in the behavior of the exchange rate. These next two chapters will consider what we might call the exchange rate effect of fixed exchange rates.

The mere classification of annual observations into those categorized as pegs and those categorized as floats (or, more accurately, nonpegs) would not matter if the governments shied away from volatility and truly limited exchange rate flexibility when countries do not peg. As discussed in chapter 4, Calvo and Reinhart (2002) argue that governments that declare they float exhibit a "fear of floating," that is, an aversion to allowing their currencies' values to be determined by the foreign exchange market. But if this is the case, then the distinction between fixed and floating exchange rate regimes discussed in part II of this book might have little economic consequence. We show in this chapter, however, that while numerous declared floats are actually pegged or heavily managed floats, countries that do float show a distinctly different pattern of exchange rate behavior than those that peg.[1] That is, we demonstrate in this chapter that after properly accounting for which countries peg and which float, there are clear differences in exchange rate volatility between these two categories.

The qualitative result that one can associate lower bilateral volatility with *de facto* pegs is not striking, and may even be viewed as tautological, but the interesting question is the quantitative implications of pegging. Currency pegs, by definition, exhibit more bilateral exchange rate stability than floating exchange rates—if the volatility of floats were identical to that of pegs, they would all be considered pegs—but how much more? The "fear of floating" result suggests that this difference is not large. We demonstrate, however, that the magnitude of bilateral exchange rate volatility between a country that has a pegged rate and its base country is distinct from bilateral volatility when a country does not peg. The focus of the chapter is to show that the size of the difference in volatility is meaningful, and that the bulk of countries that are coded as floats look more like a classic float rather than just a loose peg. These results are obtained even when controlling for country and year fixed effects, and for inflation behavior and capital controls.

Another important point established in this chapter concerns the continuing effects of a peg. Many economic decisions regarding exchange rates incorporate forward-looking behavior; for example, contracts for international trade are signed six months to two years before actual delivery and payment takes place. Thus today's peg must tell us something about the future to affect actions initially undertaken today that have implications for future transactions. We find that differences in volatility between pegged and floating exchange rate arrangements persist into the future. A peg in one year predicts lower volatility for a number of subsequent years.

The skepticism of the fear of floating school runs against the well-known results of Mussa (1986) which show that bilateral real exchange rate volatility was distinctly different across exchange rate regimes. This result stems primarily from differences in bilateral nominal exchange rate volatility. Mussa's results were revisited and confirmed in numerous studies, such as Baxter and Stockman (1989) and Liang (1998).[2] We focus in this chapter on bilateral nominal volatility as it directly addresses the question of whether pegs matter and because the real exchange rate result has already received much attention.

Thus, before we move on to consider the effects of exchange rate regimes in part IV, we establish an economically relevant distinction between the exchange rate behavior of fixed and floating exchange rate regimes. In this chapter we focus on the bilateral exchange rate between a country and its natural base. In the next chapter we consider a similar set of questions for multilateral exchange rates.

6.1 Indisputable and Disputable Floats

Some countries indisputably allow their currencies to float. Calvo and Reinhart (2002) often cite the benchmark of Australia and Japan as examples of idealized floats. An examination of the behavior of their dollar exchange rates supports this judgment. For example, the Japanese yen has moved considerably over the past three decades, appreciating from ¥360/US$1 in the early 1970s to a rate as strong as ¥80/US$1 in 1995, back up to over ¥140/US$1 in 1998, and dipping below ¥100/US$1 a decade later. This might well be taken as prima facie evidence that Japan has a floating exchange rate regime, even though the Bank of Japan has used its foreign exchange reserves to intervene in the market. Similarly the Australian dollar began the modern era at $0.71/US$1 in March 1973, depreciated to $1.63/US$1 about a dozen years later, and further to almost $2.00/US$1 at the beginning of this century, before strengthening to within four cents of parity in 2008.

But how typical are these experiences? Calvo and Reinhart argue that the dollar exchange rates of the yen and the Australian dollar (along with some other currencies, like the deutsche mark in the pre-euro period) behave differently than the bulk of other flexible exchange rates, and that "fear of floating" is pervasive. One way to judge this argument is to compare the historical volatility of the dollar exchange rates of the yen, the Australian dollar, and the deutsche mark to those of other floating currencies. This requires a calculation of volatility and also a classification that gives us a set of country–year observations for which the exchange rate is judged to be floating. We calculate volatility as the standard deviation of the monthly percentage change in the exchange rate, which is the formula typically used (e.g., see Lane and Devereux 2003; Rose 2000).[3] We use the Klein–Shambaugh classification scheme described in chapter 4 to obtain a set of country–year observations that are classified as floating from the full sample of 125 countries in the 1973 to 2004 period.[4]

This exercise shows that the average exchange rate volatility of the currencies of Australia, Japan, and Germany are not outliers in this set of floating exchange rate observations. In particular, the average volatilities of the bilateral dollar exchange rates of these countries fall within the 50th and 60th percentiles of the set of country–year volatility statistics for the set of floating observations. If we drop the first year of float spells, observations that are typically more volatile than other years in spells, the average volatilities of these three countries are within the 60th and 70th percentiles, a higher level, to be sure, but far from atypical of the set as a whole.

6.2   Volatility in Floats and Pegs

Placing the volatility of the bilateral US dollar exchange rates of Australia, Germany, and Japan in context shows that these acknowledged paradigms of floating actually exhibit fairly typical behavior for the set of floating observations as a whole. In this section we consider the volatility of the entire set of floating observations as compared to the entire set of pegged observations. It will not be surprising, of course, that we find that the volatility of the floating observations is greater than that of the pegged observations; the question is the extent to which the former exceeds the latter, and whether there is a meaningful distinction between the two groups.

We begin by considering the extent of the overlap in measured volatility between the set of float observations and the set of peg observations where, once again, the Klein–Shambaugh classification system is used to distinguish pegs from floats. We sort the set of annual observations by exchange rate volatility. We then divide these observations into quintiles, and determine the number of peg observations in each of the five quintiles.[5]

If volatility between peg observations and float observations were roughly equal, we would expect to find that each quintile would have about half peg observations and half float observations, since the sample is roughly divided evenly between pegs and floats. If pegs and floats are truly distinct, we expect to see all the pegs in low volatility quintiles and all the floats in high volatility quintiles. Figure 6.1 shows the percentage of observations pegged in each volatility quintile. The lowest quintile of bilateral volatility among country–year observations consists exclusively of pegs. The second quintile includes 87 percent annual peg observations. The third quintile is a middle ground and is more evenly split between peg and float observations.[6] But the fourth and fifth quintiles are almost exclusively the province of floating observations. Thus pegs and floats demonstrate distinctly different volatility.[7]

While these results show that pegs and floats occupy different parts of the volatility distribution, the question remains about the magnitude of the difference in volatility across these regimes.[8] We examine this by

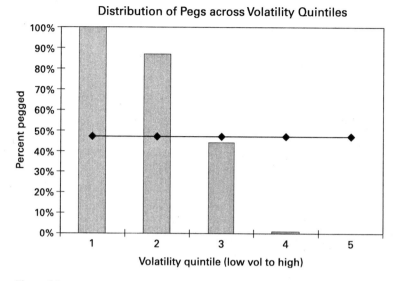

Figure 6.1
Columns show the percent of observations which are pegged within each quintile of the exchange rate volatility distribution. Line represents the total percentage pegged in the sample (47%).

regressing exchange rate volatility on a dummy variable that indicates whether an exchange rate regime spell or country–year observation represents a peg, as well as dummy variables for each country (but one), that controls for country fixed effects (CFE) and, in some specifications, time-varying covariates such as inflation and capital controls. Country fixed effect estimation addresses potential concerns that pegs and floats are simply different types of countries, and this fundamental difference drives both the volatility and the exchange rate regime. We saw in chapter 5 that pegs and floats may differ in certain long-run characteristics, and fixed effects estimation will control for this feature of the data (of course, CFE precludes the use of most covariates used in other studies, for example, distance, colonial relationship, and common language). For example, if countries have no logical base, or if they are generally unstable, they could both have high volatility and rarely peg. Without including fixed effects, this set of countries would tilt results toward a finding that floats have high volatility. Likewise, countries that often peg may maintain their pegs because they have naturally low volatility and there is little cost to pegging. In this case as well, this set of countries tilts results toward a finding that peggers have low volatility. In contrast, the inclusion of country fixed effects will take into account a country's relationship with its base, and identification will come from strictly comparing the times it is pegged to the times it is not. Thus we lose any information from countries that always peg, or never peg, and rely on how volatility changes across peg and float spells for the same country. The basic specification is

$$EVOL_{it} = a + a_i + bPEG_{it} + u_{it} \tag{6.1}$$

where $EVOL_{it}$ is the average annual standard deviation of the monthly percentage change in the exchange rate for country i in either spell t (in the spell-based regressions presented in table 6.2) or in year t (in the panel regressions with country–year observations presented in table 6.3).[9]

We focus on the coefficient b, which represents the difference in conditional means across the two groups. A limited number of spells and annual observations show very high volatility, skewing the data set, so we pay particular attention to the effect of outliers. For this reason we cannot suggest that a typical country will see a reduction in volatility if they switched from a float to a peg based on the size of the coefficient. Also we cannot claim that a choice to peg is the only policy in place or is even a feasible choice. Clearly, some countries may be unable to peg due to policy weakness or chaos, so in some instances a float may represent a combination of a choice not to peg and an inability to peg. We are instead demonstrating the average difference of volatility across pegs and nonpeg spells, trying to eliminate very atypical examples.

Table 6.1 includes regressions in which the unit of observation is the average annual volatility during a peg spell or a float spell. Because the data are spell based, other controls, such as world wide year effects, cannot be included since the spells vary in their length and year coverage. In the full sample the coefficient on PEG shows that, even when including country fixed effects, pegs on average have an annual volatility 16 percentage points lower than nonpegs and the coefficient is highly statistically significant. In the lower panel of the table we see that the average volatility for a peg is roughly zero and that of a float is roughly 16 percent. The lower panel of the table also shows the standard deviation for the full sample of spells. It is large (roughly 70 percent) mainly due to the presence of outliers with very high volatility.

To put the numbers in context, if we assume that half the monthly exchange rate changes are at one extreme and half are at the other

Table 6.1
Exchange rate volatility in spells

Sample	1 Full	2 Drop 1%
Peg	−0.158** (0.051)	−0.068** (0.008)
Constant	0.161** (0.026)	0.071** (0.004)
Observations	792	785
R^2	0.170	0.310
Sample standard deviation	0.689	0.086
Peg mean	0.004	0.004
Peg med	0.003	0.003
Nonpeg mean	0.161	0.069
Nonpeg med	0.025	0.024

Note: Standard errors are clustered at the country level; country fixed effects are included. Column labeled "Drop 1%" drops the 1% largest volatility observations to reduce the impact of outliers. *represents a statistically significant difference from zero at the 95% confidence level, **at the 99% level. Sample: spells covering 125 countries from 1973–2004.

extreme, the estimated intercept and slope coefficients suggest that monthly changes in the −1 to 1 percent range for pegged observations and the large range of about −16 to 16 percent for floating exchange rates. The ranges consistent with these estimated coefficients could in fact be larger if some monthly changes are not at the extreme values.[10]

A sample without outliers gives us a better picture of a typical float. We use a sample that excludes spells that represent the top 1 percentile of volatility. As seen in column 2 of table 6.1, the standard deviation of this sample drops considerably, even though we have only eliminated 1 percent of the observations. In this case the coefficient on PEG is less than half as big as in the full sample regression (though it remains statistically significant) and its (absolute) value of 0.07 is now nearly equal to the standard deviation of the dependent variable. That is, once outliers are removed, pegs have a roughly one standard deviation lower volatility than floats when we have controlled for country fixed effects. Also, once outliers are removed, the R^2 jumps up to 0.31 with only the dummy for pegging and country fixed effects in the regression. This is notable given that the peg variable, by definition, only distinguishes between pegs and floats and cannot help explain differences within the floating group. The bottom panel of the table shows that pegs have roughly zero volatility and nonpegs (excluding the top 1 percentile group) have volatility close to 7 percent. Many floats with an annual volatility of 7 percent typically show a range in the monthly change in the level of the exchange rate of −3 percent to 5 percent, with one month in the mid 20 percent range (e.g., Spain 1977, New Zealand 1984, and Fiji 1998).[11] The message from these results is that, while there may be fear of floating behavior, the typical floating country has considerably more exchange rate volatility than a peg.[12]

The estimates in table 6.2 are based on regressions in which the unit of observation is a country–year data point rather than a peg spell or a float spell. These data allow us to include year effects (to take into account that some years may have seen broad volatility across the globe) and annual covariates that align directly to our data. This analysis also allows for estimating whether the first year of a floating spell is marked by an unusually high level of volatility; thus the estimates on the peg dummy in specifications that include a first-year-of-float dummy are interpreted as the effect of a peg as compared to a second or subsequent year of a float. As in table 6.1 we seek to eliminate the effect of a few extreme outlier cases, so our estimates in table 6.2 are based on samples that drop the 1 percent most volatile country–year observations.[13] Once again, we include country fixed effects. Combined with year fixed effects, which control for differences in world volatility from year to year, CFE allow us to isolate the differences in volatility across pegs and nonpegs controlling for differences in country behavior.

The estimates in the first column of table 6.2 indicate that annual volatility is 5 percentage points lower for peg country–year observations than for float country–year observations. The estimate in the second column shows that annual volatility for pegs is 4.2 percentage points lower for pegs than for non-first-year floats, and volatility is 2.4 percentage points higher during the first year of a float than during subsequent years. The median for bilateral float volatility is close to that of Japan in 1984 (2 percent volatility) when its monthly percentage changes ranged from −4 percent to 3 percent and the yen/dollar rate, beginning the year at ¥235/US$1, went as low (in the end-of-month data) as ¥220/US$1 and as high as ¥250/US$1. The mean for non-first-year float floats was 3.8 percent, which is similar to Germany in 1981 when monthly changes ranged from 8 percent to −4 percent and the DM ranged from DM2.1/US$1 to DM2.46/US$1. These were not crisis-driven years, but represent the average volatility of floats, considerably

Table 6.2
Exchange rate volatility in annual panel data

	1	2	3
Peg	−0.049**	−0.042**	−0.031**
	(0.005)	(0.004)	(0.003)
First-year float		0.024**	0.033**
		(0.006)	(0.007)
Inflation			0.074**
			(0.010)
Capital controls			0.006
			(0.004)
Constant	0.035**	0.032**	0.014**
	(0.002)	(0.002)	(0.005)
Observations	3,816	3,816	3,546
R^2	0.25	0.26	0.37
Sample standard deviation	0.056	0.056	0.055
Peg mean	0.002	0.002	0.002
Peg median	0	0	0
Nonpeg mean	0.042	0.042	0.041
Nonpeg median	0.02	0.02	0.02

Note: Standard errors are clustered at the country level and are shown below the coefficients. Country fixed effects and year fixed effects are included in all specifications. The sample drops the 1% largest volatility observations to reduce the impact of outliers, and column 3 drops the 1% largest outcomes of inflation. * represents statistically significantly different from zero at the 95% confidence level, ** at the 99% level. Sample: 125 countries from 1973–2004.

different than the pegged countries staying in the 2 percentage bands where behavior is usually close to 1 percent up or down a month. By definition, the maximum annual range of the exchange rate for pegs was ±2 percent, the median was less than ±0.5 percent. For floats, the average range was ±12 percent (median ±6 percent). For example, a year when the yen/dollar exchange rate ranged from 120 to 135 would be at the median range and between 120 and 150 would be the average range. It is important to note that these "classic" floats, as mentioned above, are near the middle of the distribution. They are not unusual floats in terms of the magnitude of volatility. They are fairly typical descriptions of the experiences of floats.

Table 6.2 also includes estimates in which we control for other aspects of a country's economy. The third column shows that inflation is positively and significantly correlated with volatility, and volatility is also higher in the presence of capital controls (although not significantly so). But, even with these covariates in the regression, a peg is substantially more stable than a nonpeg with relatively little change to the magnitude of the coefficient on the peg dummy. Results hold across industrial countries and nonindustrial countries with means and coefficients smaller for industrial countries and first-year floats not associated with higher volatility for rich countries.

6.3   Persistent Effects of Pegging

Section 6.2 demonstrates that the exchange rate matters for current year exchange rate volatility. However, for the exchange rate regime to matter to a number of outcomes that we explore later in the book, it is important to discern whether a peg today suggests lower volatility in future years.

We investigate this question by running a series of regressions of exchange rate volatility on peg status (with year and country fixed effects included) that are similar to those in column 1 of table 6.2 but for successive lags of the peg dummy variable, rather than its contemporaneous value. That is, we first test the impact of being pegged today on today's volatility, and then separately test the impact of being pegged today on volatility next year, and in subsequent years, regardless of what happens to the exchange rate regime in those future years.

The estimates from this analysis are presented in figure 6.2. The numbers along the horizontal axis in these figures represents the number of years that the peg variable is lagged in a regression of country–year volatility on a peg dummy. Thus, the point associated with the zero value in each of these figures represents the current year effect of a peg on exchange rate volatility, that is, the coefficient reported in column 1 of table 6.2. The associated horizontal lines around these points represent a confidence interval equal to two times the standard error.[14] The other points and lines represent point estimates and standard errors from the regressions using 1, 2, 3, 4, and 5 year lags of the peg variable. The regressions are estimated using the lagged peg dummy variable regardless of the subsequent history of the peg spell.

Figure 6.2 shows that the effect of a peg extends, in a significant way, up to two years in the future. Both the one- and two-year lags of pegs are associated with significantly lower bilateral volatility. Earlier lags than these, however, have relatively small impacts on volatility.[15] Thus a peg today suggests lower volatility today, next year, and the year after that, but this effect fades once one moves out beyond two years.

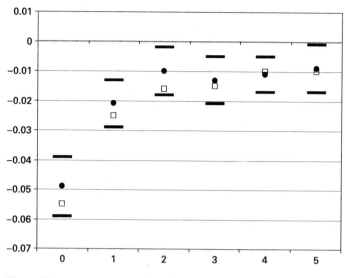

Figure 6.2
Bilateral volatility over time. Time 0 represents the contemporaneous coefficient of exchange rate volatility on pegging, time 1 represents the coefficient on a lagged peg, and so on. Thus the point at time 2 represents the difference in volatility for a country that was pegged two years ago (whether it has remained pegged or not). Country- and year-fixed effects are included. The dark lines represent 2 times standard error bands around the main point estimates, where standard errors are clustered on country. To ensure that the comparison is with nonpegged observations, new pegs that are not re-pegs are excluded (see text). Squares represent the point estimate if the first year of pegging is excluded.

Given the results of chapter 4 that pegs often break, it is no surprise that a peg today does not suggest lower volatility indefinitely. Yet we also saw that pegs became more durable over time. First-year pegs were the most fragile. Reestimating these results without the first year of pegs (which eliminates one-year pegs) increases the persistent effect of a peg on subsequent bilateral volatility for the one- and two-year horizons, as the remaining pegs are more durable and more likely to re-form if broken (these points are shown as squares on the figures), but makes no difference after that.

These results are important in exploring how pegs could have an impact on forward-looking economic behavior. A peg today does suggest lower volatility in the future. These results suggest why, for example, Klein and Shambaugh (2006) find an increase in bilateral trade from pegging even when controlling for contemporaneous volatility, since a peg today implies lower exchange rate volatility in the future.[16]

Table 6.3
Percentage pegged by exchange rate volatility quintile

	KSpeg	JSpeg	RRpeg	DJpeg	LYSpeg
1	100%	99%	71%	89%	99%
2	87%	83%	58%	66%	93%
3	44%	31%	16%	21%	41%
4	1%	1%	7%	9%	39%
5	0%	11%	11%	20%	21%
Total	47%	45%	33%	41%	58%

Note: As in figure 6.1, the table shows the percentages of annual observations that are pegged in each quintile of exchange rate volatility. The bottom row shows the total share of pegs in the entire sample for each classification. KS = Klein–Shambaugh, JS = Shambaugh, RR = Reinhart–Rogoff, DJ = de jure, LYS = Levy–Yeyati and Sturzenegger.

6.4 Exchange Rate Outcomes across Classifications

We also examine our volatility results across the different exchange rate regime classifications that were discussed in chapter 3. For some questions such an exercise could be considered merely a robustness test—examining if the results are sensitive to the definition of a peg. In this case, however, the results go beyond robustness to shed more light on the variation of conceptions undergirding classifications schemes.

Table 6.3 demonstrates the broad similarity of the overall pattern across schemes. Pegs tend to fill most of the lower volatility quintiles and are found less frequently in the top two. The differences across the columns are nevertheless informative. A source of the difference between the Klein–Shambaugh based results presented in sections 6.1 through 6.3 and those obtained when the peg dummy is defined using the Shambaugh classification is that the latter allows a peg to continue through a one-time devaluation, and consequently more volatile exchange rate outcomes can be called pegs. Likewise pegs can last through devaluations in the Reinhart–Rogoff classification, and for this reason the Reinhart–Rogoff results look similar to the Shambaugh results with regards to the percentage of high volatility outcomes that are pegs (11 percent). Also, the Reinhart–Rogoff classification does not count all stable official rates as pegs (due to the use of secondary market rates), and thus many of the most stable outcomes are nonpegs (100 percent − 71 percent = 29 percent). Reinhart–Rogoff is the only *de facto* classification that has many stable observations labeled as floats. There are also instances of low-volatility observations labeled as *de jure* non-

Table 6.4
Exchange rate volatility in annual panel data across classifications

	1	2	3	4
Classification	JS	RR	DJ	LYS
Peg	−0.025**	−0.013**	−0.001	−0.033**
	(0.004)	(0.004)	(0.005)	(0.004)
First-year float	0.027**	0.017	0.035**	0.034*
	(0.007)	(0.012)	(0.010)	(0.007)
Constant	0.020**	0.025**	0.013**	0.031*
	(0.003)	(0.005)	(0.003)	(0.003)
Observations	3,816	3,101	3,704	3,088
R^2	0.18	0.16	0.15	0.31

Note: this table reproduces column 2 from table 6.2, for bilateral exchange rate volatility, across classifications. There are country and year fixed effects included, 1% outliers are dropped, and standard errors are clustered at the country level. The change in the number of observations across columns is due to different availability of the classifications. * represents statistically significantly different from zero at the 95% confidence level, ** at the 99% level.

pegs, as some countries that declare a float actually limit exchange rate volatility tightly. In addition a fifth of the *de jure* pegs are highly volatile since some countries declare pegs that do not hold. The LYS classification scheme also has a large number of volatile pegs; 21 percent of the high-volatility outcomes are labeled pegs, a higher percentage basis then even the *de jure* classification. These high-volatility pegs are not discrete devaluations but simply moderate to high volatility outcomes that are labeled pegs in their cluster analysis technique.

We also examine regressions such as those in table 6.2 for the different classifications. The most notable difference on the exchange rate effects of pegging across classifications is that with the *de jure* classification the coefficient on PEG variable is not significantly different from zero. This result, and others using the Reinhart–Rogoff, Shambaugh, and LYS classifications, are presented in table 6.4. This table includes specifications matching those in column 2 of table 6.2 to show how the effect of a peg on exchange rate volatility depends on the classification employed. The results in columns 1 and 2 show that the Shambaugh and Reinhart–Rogoff classification schemes, which allow peg spells to continue through one-time devaluations, result in weaker results for the coefficient on PEG than is the case with the Klein–Shambaugh classification scheme used in table 6.2 (the coefficient is −0.042 with Klein–Shambaugh, but −0.025 with Shambaugh and −0.013 with Reinhart–Rogoff). The result in column 3 shows that the misidentification of regimes that occurs with *de jure* classifications results in insignificant coefficients on PEG.[17] The result in column 4 demonstrates that the coefficient on PEG is weaker when using the LYS classification than that obtained with the Klein–Shambaugh classification (as in table 6.2) since the LYS classification includes more volatile observations as pegs. However, the results using LYS classification are stronger than those with the Reinhart–Rogoff or Shambaugh classifications because Levy-Yeyati and Sturzenegger do not classify cases with very large devaluations as continuing pegs.

6.5   Volatility and the End of Exchange Rate Pegs

We consider one final question regarding volatility. Does a peg simply bottle up volatility until a crash? If so, pegs only delay, not repress, exchange rate volatility. This was a key contention of Friedman (1953) in part of his argument as to why floats would not be more volatile than pegs. He argued that smoothly floating exchange rates would generate less volatility than the large devaluations within adjustable peg regimes.[18] One might also worry that the longer a peg exists, the more spectacular will be its collapse. To test this idea, we look at whether high volatility is tied to the end of a peg regime in three different ways.

Panel A of table 6.5 divides the 37 top 1 percent volatility outcomes and the 187 top 5 percent volatility outcomes according to whether the preceding year was one in which the exchange rate was pegged or whether it floated. There is nearly an even division between these categories, with slightly fewer high volatility observations following a peg and slightly more following a float. The 37 top 1 percent volatility outcomes are divided between 21 that followed a float year (which is 1.1 percent of the float observations) and 16 that followed a peg (which is 0.9 percent of the peg observations). Similarly 118 of the 187 top 5 percent volatility observations followed a float (representing 5.9 percent of the float observations) while the remaining 69 followed a peg (4.0 percent of the peg observations). Thus an extremely high volatility outcome is not significantly more likely to follow a peg than it is to follow a year in which the exchange rate was not pegged.[19]

The statistics presented in panel B of table 6.5 allows us to consider whether a year in a pegged regime of a particular length is followed by a high-volatility year, regardless of whether these dates in the peg spell actually represented the terminal year of the peg. There is a slightly higher value for the percentage of extremely high (top 1 and

Table 6.5
Exchange rate regime status in year prior to high-volatility outcomes

	Observations[a]	In top 1%[b]	Percent	In top 5%	Percent
Panel A					
Full sample	3,738	37	1.0%	187	5.0%
Nonpeg in previous year	1,998	21	1.1%	118	5.9%
Peg	1,740	16	0.9%	69	4.0%
Panel B					
Pegged in previous year with peg representing:					
First year of pegging	388	6	1.5%	18	4.6%
2–5 years of pegging	575	5	0.9%	20	3.5%
>5 years of pegging	777	5	0.6%	31	4.0%
Panel C					
Final year of peg	342	16	4.7%	69	20.2%
One-year peg spell	173	6	3.5%	18	10.4%
2–5-year peg spell	112	5	4.5%	20	17.9%
>5-year peg spell	57	5	8.8%	31	54.4%

a. Total number of observations following a given exchange rate regime status.
b. Number of observations in the top 1% of the volatility distribution.

top 5 percent) volatility observations that follow in the wake of a one-year peg (1.5 and 4.6 percent respectively), but the differences are not especially notable. Thus we see that at the start of a year, regardless of how long a peg has lasted, the odds of a spectacular collapse are about the same (and again, as seen in panel A, are roughly the same as for a floating observation).

A striking difference across the length of a peg does arise, however, when we look at exchange rate pegs that break. This is shown in panel C of table 6.5. The statistics in this part of the table show that 8.8 percent of the years immediately following the breakup of a long (i.e., longer than five-year) peg are in the set of the top 1 percent volatility observations, and more than half (54.4 percent) of these long peg collapses are in the set of the top 5 percent volatility observations. The comparable numbers for one-year pegs and for pegs that last between two and five years are much smaller. Because long pegs are more likely to survive, a randomly drawn long peg observation is no more likely than any other to be followed by a high volatility outcome. But, once a long peg does collapse, it is far more likely to collapse in a chaotic fashion.

Thus, the message from table 6.5 is that high volatility outcomes are no more likely to follow a year in which a currency was pegged than a year in which a currency floats. Also the number of years that a peg has been ongoing is not especially informative for predicting whether, in the next year, there will be an extremely high volatility outcome. But if we know that a peg ends after a particular number of years, we can predict that volatility is higher if the peg has lasted longer.[20] The distinction between the second and the third statements reflects the fact that there is a decreasing hazard for pegs; the longer the peg lasts, the less likely that it will break in a subsequent year, but if it does break, it does so in a more spectacular fashion if it is older than if it is younger.

6.6   Conclusion

As our discussion in chapter 3 makes clear, it is unquestionable that many countries limit their exchange rate volatility, despite their claims that they allow their currencies to float. But this leaves open the question of how different actual pegs and floats are. We find that the magnitude of the gap in volatility is substantial. The average or median float does conform to our standard view of a float—one where the exchange rate can move a fair bit over the course of a year. Classic floats such as the yen or Australian dollar are not atypical but stand in the middle of our volatility distribution. A typical floating observation simply has a considerable amount more volatility than a peg, even when we control for country and year fixed effects and the first year of floating. In addition, despite the fragility of pegs, enough pegs last (or re-peg quickly) such that pegging today is a good predictor of low volatility in the future, suggesting that we might expect pegs to have a real effect on economic outcomes. Further, these pegs have not simply bottled up volatility until a spectacular collapse since floating countries also find themselves thrown into very high volatility outcomes at roughly the same rate. The next chapter extends this analysis to consider exchange rate indexes that look at the movement of the exchange rate against some weighted average of currencies as opposed to strictly the base currency.

7 Exchange Rate Regimes and Multilateral Exchange Rates

You can only do one thing at a time.

—Maxwell Maltz, *Pyscho-Cybernetics* (1960)

An exchange rate is inherently bilateral. That is, one cannot speak precisely about the dollar depreciating or appreciating without specifying the currency against which it moves. The dollar could be rising against one currency and falling against another at the same time. This seemingly simple observation is a crucial one for the economics of exchange rate regimes in the modern era. It also distinguishes the modern era from the gold standard or Bretton Woods periods when the use of a common anchor by nearly all countries meant that pegs in those eras would almost automatically be stabilizing the multilateral as well as the bilateral exchange rate.

In the modern era, the general rule is that a country can only peg its exchange rate against one particular currency or, in some cases (e.g., with the euro, post-1999), against the currency used by a set of countries. For example, in the 1990s Argentina pegged to the US dollar. This stabilized its dollar exchange rate, but as the dollar appreciated against European currencies in the latter part of that decade, so did the Argentine peso.

Chapter 6 demonstrated that exchange rate pegs significantly reduce bilateral exchange rate volatility, and that floats have considerably more bilateral volatility than pegs. But a country with trade and investment across the globe will worry about many different exchange rates. Since a country cannot stabilize its exchange rate against all countries, just against one other currency, we are left wondering whether a bilateral exchange rate peg stabilizes a broader measure of the value of a currency.[1]

The need to summarize the value of a currency, rather than speak of how the exchange rate has moved against each partner currency, leads us to study an average value—or index value—of a currency. A multilateral exchange rate index weights the value of a currency against all partner currencies, typically using trade shares to weight the various bilateral exchange rates. Thus, if half of US trade is with the euro area, a quarter with Japan, a quarter with Canada, we would take the value of the dollar against each currency and create an average using these weights. Then we could track the weighted average value of the dollar. These indexes are sometimes referred to as effective exchange rate indexes.

The usefulness of an index goes beyond the ability to simply summarize a currency's standing. While some outcomes depend on the stability of a bilateral exchange rate with the base (e.g., trade with the base or the stability of the nominal anchor), many others are probably more dependent on the stability of a properly weighted index of the exchange rate, for example, overall trade or import price stability. A stable bilateral rate coupled with an unstable multilateral rate could be associated with instability in the overall prices of imports and exports.

A fixed bilateral exchange rate could affect the multilateral index through three routes. First, it can stabilize one part of the index, the exchange rate against the base country. If the base country is a substantial part of the index, this may importantly contribute to the stabilization of the index. Second, other countries may peg to the base as well which would lead to even more stability in the index. This was more important during the gold standard and the Bretton Woods eras than during the modern era when there has been heterogeneity in both base countries and exchange rate arrangements. Finally pegs may avoid very high volatility outcomes, especially for emerging market and developing countries, by providing a nominal anchor. This stabilizes that country's currency to a wider set of industrial countries than just its own base, since most volatility among the currencies of industrial countries is relatively low compared to that of some emerging market and developing countries.

This chapter shows how the exchange rate regime can, and does, affect the overall exchange rate index. We will examine the nominal effective exchange rate, representing the relative price of monies across countries, as well as the real effective exchange rate, representing the relative price of goods and services across countries.

7.1   Literature on Multilateral Volatility

The literature on the exchange rate effects of a fixed exchange rate has tended to focus on the bilateral rates. As discussed in the previous chapter, the work of Mussa (1986) and those that followed saw a considerable effort to document the way the bilateral real exchange rate varies across exchange rate regimes. The work on multilateral exchange rates is more limited. Klein and Shambaugh (2008) examine this topic, and we return to empirical work based on those estimates in section 7.2.

Some authors present limited discussions of multilateral volatility in broader surveys of the impact of exchange rate regimes. Ghosh et al. (2002) present averages of nominal and real multilateral volatility across exchange rate regimes. They show that nominal volatility is larger for floating countries than for countries that peg. The differences across sets of countries, based on their exchange rate arrangements, are less marked for real exchange rate volatility. These results do not control for country effects or other covariates, but rather represent descriptive statistics. Similarly Husain, Mody, and Rogoff (2005) present simple averages of real effective exchange rate volatility across regimes. They demonstrate that as *de facto* flexibility increases, so does real effective exchange rate volatility. This effect is less apparent when making distinctions based on *de jure* classifications.

A small number of working papers have examined multilateral volatility in more detail. Canales-Kriljenko and Habermeier (2004) explore various institutional determinants of exchange rate volatility and present some evidence that pegs have lower nominal multilateral exchange rate volatility than floats. They focus on the institutional features of the foreign exchange market, but also include exchange rate regimes, and argue that floating countries experience higher multilateral nominal volatility. Kent and Naja (1998) examine real multilateral volatility and argue there is some limited evidence of lower real volatility for pegs. Finally, Carrera and Vuletin (2002) argue that floating regimes may not experience substantially more volatility than pegged regimes, and that only intermediate regimes truly show more volatility.[2]

One could also consider multilateral rates based on something other than trade weights. Lane and Shambaugh (2009) create a set of exchange rate indexes weighted by the currency denominations of the external assets and liabilities of a set of a hundred countries for the last fifteen years. These weights generate indexes that move considerably differently from trade weighted indexes. One notable feature is that many countries with fixed exchange rates that have a fairly volatile trade-weighted multilateral index (such as China) have a very stable financially weighted multilateral index because all their assets and liabilities that are not in local currency are in the currency to which they peg.[3]

In the following section we try to formalize and synthesize results in this research area. We use the regime classification described in chapter 3 and many of the same techniques used in the previous chapter to determine whether a fixed exchange rate has had a substantial impact on multilateral volatility during the modern era.

7.2   Empirical Evidence on Multilateral Volatility

As in chapter 6, we begin our analysis of the link between the exchange rate regime and exchange rate volatility by examining the exchange rate regime status of countries at different levels of volatility. In this chapter, we use both real and nominal multilateral volatility indexes. These are based on nominal and real multilateral exchange rate indexes from the IMF's International Financial Statistics. The indexes are constructed using trade weights. Data are available for the time period 1979 to 2004.[4]

Volatility is defined as the annual standard deviation of the monthly percentage change in the exchange rate, as it was in the previous chapter. We sort the observations by volatility and arrange them in five groups (quintiles) from lowest to highest volatility. Figure 7.1 shows the percentage of peg observations in each quintile of volatility for both nominal and real multilateral volatility. If there were no difference between peg and float observations, we would expect to see each quintile consisting of 35 percent peg observations, since this is the percentage of pegs in the overall sample. Instead, we see more pegs in the two low-volatility quintiles and a lack of pegs in the highest volatility quintile.

Pegs make up over 50 percent of the lowest multilateral volatility quintile. Nonpegs represent a much larger portion of the low multilateral volatility quintiles than is the case when considering bilateral volatility, where there are no nonpegs in the two lowest bilateral volatility quintiles. In the case of multilateral volatility, however, while nonpegs are relatively underrepresented in the two lowest quintiles, they do ac-

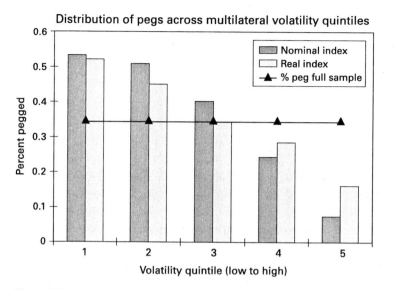

Figure 7.1
Columns show the percent of observations which are pegged within each quintile of the exchange rate volatility distribution. The line represents the total percentage pegged in the sample (35%). The number of pegs is smaller than in most samples because the real exchange rate data are only available for a limited set of countries and are skewed toward larger countries that tend not to peg. The same sample is used for both the *neer* and *reer*. If the larger sample for *neer* alone is used, the figure looks quite similar.

count for nearly half the observations. Thus pegging appears to lower multilateral volatility, but nowhere as starkly as it does with bilateral volatility. Further, while pegging eliminates any possibility of being in the top two quintiles of bilateral volatility, many pegs are found in the higher multilateral volatility groupings. In fact, 21 percent of pegs are in the two highest volatility quintiles for nominal volatility and 25 percent are in the two highest volatility quintiles for real volatility. Very high multilateral nominal volatility outcomes, however, remain largely the province of floats, with pegs making up less than 10 percent of these observations. Real multilateral volatility is less successfully tempered by a bilateral nominal peg, as 16 percent of the highest volatility quintile are pegs. Thus, overall, we see a slight tilting of multilateral volatility away from pegged observations, but the impact is far less clear for multilateral nominal volatility than bilateral nominal volatility, and even less clear for real multilateral volatility.

We further explore these results by regressing volatility on exchange rate regime status and a series of controls for both exchange rate regime spells and annual observations, in the same manner as in chapter 6. This will allow us to check the statistical significance of the differences seen in the figure as well as allow us to determine the magnitude of any potential impact. Thus we run regressions of the form:

$$EVOL_{it} = a + a_i + bPEG_{it} + u_{it} \tag{7.1}$$

where $EVOL_{it}$ is the standard deviation of the monthly percentage change in the exchange rate for either spell t (for estimates presented in table 7.1) or time t (for estimates in table 7.2). As with the bilateral volatility, we will take care to monitor the impact of outliers, typically by dropping the observations representing the top 1 percent of volatility outcomes (a set in which all observations represent floats).

Table 7.1 shows the regressions for spells. As with our analysis in chapter 6, we are limited in our ability to include year controls or other general controls because the length and timing of the spells vary. We include country fixed effects, which means identification comes from differences of being in a peg spell versus a float spell for a given country.[5] The results in this table show that peg spells have significantly

Table 7.1
Multilateral volatility in spells

	1	2	3	4
Sample	Full	Drop 1%	Full	Drop 1%
Dependent variable	Nominal volatility	Nominal volatility	Real volatility	Real volatility
Peg	−0.0250**	−0.0214**	−0.0289**	−0.0253**
	(0.0033)	(0.0028)	(0.0070)	(0.0063)
Constant	0.0365**	0.0330**	0.0471**	0.0410**
	(0.0017)	(0.0014)	(0.0035)	(0.0032)
Observations	568	562	318	314
R^2	0.42	0.45	0.37	0.43
Sample standard deviation	0.031	0.025	0.058	0.043
Peg mean	0.013	0.013	0.020	0.017
Nonpeg mean	0.035	0.032	0.045	0.039

Note: Column labeled "Drop 1%" drops the 1% largest volatility observations to reduce the impact of outliers.
Robust standard errors shown below coefficients (clustered by country); *significant at 5%; **significant at 1%.
Country fixed effects are included in all regressions.
Sample: 119 countries from 1979–2004 for columns 1 and 2; 68 countries for columns 3 and 4.

lower multilateral volatility than float spells, even when we control for all differences across countries with country fixed effects. We see that the estimated coefficient on the peg variable is negative and highly significantly different from zero.[6] Pegs have a mean nominal volatility of 0.013 and nonpegs roughly 0.035, and hence in a simple regression, the coefficient on peg is −0.025.[7] The coefficients on peg for real and nominal volatility are very close, but the overall volatility outcomes have a slightly larger range for the real volatility (the standard deviation of volatility in the sample is higher). Thus the impact on volatility—relative to the variance of volatility—is slightly smaller for real multilateral volatility.

We can control for more features of the data by analyzing annual observations rather than spells. For example, we can take into account the possibility that many first-year floats may be crisis observations, and hence atypical. We can also control for various annual covariates like inflation, capital controls, and year effects. Table 7.2 shows the results.[8] With just the peg and country fixed effects included, the estimated peg coefficient is 70 percent of the standard deviation of nominal volatility and 40 percent of the standard deviation of real volatility in the respective regressions. In both cases the coefficient is highly statistically significantly different from zero.[9]

The coefficients on the first year of floating variable show that volatility is higher immediately after a peg breaks. But, even controlling for this high volatility first year of floating, pegs are still considerably less volatile than floats. Thus floats are not simply more volatile because of crises observations following a peg; rather both nominal and real multilateral exchange rate volatilities are lower for pegs (also recall that these results do not include the very high volatility observations). This result still holds when controlling for both inflation and capital controls, as demonstrated in the regressions presented in columns 3 and 6. These regressions also show that high-inflation countries have significantly more nominal and real volatility, but capital controls do not significantly affect volatility.[10]

This significant effect of inflation on multilateral volatility could suggest that any sensible macro policy, and not just pegging, lowers multilateral volatility. Rose (2007) argues that countries that target inflation do not face higher volatility than a control group of countries. To explore this issue, we examine the multilateral exchange rate behavior of countries that have inflation targets, countries that peg, and countries that float.

Table 7.2
Multilateral volatility in annual data

Dependent variable	1 Nominal volatility	2 Nominal volatility	3 Nominal volatility	4 Real volatility	5 Real volatility	6 Real volatility
Peg	-0.0178**	-0.0152**	-0.0125**	-0.0163**	-0.0114**	-0.0093**
	(0.0020)	(0.0019)	(0.0016)	(0.0037)	(0.0028)	(0.0027)
First-year float		0.0100**	0.0114**		0.0184*	0.0196**
		(0.0027)	(0.0027)		(0.0075)	(0.0074)
Inflation			0.0365**			0.0469**
			(0.0056)			(0.0091)
Capital controls			0.0011			0.0036
			(0.0020)			(0.0041)
Constant	0.0284**	0.0264**	0.0186**	0.0313**	0.0281**	0.0178**
	(0.0009)	(0.0008)	(0.0016)	(0.0013)	(0.0011)	(0.0033)
Observations	3,007	3,007	2,849	1,626	1,626	1,561
R^2	0.25	0.26	0.36	0.22	0.23	0.35
Sample standard deviation	0.025	0.025	0.024	0.037	0.037	0.035
Peg mean	0.012	0.012	0.012	0.016	0.016	0.016
Nonpeg mean	0.027	0.027	0.027	0.031	0.031	0.030

Note: * significant at 5%, ** significant at 1%.
Standard errors clustered by country and are shown below coefficients.
All regressions include country fixed effects and drop the 1% largest volatility outliers and columns 3 and 6 drop 1% outliers in inflation.
Sample: for columns 1–3, 120 countries from 1979–2004. For columns 4–6, 68 countries from 1979–2004.

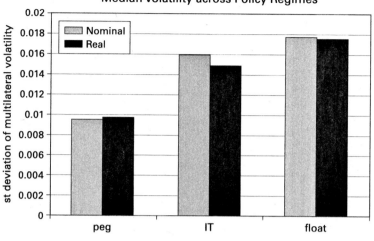

Figure 7.2
Median volatility across policy regimes.

Figure 7.2 shows that observations associated with a pegged exchange rate have lower median volatility than both observations associated with a floating exchange rate and observations representing years in which countries target inflation. Countries that target inflation do not appear to have more volatility than a typical float (as Rose suggests), but this method of reducing inflation and stabilizing monetary policy does not have the same impact on multilateral volatility as pegging the exchange rate.

Table 7.3 extends these results by testing inflation targeting in the broader regressions shown in table 7.2. Controlling for inflation targeting makes no difference to the results—the coefficient on peg is unchanged from table 7.2—and the coefficient on inflation targeting is not significantly different from zero. Rose's results suggest that countries that target the inflation rate are not different than a typical country. Here we see, however, that volatility is higher during episodes of inflation targeting than during years in which a country pegs its exchange rate, but is not significantly different from years in which a country's currency floats. When controlling for first-year floating, inflation, and capital controls, the coefficient on the peg is also the same as in table 7.2. When controlling for inflation, countries that target inflation show slightly elevated nominal exchange rate volatility (column 2). One reason they have low volatility is that they have low inflation, so controlling for low inflation may cloud the results.

Table 7.3
Comparisons with Inflation Targeting (IT)

Dependent variable	1 Nominal volatility	2 Nominal volatility	3 Real volatility	4 Real volatility
Peg	−0.0178**	−0.0125**	−0.0163**	−0.0093**
	(0.0020)	(0.0016)	(0.0037)	(0.0027)
IT	−0.0035	0.0058*	−0.0041	0.0041
	(0.0019)	(0.0026)	(0.0026)	(0.0024)
First-year float		0.0115**		0.0196**
		(0.0027)		(0.0074)
Inflation		0.0371**		0.0473**
		(0.0054)		(0.0091)
Capital controls		0.0017		0.0042
		(0.0020)		(0.0043)
Constant	0.0285**	0.0178**	0.0316**	0.0170**
	(0.0009)	(0.0016)	(0.0013)	(0.0035)
Observations	3,007	2,849	1,626	1,561
R^2	0.25	0.37	0.22	0.35
Sample sd	0.025	0.024	0.037	0.035
Peg mean	0.012	0.012	0.016	0.016
Nonpeg mean	0.027	0.027	0.031	0.030

Note: Robust standard errors shown below coefficients (clustered by country); * significant at 5%; ** significant at 1%.
All columns include country fixed effects and drop 1% outliers, and columns 2 and 4 drop 1% outliers in inflation.

While the book focuses on direct pegs to a single base—as opposed to basket pegs (see chapter 3 for discussion)—one place where it would be logical for basket pegs to be relevant is the multilateral exchange rate. As discussed in chapter 3, a basket peg assigns weights in an index to a variety of currencies and then commits to stabilizing that index. In theory, a basket peg using the same index as the multilateral nominal effective exchange rate index could perfectly stabilize that index. Two issues suggest caution in following this argument, however. First, as noted in chapter 3, basket pegs are quite difficult to discern on a *de facto* basis.[11] Second, declared baskets are frequently either *de facto* single-currency pegs or flexible arrangements in which the monetary authority changes weights without announcement and, therefore, are effectively managed floats. Thus we are left to examine *de jure* basket pegs, while recognizing many of them may be imperfect examples of *de facto* basket pegs.

In table 7.4 we augment our basic regressions on annual data with dummy variables for a declared basket peg. The results show that for both nominal and real multilateral volatility the basket pegs have a much smaller impact on volatility than a direct peg to a base. Thus, either because the basket is simply declared but not actually stabilized, or because the basket is not matched to the trade weighted index, multilateral pegs are less effective than direct pegs at stabilizing the exchange rate. For example, the results in column 1 include a dummy for a *de jure* basket peg, and thus represent a direct parallel to the regression in column 1 in table 7.2. The coefficient on the basket peg is close to zero and statistically insignificant. This specification, however, is asking whether basket pegs have lower volatility than all other exchange rate arrangements.

A distinct question is whether basket pegs have lower volatility than floats. This requires controlling for direct pegs. But we need to account for the fact that 134 out of the 512 declared basket pegs are also *de facto* direct pegs. For example, Jordan declared a basket peg from 1989 to 1997 but also had a *de facto* peg to the US dollar from 1990 to 1997 (including two years with precisely zero change against the dollar). We thus include three separate dummies: direct pegs that are not declared baskets; declared baskets that are not direct pegs; and direct pegs that are declared baskets. In this specification we see that declared baskets that are not actually direct pegs do show less volatility than floats (the coefficient is significant and negative), but the impact is less than half of a direct peg. Direct pegs—whether or not declared as baskets—both show significantly less volatility than either floats or declared baskets. When controlling for other factors, such as capital controls, inflation, and first year of floating, the pattern is the same.

When we consider real effective exchange rate volatility, the basket pegs have no statistically significant impact regardless of controls, or whether we compare them to all other exchange rate arrangements, or only compare them to floats. The coefficient on the declared basket pegs and on the declared basket pegs that do not qualify as direct pegs are never statistically significantly different from zero, and the point estimates are always close to zero. These results, in part, justify the book's emphasis on the direct pegs to single currencies (or systems of fixed exchange rates). Basket pegs are difficult to verify and in many cases seem to differ little from either a direct peg (if the basket is weighted heavily to one country) or managed floating (if it is changed

Table 7.4
Basket pegs

	1 Nominal volatility	2 Nominal volatility	3 Nominal volatility	4 Real volatility	5 Real volatility	6 Real volatility
De jure basket	-0.0036 (0.0024)			0.0017 (0.0038)		
Direct peg (nonbasket)		-0.0216** (0.0025)	-0.0153** (0.0020)		-0.0186** (0.0046)	-0.0108** (0.0034)
De jure basket (not peg)		-0.0093** (0.0029)	-0.0087** (0.0026)		-0.0021 (0.0047)	-0.0014 (0.0050)
De jure basket and peg		-0.0162** (0.0022)	-0.0125** (0.0020)		-0.0095** (0.0033)	-0.0044 (0.0032)
First-year float			0.0114** (0.0027)			0.0196* (0.0074)
Inflation			0.0357** (0.0057)			0.0467** (0.0092)
Capital controls			0.0020 (0.0021)			0.0036 (0.0044)
Constant	0.0212** (0.0004)	0.0310** (0.0013)	0.0203** (0.0017)	0.0254** (0.0007)	0.0323** (0.0019)	0.0183** (0.0034)
Observations	2,900	2,900	2,849	1,574	1,574	1,561
R^2	0.20	0.27	0.37	0.2	0.22	0.35

Note: * significant at 5%; ** significant at 1%.
Standard errors are clustered at the country level and are reported below coefficients. All columns include country fixed effects and drop 1% volatility outliers. Columns 3 and 6 also drop 1% inflation outliers.

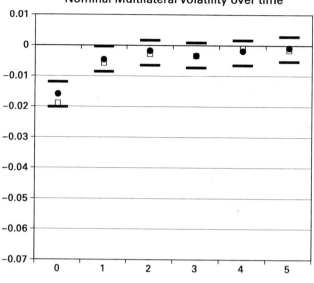

Figure 7.3
Time 0 represents the contemporaneous coefficient of exchange rate volatility on pegging, time 1 represents the coefficient on a lagged peg, and so on. Thus the point at time 2 represents the difference in volatility for a country that was pegged two years ago (whether or not it has remained pegged). Country- and year-fixed effects are included. The dark lines represent 2 times standard error bands around the main point estimates where standard errors are clustered on country. To ensure that the comparison is with nonpegged observations, new pegs that are not re-pegs are excluded. The squares represent point estimates if the first year of pegging is excluded.

often). Thus, strikingly, simply pegging to one currency has a bigger and more significant impact on multilateral exchange rate volatility than a basket peg.

Overall, these results show that the multilateral volatility of both real and nominal exchange rates is lower when a country pegs than when it floats. This is true even when controlling for country effects, outliers, or many other features and policies.[12]

We close this chapter by briefly considering whether these results for the contemporaneous effect of pegs on multilateral volatility extend over time, along the lines of our inquiry in the previous chapter. Figure 7.3 repeats the exercise of figure 6.2 and examines volatility outcomes in years after a pegged observation, regardless of whether a country stays pegged. This represents the best guess of future volatility for an observer knowing nothing more than the fact that the country is pegged today. We see in figure 7.3 that, while a pegged observation has lower nominal multilateral volatility in the year it is pegged, the likelihood of a break in the peg—combined with the relatively weak impact of pegging—means that just one year out, multilateral volatility is not necessarily lower, and two years out there is no distinguishable impact—on average—for pegs versus floats. Even dropping the first year of pegging (and hence dropping the unstable single-year pegs) has little impact.

7.3   Conclusion

By definition, an exchange rate can only be fixed against one currency. The results in chapter 6 show that fixed exchange rates lower bilateral volatility. But this result has limited implications for the economic effects of pegging. Many economic outcomes depend more on the multilateral exchange rate than the bilateral exchange rate. This chapter shows that a peg does stabilize the multilateral exchange rate relative to a nonpeg. Unlike bilateral volatility, pegs are not the only observations with low volatility. Many nonpegged observations have very low multilateral volatility. Also many pegged observations have high volatility. Thus pegging is neither necessary for low multilateral volatility nor is it a guarantee for low volatility. But the typical peg has lower volatility than the typical float even when we control for country effects and other behavior, meaning that a given country has lower multilateral volatility when it is pegging. The effect of the peg on volatility is stronger than that of other policies that might generate broad macro stability, such as inflation targeting or pegging to a basket of currencies. The latter result is particularly surprising since one might expect that a basket peg stabilizes the multilateral rate completely. It suggests that *de jure* baskets either do not truly follow the basket or the basket weights do not match the trade weights.

Overall, the results in chapters 6 and 7 show that exchange rate regimes do have a material impact on the exchange rate. Pegging stabilizes the bilateral rate in a substantial way relative to floats. This difference in volatility spills over into multilateral volatility as well. Thus it seems reasonable that exchange rate regimes may have impacts on other macroeconomic outcomes. We turn to these topics in chapters 8 through 11.

IV   Economic Consequences of Exchange Rate Regimes

8   Exchange Rate Regimes and Monetary Autonomy

The greater the attention given to the exchange rate, the more constrained monetary policy is in pursuing other goals.

—Maurice Obstfeld, "The global capital market, benefactor or menace," 1998

Chapter 2 introduced the concept of the trilemma. A country cannot pursue more than two of the three options of a fixed exchange rate, open financial markets, and domestic monetary autonomy. This core concept of international macroeconomics is very general, and it is an implication of a wide range of macroeconomic models that allow for international trade in assets, but it also follows from fairly basic intuition.

The trilemma is sometimes summarized to mean that countries can operate with an open capital market, a peg and zero autonomy; a closed capital market, a peg with autonomy; or an open capital market, a float with autonomy. More accurately, however, the concept is about trade-offs. A country does not have to operate purely at any of these corner solutions, but if it wants to stabilize the exchange rate and allow some capital mobility, some compromise in domestic monetary autonomy will be necessary. Countries can give up varying amounts of all three options, the only stricture being they cannot pursue all three at the same time.

The focus of this chapter is the important question of whether the predictions of the theory of the policy trilemma tend to be borne out in practice. We will present tests that focus on the extent to which there is a systematic difference in monetary policy independence across sets of countries according to their exchange rate and capital mobility policies. In particular, we focus on whether exchange rate pegs limit monetary autonomy. As is the case with other exchange rate issues, countries' experiences during the modern era offer an interesting and useful sample for these tests due to the heterogeneity of policies during this period. We can also use tests based on the gold standard era and Bretton Woods era to provide context for the results of the modern era.

8.1 Exchange Rates, Interest Rates, and the Policy Trilemma[1]

Before presenting empirical tests, we discuss the general principle of the trilemma, the link between exchange rates and interest rates under a peg with capital mobility. If investors can move money to either of two countries (open financial markets), and they believe that the price of one currency for the other will stay constant over time (fixed exchange rates), then the only way for there to be equilibrium in the exchange rate market is if the interest rate is the same in both countries. If a riskless asset paid more in country A than in country B, and the exchange rate at the end of the period will be the same as the one at the start, there would be no reason to ever hold the lower return country B asset. Everyone would try to sell the asset in country B and change their money to country A's currency—causing an increase in the price of country A's currency and hence the exchange rate peg to break.[2] Thus we expect the interest rate in one country to equal the interest rate in the other when there is a peg.

Alternatively, if the exchange rate is not fixed, interest rates do not have to be equivalent across countries. If an investor expects country B's currency to be worth less at the end of the year by 5 percent, she would no longer want to hold country B's asset in her portfolio unless she received an extra 5 percent in interest over the year to compensate her for the loss in value due to the depreciation of the foreign currency, which causes the domestic-currency price of the foreign asset to decrease by 5 percent. Thus, if a country has a fixed exchange rate, but people worry it may not last, there may be higher rates in the pegged country than in the base.

An equation that captures these ideas is the familiar uncovered interest parity relationship,

$$R = R^* + \%\Delta E^e, \tag{8.1}$$

where $\%\Delta E^e$ represents the expected change in the exchange rate over the maturity of the bonds. The equation implies that the home interest rate R must equal the foreign interest rate R^* plus any expected depreciation in the home currency. If this condition is satisfied, investors expect to earn the same amount of money in either country, and thus there is no excess demand in one direction or the other. Capital mobility is a precondition for the equation to hold; that is, the ability to purchase foreign bonds is a relevant consideration for the domestic investor. It is, of course, possible that new information will appear and expectations will have been wrong, but we expect this equation to hold on average. If currencies are floating, then $\%\Delta E^e$ represents the expected depreciation; if they are pegged, then we can think of it as encompassing some probability of breaking the peg combined with the expected extent of a depreciation if the peg breaks. Thus, if there is some chance of the peg breaking, we will not expect $R = R^*$ to hold perfectly.

In addition, if the assets are not identical, we do not expect R and R^* to be the same even if there is no chance of a depreciation or a devaluation. Consider a comparison of US Treasury bills (highly unlikely to default) and Argentinean Treasury bills (likely to default) in late 2001. The Argentine bonds are more risky and would have to pay a higher interest rate due to a higher "risk premium" on the Argentine bonds.

Thus we expect R to equal R^* plus any expected depreciation and any risk premium. Therefore we would not conduct an empirical test of the trilemma that requires interest rates to be identical. Rather, an appropriate test would examine whether the interest rate of countries that peg move one-for-one with the foreign or base interest rate. This test allows for a gap in the levels on interest rates across countries, and assumes that the risk premium and the odds of a peg breaking are relatively static, or at least do not change systematically with changes in the base interest rate. The regression specification for such a test is

$$\Delta R = \alpha + \beta\Delta R^*. \tag{8.2}$$

We expect β to equal 1 for a sample of pegged countries with open financial markets. If an increase in the base interest rate makes it more likely that the home country will break its peg (because the home country may not want to raise its interest rate), depreciation expectations rise when R^* rises. In this case, R would have to increase by more than R^* to preserve the peg, and β would be greater than one. On the other hand, as we have noted before, pegs are rarely perfectly fixed, but tend to have some small room for discretion. Thus countries may be able to allow a small depreciation if R^* goes up, rather than respond entirely with interest rate changes. If this is the case, β may be less than one.

For a sample of floating countries, we may expect a β of zero. This would be the case if floating countries ignored the base interest rate when setting monetary policy and their economies were independent. On the other hand, countries may experience common shocks. In this case they may coincidentally increase or decrease interest rates together such that β is greater than zero. In addition floats may try to temper exchange rate changes and hence respond to changes in the base interest rate to try to partially stabilize the exchange rate. This "fear of floating" behavior will also generate a β greater than zero.

Capital controls are crucial to this discussion. A country that limits capital flows and administratively sets the price of the exchange rate has a wide latitude in setting its interest rate since capital controls prevent international capital flows from forcing a break in the exchange rate peg. Thus the expected response of home interest rates to the base interest rate outlined in this section would hold—or at least would hold most strongly—for countries with open capital markets.

8.2   Literature on the Trilemma

While the general prescriptions of the trilemma fall straight from basic theory, room for discretion provided by target zones or transaction costs could limit the loss of autonomy from pegging. On the other hand, even floating countries may have a limited amount of autonomy if there is a correlation of depreciation expectations or risk premia with the base interest rate in which case countries may follow the base to some extent to avoid large movements in the exchange rate even if they are floating. Thus the extent that a fixed exchange rate truly limits monetary autonomy becomes an empirical question.

Both possible caveats to the trilemma have been explored empirically. The first question—is there really enough room for discretion to make the constraint irrelevant?—has been explored chiefly in the gold standard era. Work by Bordo and MacDonald (1997) suggested that countries on the gold standard had some flexibility in their monetary policy. These results are considered by Obstfeld, Shambaugh, and Taylor (2005), who show that, while the trilemma does not bind entirely, there is still a significant difference between the loss of monetary policy autonomy under pegs as compared to under floats. More recently Jansen (2008) argues that the Dutch still had some limited autonomy despite pegging to Germany due to its tight target zone against the deutsche mark and argues a target zone can provide some autonomy.

Alternatively, the fear of floating school of thought suggests that even countries that do not truly peg have limited monetary policy autonomy (see chapters 4 and 6). It is important to make a distinction in this argument. If one simply claims that some countries declare a float but actually peg, and those countries lose autonomy, this is not evidence against the trilemma but just reflects mis-declaration of the true exchange rate regime, as noted in chapter 3. The real question of the trilemma is to what extent actually following a peg limits monetary autonomy. Fear of floating is relevant to the trilemma if countries that actually do float still manage their exchange rates and give up autonomy as a result.

Some research points to a failure of empirical support for the policy trilemma. Frankel (1999) suggests that, in some cases, floats may follow the base rate even more than pegs. Frankel, Schmukler, and Serven (2004) suggest that their results show limited autonomy for all but the largest floating countries. Forssbæck and Oxelheim (2006) examine EU nations in the 1979 to 2000 period and argue there is not clear evidence of monetary policy constraints differing across exchange rate regimes. But they focus on testing elasticities rather than more straightforwardly testing differences in interest rates. This leads to very large error bands around the results, and thus they cannot reject any reasonable null hypothesis about the data.

Other research supports the empirical relevance of the policy trilemma. Shambaugh (2004) and Obstfeld, Shambaugh, and Taylor (2005) suggest that the gap between pegs and floats becomes clear when actual pegs and floats are carefully distinguished and when using an empirical specification appropriate for the time-series properties of the data and eliminating hyperinflation countries. Floating countries appear to respond less, and with more delay, to movements in the base rate. Clarida, Gali, and Gertler (1999) analyze whether the policy interest rate of different major countries is driven by local conditions or international interest rates. They find that while the United States, Germany, and Japan (all floaters) follow their own shocks, even large countries participating in the EMS significantly curtail the extent that they follow their own shocks and instead follow the German interest rate.[3]

Other recent research has tried to consider the type of interest rate shock coming from the base country. Basic theory suggests that any interest rate movement by the base country should be followed by a pegged country. Much research on monetary policy, though, prefers to eliminate any "endogenous" monetary policy changes—where the central bank is responding to local conditions. If one worried that some countries more naturally followed the base country interest rate due to similar economic circumstances (more common shocks), one might prefer to see responses to exclusively exogenous monetary policy shocks. Borenzstein, Zettelmeyer, and Philippon (2001) examine the responsiveness of a variety of countries to identified US monetary policy shocks. They find that Hong Kong reacts more than Singapore though Mexico and Argentina are somewhat similar. In addition they find that Hong Kong responds significantly more to exogenous US interest rate movements than a variety of industrial countries, which is consistent with pegging generating a loss of monetary autonomy. Miniane and Rogers (2007) derive monetary policy shocks based on a vector autoregression, and while their results are focused on the capital control side of the trilemma, their results regarding exchange rate regimes are also supportive of the idea that pegged open financial market countries follow base shocks more closely. Bluedorn and Bowler (2008) describe in detail how correlations between the base interest rate and exchange rate expectations may vary depending on the character of the interest rate change (whether or not it was expected and whether it responded to economic conditions or was exogenous). Their results suggest that open capital market pegs may respond even more strongly to exogenous shocks to the base interest rate.

We next consider results that test the basic premises of the trilemma described in section 8.1. These results are based on results in Shambaugh (2004) and Obstfeld, Shambaugh, and Taylor (2005).

8.3 Empirical Evidence on the Trilemma

In this section we present tests of monetary autonomy across different exchange rate policy regimes. We use the co-movement of home and base-country interest rates as an indicator of monetary autonomy. The exchange rate regime status is based on the *de facto* Shambaugh (2004) classification.[4] We also employ a measure of capital controls from the IMF annual yearbooks since, as discussed above, the exchange rate—interest rate trade-off is most relevant for countries with open capital markets.[5]

We test the basic equation outlined in section 8.1 across different types of exchange rate regimes. Our focus is on the modern era (as in Shambaugh 2004), a time period where there is adequate variability in regimes to test different arrangements. We also present results from the Bretton Woods and gold standard periods (as in Obstfeld, Shambaugh, and Taylor 2005). These earlier eras provide helpful benchmarks and a useful context because many countries took similar positions within the trilemma framework during these periods.[6] In the gold standard era most countries were pegged and there were no capital controls, while during the Bretton Woods period most countries pegged but capital controls were pervasive. In contrast, the modern era is marked by a mixture of policy regimes.

Each of these three eras demands its own method for classifying observations as either pegs or floats. For the gold standard era, countries are considered pegged if they have a stable exchange rate against gold. Thus, for the gold standard era, we use a *de facto* gold peg classification that parallels those used in the Bretton Woods era and the modern era. The base interest rate for the gold standard era is the UK interest rate (the London call money rate) because sterling was considered the base currency at that time. Home interest rates are call money rates for a variety of countries from 1878 to 1914. For the Bretton Woods era, the base interest rate is the US dollar interest rate since the United States was the center country in the Bretton Woods system (the sample that we use for this period is from 1959 to 1970). Obstfeld, Shambaugh, and Taylor (2005) provide details of the data for these eras. The modern era involves a variety of base interest rates as different countries peg to different bases in this era (the sample for this period is 1973 to 2000, as in Shambaugh 2004).[7]

The basic analysis examines the changes in annual interest rates across a panel of countries using OLS regressions. Results in figure 8.1 present the β coefficients (and the associated 95 percent confidence intervals) from the regressions based on equation 8.2 for a panel of countries across each of the three eras.[8] We expect the β coefficient to be larger (and near 1) for the estimates using the gold standard era sample, when countries pegged to gold and there were few constraints on international capital flows, and, to be close to zero for estimates using the Bretton Woods era sample, when there were significant capital controls. The legend to this figure reports the R^2 statistics for these regressions; we expect these to be higher for periods when the dominant determinant of the home interest rate is the base interest rate. The results in this figure match these expectations. For the gold standard countries, countries follow the base to a large degree and a reasonable portion of interest rate changes can be explained by changes in the

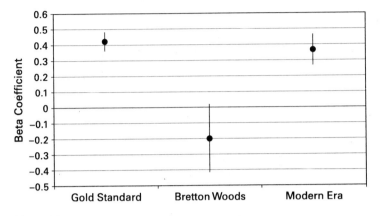

Figure 8.1
Response of local interest rate to base interest rate in different eras. Figure shows the response of local rates to base rates as well as two standard error bars. The R^2 for the gold standard is 0.26, for Bretton Woods 0.02, and for the modern era 0.03.

base. In the Bretton Woods period, capital controls shut down any interest rate pass-through. There is a tendency for home interest rates to follow the base interest rate in the modern era, but less of the home interest rate behavior is explained by the base interest rate during this period than in the gold standard era.

Another way to analyze the impact of the exchange rate regime on monetary autonomy is by estimating equation (8.1) separately for pegs and nonpegs in the gold standard and modern eras (we cannot undertake a similar exercise for the Bretton Woods era since all countries in our sample pegged during that time). The results of this exercise, reported in table 8.1, again support the core idea that pegging the exchange rate leads to a loss of monetary autonomy. The results here are even stronger than those represented in figure 8.1. Gold standard pegs move with the base considerably and the R^2 is quite high. On the other hand, nonpegged countries during that era show no propensity to follow the base, and the R^2 is zero. The gold standard results provide an important context for the results from the modern era. In the earlier period, when there were no capital controls and there was strict adherence to the peg, the β coefficient is only 0.5. The results in the modern era are similar. As in the gold standard, pegged countries moved their interest rates roughly half a point for every point move by the base. Nonpegged countries move considerably less, although nonpegs follow the base more in the modern era than in the gold standard. In ad-

Table 8.1
Results across exchange rate regime status

	Gold standard peg	Gold standard nonpeg	Modern era peg	Modern era nonpeg
ΔR^*	0.52**	0.05	0.46**	0.27**
	(0.04)	(0.09)	(0.04)	(0.08)
R^2	0.41	0.00	0.19	0.01
Observations	350	140	748	1,103

Note: dependent variable: ΔR. Gold standard results for 1880–1914, Modern era results from Shambaugh (2004) using 150 countries from 1973–2000.
Standard errors underneath coefficients. *denotes statistically significantly different from zero at the 95% confidence level, and ** denotes 99% level.
See Obstfeld, Shambaugh, and Taylor (2005) for details on sample.

dition the R^2 for pegged countries is substantial, but essentially zero for nonpegs. Effectively, a change in the base interest rate has no information about what will happen to the local interest rate for nonpegs.

Is a value of β of 0.5 too low to imply that pegs impose a meaningful constraint on monetary autonomy? Is a statistically significant value of β equal to 0.27 too high to imply monetary autonomy for nonpegs? These questions are addressed by Obstfeld, Shambaugh, and Taylor (2005). In one exercise, they generate data from a simulated target zone model with a 2 percent band. They find that a coefficient of 0.5 and an R^2 statistic below 0.2 are consistent with this tight exchange rate band. They also find that a correlation of shocks between the home and foreign countries can result in coefficients on the order of 0.3 even when there is a floating exchange rate and monetary autonomy (although the R^2 statistic remains near zero in this case).

An alternative approach to this data involves pooling the sample across pegs and nonpegs in order to check the statistical significance of the difference in the response of R to R^* across exchange rate regimes. This involves estimating the equation:

$$\Delta R_{it} = \alpha + \beta_1 \Delta R^*_{it} + \beta_2 (Peg_{it} \times \Delta R^*_{it}) + \varepsilon_{it}. \tag{8.3}$$

The β_1 coefficient represents the extent of common shocks and fear of floating in home interest rate movements, and the β_2 coefficient reflects monetary constraints due to pegging. This specification allows us to test whether the response of home interest rates to base rates is significantly different between countries that peg and countries that do not

Table 8.2
Pooling pegs and nonpegs

	Pooled	Gold standard	Modern era	Modern era
ΔR^*	0.19	0.05	0.28**	0.18
	(0.10)	(0.10)	(0.08)	(0.11)
$(\text{peg} \times \Delta R^*)$	0.24*	0.47**	0.30**	0.33**
	(0.09)	(0.09)	(0.10)	(0.10)
$(\text{FinOpen} \times \Delta R^*)$	0.31*			0.37**
	(0.09)			(0.10)
R^2	0.03	0.33	0.03	0.03
Observations	2,305	484	1,598	1,598

Note: Standard errors underneath coefficients *denotes statistically significantly different from zero at the 95% confidence level, and **denotes 99% level. FinOpen is a dummy representing having an open financial account (see text). Pooled regression includes data from all three eras.

peg. In addition the pooled approach allows us to augment the specification with an indicator of financial account openness to see if it affects the responsiveness of the local rate to the base rate.

The pooled results presented in table 8.2 support the basic message of the trilemma.[9] Only countries that have open capital markets or peg show a statistically significant relationship between their own interest rate and that of the base country (that is, the change in the base interest rate only has a significant impact on the local rate when interacted with the peg or financial market openness indicator).[10] This result is strongest for the gold standard era. The estimates using the modern era sample show evidence that the home interest rate moves significantly with the base country interest rate under both pegs and nonpegs if the financial account openness indicator is not included in the regression (though the pegs move more, as their response is $\beta_1 + \beta_2$). But the significance of β_1 disappears when controlling for financial account openness by augmenting equation (8.3) with the term $(FinOpen_{it} \times \Delta R^*_{it})$ where $FinOpen_{it}$ is an indicator of financial account openness, and its coefficient is β_3. In this case, the results are very similar to those for the full pooled sample and show that, during the modern era, a peg or an open financial account limits monetary autonomy.[11]

Rather than relying exclusively on panel results based on changes in the interest rate, we could take two alternate routes to examining the way fixed exchange rates affect monetary autonomy. First, we could run individual regressions of country interest rates on the base country for different country/regime episodes and then test whether the responsiveness to the base interest rate is altered by the exchange rate regime. That is, for any set of years where a particular country is either pegged or nonpegged, we label that an episode and then look at the responsiveness of monthly interest rates to the base interest rate over that episode. Then we can take these coefficients and see what country characteristics drive the relationship. Shambaugh (2004) pursues this strategy and finds that the peg variable is always a significant determinant of the coefficient on the base interest rate.[12]

In addition we could examine the dynamics of the way local interest rates move when the base interest rate does. To do this, we can use a technique used first in this literature by Frankel, Schmukler, and Serven (2004) and also by Shambaugh (2004) and Obstfeld et al. (2004, 2005). In this technique we can examine if the interest rates really move together and also how fast the local country responds to the base country interest rates.[13] Because the dynamics are almost certainly different across individual countries, we must run these procedures on individual country episodes. We focus on a few key statistics from the results: what is the average long run responsiveness of the local rate to the base rate (how much of a change in the base rate is eventually passed through to the local rate), how fast does the local rate adjust to the base rate (specifically what is the half-life of adjustment), and what percent of the episodes show a statistically significant relationship.

Table 8.3 presents results using this second alternative strategy. The results show that there are no significant links between home and UK interest rates for the few nonpegged episodes in the gold standard era. In fact, the negative average level relationship implies that home interest rates diverge from the UK rate rather than move toward it. Gold standard pegs, on the other hand, typically have a statistically significant relationship, and the home rate adjusts to 0.43 of any base rate shock (consistent with the panel analysis) and the adjustment is relatively quick (4–5 months). In the Bretton Woods era, far fewer pegs are significantly linked to the base, and while the coefficient is similar, the adjustment speed is roughly twice as high.

The analysis of the modern era divides the sample into countries that peg, countries that do not peg, and countries that flip between these two categories. The time samples are generally shorter (especially for the pegs), and hence the frequency of statistical significance is lower than in other eras. Nevertheless, we do see a levels relationship of almost 1 for the pegs as opposed to less than 0.7 for the flippers and a

Table 8.3
Levels analysis of individual country episodes

	Level relationship	Convergence speed	Positive and significant levels relationship	Number of episodes
Gold standard nonpegs	−0.18	4.4 months	0	5
Gold standard pegs	0.43	4.8 months	70%	20
Bretton Woods pegs	0.51	9.3 months	20%	20
Modern era pegs	0.93	7.8 months	25%	70
Modern era flips	0.68	10.6 months	16%	25
Modern era nonpegs	−0.43	35.2 months	16%	32

Note: The results are from a Pesaran, Shin, and Smith test on individual country episodes. The level relationship reports the average levels relationship found across the episodes; convergence speed reports the half-life of convergence speed toward the levels relationship after a shock. See Obstfeld, Shambaugh, and Taylor (2005) for details on specific episodes used.

negative relationship for the nonpegs. Similarly more pegs are statistically significant and the adjustment is faster for pegs. In general, the individual country level analysis is consistent with the panel analysis; pegs respond more to the base than nonpegs, and tend to do so more quickly. In short, pegs demonstrate less monetary autonomy.

The presence of the policy trilemma does not only affect monetary policy, but economic outcomes as well. This is, in fact, closer to our ultimate concern. It is a topic explored by di Giovanni and Shambaugh (2008), who base their analysis on the fact that an increase in a base country interest rate raises the local interest rate of a pegging country. This represents an adverse exogenous shock to the monetary policy of that country, which leads to a reduction in growth. A similar effect would not be expected in countries that do not peg, since interest rates in these countries do not follow those of the base country. It is possible for countries that do not peg to be affected by the base country rates in other ways, but not directly through monetary policy. These results by di Giovanni and Shambaugh show that the growth rates of pegged countries are reduced when the base country raises rates, but that effect is not present in countries that do not peg.

8.4   Conclusion

The policy trilemma offers an appealingly straightforward theoretical framework. If money flows across borders and the exchange rate is pegged, the return on simple bonds should be equal in the base and pegging countries. This would limit the monetary autonomy of the pegged country. There obviously may be benefits to pegging, but they will come at a cost—the loss of monetary independence.

There are very important implications of this theory if it, indeed, holds. While there has been some controversy over the empirical relevance of the policy trilemma, the results presented and surveyed in this chapter show that countries actually do face the tradeoffs associated with the trilemma. This is true both across eras and in the modern era itself. Countries that peg, especially those with open financial markets, lose some of their monetary autonomy as compared to countries that do not peg.

The loss of monetary autonomy is not necessarily a bad thing. A country that has not conducted monetary policy in a responsible and reasonable manner, and therefore would have little prospect of monetary policy credibility if the central bank were left to its own discretion, can peg in order to "import" the monetary policy (and credibility) of a base country central bank. In this case, the strictures of the policy trilemma may even be a blessing since forgoing monetary independence may be welfare enhancing.[14] But many countries can, and do, run sensible monetary policy that responds to domestic economic conditions and stabilizes the economy. The results in this chapter show that this option is not open to countries with fixed currencies that allow for international financial flows.

9 Exchange Rate Regimes and International Trade

Freely fluctuating exchanges...create an element of risk which tends to discourage international trade. The risk may be covered by "hedging" operations where a forward market exists; but such insurance, if obtainable at all, is obtainable only at a price and therefore generally adds to the cost of trading.[1]

—Ragnar Nurkse, 1944

The creation of a single currency area would add to the potential benefits of an enlarged economic area because it would remove intra-Community exchange rate uncertainties and reduce transactions costs, eliminate exchange rate variability and reduce the susceptibility of the Community to external shocks.[2]

—Committee for the Study of Economic and Monetary Union (Delors Committee), 1989

Slogans are meant to rally opinion, not to reflect subtleties. Thus the slogan "One market, one money" was an effective, if not totally convincing, call by the European Commission for a single currency in Europe in order to solidify the continent's trade integration.[3] At the time the 1989 Delors Report was prepared by the European Commission (headed by its president, Jacques Delors), there was actually little systematic empirical evidence that a single currency would promote international trade.

The empirical regularity that the slogan did reflect was the longstanding view of the importance of exchange rate stability in Europe. The memory of the competitive devaluations of the interwar period, and the collapse of trade at that time, cast a long shadow over thinking about European economic issues. The 1944 quote from Ragnar Nurkse above demonstrates the concern that exchange rate fluctuations would adversely affect trade. As noted in chapter 2, this concern contributed to the establishment of the Bretton Woods bilateral dollar pegs. From a European perspective, these bilateral dollar pegs had the detrimental effect of limiting monetary policy autonomy in Europe (as discussed in the previous chapter), but they also had the salutary effect of fixing European cross-exchange rates. This was seen as contributing to the expansion of European trade during the postwar period, which in turn was viewed as contributing to both prosperity and peace.

For these reasons there was a quick response in Europe to the collapse of the Bretton Woods system in an effort to stave off exchange rate instability among the continent's countries. Initial efforts, however, were either short-lived or limited in their membership. But with the establishment of the European Monetary System in March 1979, countries began their long, fitful march toward a single currency. The 1989 Delors Report proposed a way toward this goal, and, as shown in the quote above, reasons to rally around its achievement. Despite many skeptics the euro did replace national currencies, beginning with the establishment of the European Central Bank in January 1999. At the time of this writing the euro serves as the common currency for 16 countries.[4]

Is trade among these sixteen European countries larger than would otherwise be the case just because each uses the same currency? More broadly, do fixed exchange rates promote trade? Nurkse offers reasons why this might be the case, and almost five decades later, the Delors Report echoed these ideas. Contracts specifying quantities and prices of international transactions are written up to a year before delivery and payment takes place. This lead time is not necessarily different from transactions that take place between a buyer and seller within a country, but exchange rate fluctuations introduce an element of uncertainty into international transactions absent from those that take place within the borders of a single country. For example, a contract specifying the dollar price of future US exports to the United Kingdom leaves the price in terms of pounds open to the vagaries of the foreign exchange market. Hedging against this risk through the use of forward markets is a possibility, but as noted by Nurkse, this hedging comes at a price, and besides, these forward contracts are not available for many currencies and for time horizons of more than one year. A central concern is that due to this uncertainty and the associated riskiness, exchange rate volatility diminishes trade. As with any other feature of an economy that adversely affects transactions, market volatility can lower welfare.

This is a reasonable view of the effects of exchange rate volatility on trade. But it was not one that was supported by empirical analysis during the first quarter century of the modern era. During all this time, analysis of this topic proceeded by estimating trade equations that were augmented with a term representing exchange rate volatility. This research consistently failed to find a compelling adverse effect of exchange rate volatility on imports, exports, or overall trade. More recent work, however, employs longer and larger data sets and, importantly, an alternative estimation method. This research, pioneered by Rose (2000), used a gravity model and included a categorical variable representing the exchange rate regime between two countries instead of simply examining the volatility of the exchange rate. Research in this branch of the literature has consistently found a statistically significant and economically large effect of currency unions on trade. Subsequently Klein and Shambaugh (2006) examined fixed exchange rates in a gravity model and found economically and statistically significant effects.[5]

In this chapter we present an overview of this research. We begin with a review of the literature, discussing the earlier estimates of import and export equations, and more recent work utilizing a gravity model. The next section then turns to an analysis of fixed exchange rates on trade, which augments a gravity model with a categorical exchange rate variable based on the Shambaugh (2004) classification scheme discussed in chapter 3. Those results show that there is a statistically significant and economically meaningful effect of exchange rate regimes on trade. All else equal, a country with a fixed exchange rate trades significantly more with its base country than with other countries. This is not necessarily an argument in favor of pegging a currency, but it does introduce an important consideration in a discussion of the effects of exchange rate regimes.

9.1 Exchange Rate Volatility, Exchange Rate Regimes, and International Trade

Volatile currencies following the collapse of Bretton Woods prompted questions about the consequences of exchange rate variability on trade. Theoretical contributions by Ethier (1973) and Clark (1973) showed how risk-averse firms would trade less with firms in other countries as exchange rate risk increased.[6] Empirical investigation based on these models augmented export and import equations with variables representing exchange rate risk.[7] The first set of published results included samples that incorporated years in both the Bretton Woods and the modern era. Hooper and Kohlhagen (1978) report that exchange rate uncertainty, measured as the absolute difference between the lagged forward exchange rate and the corresponding spot rate, had no significant effect on the volume of bilateral trade between the United States and Germany, or on the multilateral trade between these countries and other industrial countries, over the period 1965 to 1975. In contrast, Cushman (1983) presents evidence that bilateral real exchange rate volatility significantly diminished US and German bilateral trade with each other and with four other industrial countries over the period 1965 to 1977.

One criticism of these early studies was that they mixed data from two periods that were potentially distinct.[8] Much of the subsequent published work restricted the sample to the modern era. Kenen and Rodrik (1986) show that manufacturing imports to the United States, Canada, Germany, and the United Kingdom are significantly diminished by real exchange rate volatility in the 1975 to 1984 period. Cushman (1988) presents evidence of a negative effect of real exchange rate volatility on US bilateral trade with six industrial countries over the 1974 to 1983 period. He estimates that, in the absence of exchange rate risk, US imports from these countries would have been 9 percent higher and US exports to these countries would have been 3 percent higher; thus, even when statistical significance was found, the economic significance was not always particularly large. Chowdhury (1993) uses an error-correction model and finds evidence that real exchange rate volatility significantly diminishes multilateral exports for each of the G7 countries in the 1976 to 1990 period. Kroner and Lastrapes (1993) use GARCH estimation and find a significant negative effect of nominal exchange rate conditional variance on multilateral exports of the United States, the United Kingdom, West Germany, Japan, and France from the beginning of the modern era to 1990. Broadening the set of countries beyond the G7, Thursby and Thursby (1987) present evidence that nominal exchange rate variability adversely affects bilateral trade of the seventeen OECD countries in their sample. Considering a completely different set of countries, Arize, Osang, and Slotthe (2000) present evidence of a negative and significant effect of real exchange rate volatility on the exports of thirteen less developed countries. Frankel and Wei (1993) shifted the analysis more toward where Rose (2000) and other authors would take it by including exchange rate volatility in a gravity model. They find statistically significant but economically small impacts from exchange rate volatility.

And yet, despite the fact that most of these studies report at least some evidence of a negative and significant effect of exchange rate volatility on trade, skepticism remained. In an early survey of the literature, the IMF (1984) concluded, "The large majority of empirical studies on the impact of exchange rate variability on the volume of international trade are unable to establish a systematically significant link between measured exchange rate variability and the volume of international trade" (p. 36).[9] In a later survey of the literature, McKenzie (1996) concludes that, with respect to the effect of exchange rate volatility on trade "a fundamental unresolved ambiguity exists" and that "where a statistically significant relationship has been derived, they indicate a positive and negative relationship seemingly at random" (p. 100). Research that fails to find a significant result is, of course, more difficult to publish than research that reports t-statistics greater than 2. But work by Gotur (1985) and Bailey, Tavlas, and Ulan (1987) report a lack of significant effects. Klaassen (2004) writes "The literature has not provided conclusive evidence for a negative effect" (p. 817), a result he attributes to wrongly associating measures of exchange rate volatility as indicators of exchange rate risk, especially among industrial countries that have been the main focus of this literature. Tenreyro (2007) reports little evidence of a significant effect of exchange rate volatility on bilateral trade for a broad set of 87 countries over the period 1970 to 1997, and argues that this failure to find a significant effect may reflect the fact that a volatile currency offers opportunities for higher profits as well as more risk.

Thus, by the end of the 1990s, there seemed to be little compelling evidence that exchange rate volatility had an economically significant adverse effect on trade. By extension, this could be interpreted to mean that exchange rate regimes alone had little influence on trade, since in this context the relevant difference between a fixed and a floating exchange rate is that the former exhibits very little currency volatility.[10]

This view changed with the influential work of Andrew Rose, beginning with his 2000 paper "One Money, One Market: The Effect of Common Currencies on Trade." In this paper, and in a series of subsequent papers with a variety of co-authors, Rose demonstrates that membership in a currency union has a statistically significant and economically large effect on bilateral trade.[11] These papers use a gravity model in which the dependent variable was the amount of bilateral trade between a pair of countries.[12] The regressors include standard gravity model variables, such as the logarithm of distance between the countries, the product of the logarithm of their GDP, and the product of the logarithm of their GDP per capita, as well as a set of dummy variables representing whether the two countries in the pair have a common language, a shared colonial history, a common border, and a free trade arrangement. The focus of interest in Rose's work, however, is the coefficient on the dummy variable reflecting whether one country had a currency union with the other member of the country pair. In his original 2000 paper, Rose estimates that, all else equal, membership in a currency union nearly triples bilateral trade, and the coefficient is very statistically significant.[13] Interestingly, in the context of the older literature on exchange rate volatility and trade, the coefficient on bilateral exchange rate volatility was not significant in these regressions.[14] This suggests that there is a fundamental difference between the effect of this type of fixed exchange rate on trade, and the effect of low exchange rate volatility on trade.

The statistical robustness and economic magnitude in this paper and others by Rose and his co-authors led to a re-examination of economists' views on the effects of currency arrangements on trade. Not unreasonably, Rose and his co-authors extrapolated their findings to consider the effects of currency unions on trade for countries that had recently entered into these exchange rate arrangements, or were considering doing so. Rose and van Wincoop (2001) conclude their paper with the statement "Reducing these [trade] barriers through currency unions like EMU or dollarization in the Americas will thus result in increased international trade." Frankel and Rose (2002) estimate that dollarization would raise the trade-to-GDP ratios substantially in many Western Hemisphere countries, including 24 percentage points in Chile, 7 percentage points in Brazil, and 93 percentage points in Mexico.

There are some potential concerns, however, when extrapolating from this stream of research results to the effects on trade of potential currency unions, or of fixed exchange rates more generally. Currency unions are a particularly strong form of a fixed exchange rate, involving the use of a transnational currency or the currency of another country (the data set developed by Rose classifies both transnational currencies and "dollarization" as currency unions). Currency unions are relatively rare in data sets that are weighted more to observations prior to 1999 when the euro was formed, and represent about 2 percent of the more than one hundred thousand country-pair–year observations in Rose's data set. This contrasts with the prevalence of fixed exchange rate observations presented in chapter 3. Also the currency union observations in the Rose data set are generally either between a very small country or a territory, like Bermuda or Réunion, with a very large country, like the United States or France, or multilateral currency unions like the Central African Franc (CFA) Zone where a series of small economies are linked. Fixed exchange rates include large base countries, but the pegging countries are often large as well.

Other published research also called into question the extent to which the results on currency unions and trade would generalize to potential currency unions, or to other fixed exchange rate arrangements. The only country pair in the samples used by Rose and his co-authors that represent a currency union between industrial countries is that of trade between Great Britain and the Republic of Ireland. Thom and Walsh (2001) examine trade between these countries and conclude that their currency union had only a negligible effect on trade. Nitsch (2002) concludes that the currency union between Belgium and Luxembourg did not lead to a significant increase in trade between these countries. Klein (2005) shows that the effect of dollarization on trade among Western Hemisphere countries was of limited significance.

These points of conjecture, on the extent to which the strong empirical relationship between currency unions and trade can generalize to an effect of a broader set of fixed exchange rate regimes, can be addressed directly by using the fixed exchange rate data presented in chapter 3 in the gravity framework developed by Rose. We next turn to this analysis.

9.2 Fixed Exchange Rate Regimes and Trade

The quotes at the beginning of this chapter reflect the view, one that informed policy, that fixed exchange rates promote trade. We have seen that empirical analysis that augments import and export equations do not offer strong support for this relationship during the modern era.[15] The literature on currency unions provides evidence that these exchange rate arrangements are associated with much higher levels of trade than would otherwise be the case, but there are questions concerning whether these results hold for fixed exchange rates more generally.[16] In this section we present an analysis of the effects of fixed exchange rates on trade and show that, in fact, there is significant evidence that fixed exchange rates promote bilateral trade during the modern era.[17] We begin with a discussion of the gravity model and its estimation in section 9.2.1, before presenting the results in section 9.2.2.

9.2.1   The Gravity Model and Its Estimation

Gravity models have been described as the most successful empirical framework in international economics. The model's name derives from the similarity between its central equation and the equation developed by Sir Isaac Newton that describes the gravitational attraction between two masses. Newton's law of universal gravitation says that the gravitational force between two objects is proportional to the product of their masses and inversely proportional to the square of the distance between them, that is,

$$F = G \frac{m_1 m_2}{d^2} \tag{9.1}$$

where F is the gravitational force, m_1 and m_2 are the masses of the two objects, d is the distance between them, and G is the gravitational constant. The economic gravity model says that the amount of trade between two countries is proportional to the product of their relative "economic masses" and inversely proportional to features that increase *trade resistance*.[18] As shown by Anderson and van Wincoop (2003), a theoretical gravity model takes the form

$$T_{i,j} = \left(\frac{y_i y_j}{y_W} \right) \left(\frac{1}{r_{i,j}} \right)^{\beta} (R_i R_j)^{\beta} \tag{9.2}$$

where $T_{i,j}$ is trade between countries i and j, y_i and y_j are incomes in these two countries, y_W is world income, $r_{i,j}$ is the trade resistance between countries i and j, R_i and R_j represent the resistance of each country to overall multilateral trade, and β is a positive parameter.[19] Geographic distance is one feature of trade resistance in that it serves as a proxy for transportation costs. The model can be augmented with any other variables that also reflect trade resistance. These include political variables such as whether one country has a colonial history with the other, social variables such as whether the two countries share a common language, geographic features such as whether the countries are contiguous, and economic arrangements such as whether the two countries are in a common free trade area or, of particular interest here, whether they have a fixed bilateral exchange rate.

Gravity models are most usually estimated using panel data with a number of annual observations for each country. The basic empirical specification of the gravity model takes the form

$$\ln(T_{i,j,t}) = \alpha_1 \ln(y_{i,t} \times y_{j,t}) + \alpha_2 d_{i,j} + \alpha_3 X_{i,j,t} + \alpha_4 Z_{i,j} + \varepsilon_{i,j,t} \qquad (9.3)$$

where $\ln(T_{i,j,t})$ is the natural logarithm of the real value of trade between countries i and j in year t, y_i and y_j are indicators of incomes in these two countries (typically the products of both income and income per capita are included separately), $d_{i,j}$ is the logarithm of distance between the two countries, $X_{i,j,t}$ represents a set of other variables associated with the (i, j) country pair that vary over time, and $Z_{i,j}$ represents a set of other variables associated with that country pair that do not vary over time. The variables included in $X_{i,j,t}$ can include dummy variables, like one indicating whether the two countries had a free trade agreement at time t and another indicating whether one country was a colony of the other country at time t. The variables used in the regressions that do not vary over time, represented by $Z_{i,j}$, include the product of the natural logarithm of the land areas of countries i and j (because larger countries tend to trade more domestically and less internationally), dummy variables representing whether or not countries i and j share a common border or a common language, and other dummy variables indicating whether one country had been a colony of the other, whether either country is landlocked, whether either country is an island, whether both countries had a common colonizer, and whether one of the countries was at one time a dependency, territory, or colony of the other.

The estimated effect of a particular type of qualitative trade resistance on trade between two countries, such as whether two countries have a fixed exchange rate or a currency union, is represented by $\exp(\alpha_k) - 1$, where α_k is the coefficient on that particular dummy variable. For example, Frankel and Rose (2002) obtain a coefficient of 1.38 on the currency union dummy variables. This suggests that a currency union triples trade, since $(e^{1.38} - 1) = 2.97$.

There is a concern in interpreting the results from these regressions that the exchange rate regime is correlated with other country characteristics that drive trade. In the gravity setting there are a variety of fixed effect specifications one could use to address this. Country fixed effects (CFE) control for constant country characteristics that affect trade. Beyond this, however, the decision to peg could occur at a particularly good (or bad) time for a country's overall level of trade rather than just an auspicious or inauspicious time for bilateral trade with the base country. Country–year fixed effects (CYFE) address this issue.[20]

Finally, despite the wide range of other variables included in the estimation of a gravity model, and CFE or even CYFE, there may be omitted variables that affect bilateral trade and are correlated with a fixed exchange rate. This can be addressed with the use of country-pair fixed effects (CPFE) estimation where there is a separate dummy for each country pair that exists.

CPFE estimation does not enable one to estimate the effects of any variables that do not vary over the sample period, such as distance or any variable denoted as $Z_{i,j}$. Of course, the CPFE regressions control for these factors, but their effects are subsumed in the dummy variables. This is of particular relevance when considering CPFE estimates of the effects of fixed exchange rates on trade. Any country pair that has a fixed exchange rate for the entire sample period will not yield information in the estimate of the impact of a fixed exchange rate on trade. Rather, CPFE estimates identify the effect of fixed exchange rate on trade only from those country pairs that switch exchange rate status during the sample period. Thus the coefficient on the direct peg variable in a CPFE regression represents the difference in trade due to a fixed exchange rate between two countries that, at one time, had a fixed exchange rate in place. But, as we have seen from chapter 4, most fixed exchange rate regimes do not last for the entire sample, so we lose information from relatively few country pairs when we use CPFE estimation rather than CFE estimation. Of the 144 country pairs that ever have a direct peg from 1973 to 1999, 118 change regime, with 56 of these switching once, 25 switching twice (i.e., both on and off a peg), and 37 switching more than twice.

9.2.2 Estimates of the Effects of Fixed Exchange Rates on International Trade

In this section we present estimates of the effects of fixed exchange rates on trade.[21] We build on the basic gravity model framework presented above, augmenting the specification with exchange rate regime variables and indicators of exchange rate volatility that could potentially affect trade resistance. The specification we use in this section is

$$\ln(T_{i,j,t}) = \alpha_1 \ln(y_{i,t} \times y_{j,t}) + \alpha_2 d_{i,j} + \alpha_3 X_{i,j,t} + \alpha_4 Z_{i,j} + \beta_1 F_{1,i,j,t}$$

$$+ \beta_2 F_{2,i,j,t} + \beta_3 CU_{i,j,t} + \beta_4 v_{i,j,t} + \beta_5 v_{i,j,t}^2 + \varepsilon_{i,j,t} \qquad (9.4)$$

where the variables that did not appear in the previous specification include the direct peg dummy variable $F_{1,i,j,t}$, the indirect peg dummy variable $F_{2,i,j,t}$, the currency union dummy variable $CU_{i,j,t}$, and the indicators of exchange rate volatility, $v_{i,j,t}$, and its square, $v^2_{i,j,t}$.[22]

The *direct peg* fixed exchange rate dummy variable $F_{1,i,j,t}$ is based on the Shambaugh (2004) classification system described in chapter 3. This variable equals 1 for the (i,j) country pair in year t if there is a fixed exchange rate between country i and country j in that year (this means one of these countries is a base). There are also *indirect pegs*, as represented by the dummy variable $F_{2,i,j,t}$. These indirect pegs can be most easily understood by comparing them to family relationships. For example, two countries pegged to the same base will also be pegged to one another in a "sibling" relationship (e.g., when India and South Africa both were pegged to the US dollar). A "grandchild" indirect peg occurs between a base country and another country pegged to a country that is itself pegged to the base (e.g., between Bhutan and the United States when Bhutan pegged to the Indian rupee, which was itself pegged to the dollar). There can also be an indirect "aunt/uncle" relationship, such as that between Bhutan and South Africa, and the indirect "cousin" relationship, such as that between Bhutan and Lesotho, whose currency was pegged to the South African rand. In our regressions we include a separate indirect peg dummy variable that equals 1 for a country pair that has any of the family of indirect pegs described here.

The currency union dummy variable $CU_{i,j,t}$ is the "strict" currency union dummy variable developed by Rose. We include it separately, rather than subsuming currency unions in the category of direct pegs, to allow for the possibility that the effect of this type of fixed exchange rate system on trade differs from the effect of other types of fixed exchange rates. Currency unions, direct pegs, and indirect pegs are all mutually exclusive, and any one observation can only be coded as one type of exchange rate regime.

The specification also includes the level and squared value of bilateral nominal exchange rate variability between country i and country j, $v_{i,j,t}$ and $v^2_{i,j,t}$. The inclusion of these variables allows us to consider whether they affect trade while controlling for a fixed exchange rate, and whether a fixed exchange rate significantly affects trade beyond its effect on reducing exchange rate volatility. Fixed rates may have an effect beyond that of reduced volatility for a number of reasons, most notably, the greater certainty they afford with respect to the domestic currency price paid at the time of a delivery when that payment is made six months or more after a contract is signed. Even though currency pegs are impermanent, as shown in chapter 4, the results presented in that chapter also indicate that a forecast of a fixed exchange rate is likely more reliable than a forecast of a continually quiescent floating exchange rate. Thus a fixed rate could provide a degree of certainty that may be helpful in trading relationships.[23]

The data set used in this chapter is based on information on 181 countries over the period 1973 to 1999, yielding 4,381 country–year observations (rather than $181 \times 27 = 4,887$ because some countries, like Estonia, did not exist for the entire sample period). There are 11,805 separate country pairs (rather than $(181 \times 180)/2 = 16,290$ because of missing observations), and over the 27 years of the sample there are 168,868 observations. The sample includes 1,562 observations with a direct peg. These direct peg relationships, while less than 1 percent of the observations, account for 11 percent of average annual world trade, since 90 percent of these pairs represent trade between a base country, which is usually an industrial country, and a developing country. The number of direct pegs in a bilateral trade data set will necessarily be a small proportion of the number of overall observations since any country can have a direct peg with only one other country while it can trade with as many as 100 other countries. A more relevant statistics therefore is that roughly half the country–year observations are coded as pegs and 135 countries are involved in a peg at some point, which is consistent with statistics presented in chapter 3. Any direct peg can create a large number of indirect pegs, and there are 13,679 indirect peg observations. The 2,055 currency union observations, 88 percent of which are for pairs between two developing countries, includes all intertwining relationships within a multilateral currency union (e.g., among the countries in the CFA), but not country pairs in which two countries have both, unilaterally, adopted the currency of a third country (e.g., the pair of Panama and Liberia).[24]

Regression results are in table 9.1.[25] The first column of this table presents estimates with only year fixed effects and gravity controls. The coefficient on direct pegs in this case is 0.58 and is statistically significant at the 99 percent level of confidence. The regression result in column 2 includes country fixed effects, and in this case the coefficient on the direct peg variable, at 0.32, is about half as big as in column 1, although it is still highly significant. The difference in these coefficients in columns 1 and 2 reflects the way in which country fixed effects control for multilateral resistance. As mentioned above, it might be important to allow these multilateral resistance terms to vary over time,

Table 9.1
Core results

	1 OLS, time	2 CFE, time	3 CYFE	4 CPFE, time
Direct peg	0.586**	0.324*	0.305*	0.194*
	(0.124)	(0.145)	(0.147)	(0.089)
Indirect peg	−0.351**	−0.031	−0.071	−0.015
	(0.050)	(0.040)	(0.048)	(0.028)
Currency union	1.341**	1.231**	1.159**	0.323**
	(0.158)	(0.155)	(0.156)	(0.132)
Exchange rate volatility	−0.262**	−0.271**	−0.143**	−0.205**
	(0.046)	(0.039)	(0.053)	(0.032)
(Exchange rate volatility)^2	0.007**	0.007**	0.004**	0.006**
	(0.001)	(0.001)	(0.001)	(0.001)
Ln(distance)	−1.212**	−1.431**	−1.436**	
	(0.025)	(0.026)	(0.026)	
Ln(Real GDP)	0.968**	0.059		0.445**
	(0.010)	(0.066)		(0.061)
Ln(Real GDP per capita)	0.392**	0.322**		0.007
	(0.015)	(0.063)		(0.058)
Common language	0.342**	0.302**	0.302**	
	(0.046)	(0.050)	(0.049)	
Border	0.582**	0.360**	0.330**	
	(0.126)	(0.123)	(0.123)	
Regional Trade Agreement	1.050**	0.529**	0.533**	0.265**
	(0.139)	(0.163)	(0.168)	(0.072)
Landlocked	−0.250**	−0.155		
	(0.035)	(0.322)		
Island	0.007	2.168**		
	(0.040)	(0.228)		
Ln(area)	−0.106**	0.628**		
	(0.009)	(0.045)		
Common colonizer	0.337**	0.547**	0.567**	
	(0.073)	(0.070)	(0.069)	
Current colony	0.741+	0.104	−0.015	−0.032
	(0.383)	(0.480)	(0.374)	(0.452)
Common country	−0.511	0.472	0.556	
	(0.877)	(0.558)	(0.507)	
Colony	1.403**	1.398**	1.388**	
	(0.120)	(0.120)	(0.120)	
Observations	168,868	168,868	168,868	168,868
R^2	0.64	0.71	0.73	0.87
Number of country pairs, FE				11,805
Impact of reducing volatility from mean to zero	−1.5%	−1.6%	−0.8%	−1.2%

Note: + significant at 10% *significant at 5%; ** at 1%. Standard errors are clustered at the country-pair level and reported below coefficients; constant and fixed effects are included but not reported.
Estimates for 1973–99. See Klein and Shambaugh (2006) for details.

which is accomplished with country–year fixed effects. Column 3 reports the results of this estimation. As noted earlier, the inclusion of CYFE dummy variables does not allow for separate estimation of the effect of any of the gravity variables that do not vary at the country-year level. The estimates in column 3 still show a significant result for the direct peg, and with a coefficient of 0.305 there is very little change from the estimated effect of the direct peg on trade when only CFE are included, as in column 2. Finally column 4 includes country-pair fixed effects. This is appropriate if there are specific country-pair omitted variables, but it does not allow for the estimation of specific country-pair variables that do not vary over time, like distance. Also, in this case, the use of pair-specific dummy variables means that the effect of fixed exchange rates on trade is identified solely through time-series information. The estimated effect of a fixed exchange rate on trade reported in column 4 is 0.19, and it is statistically significant at the 95 percent level of confidence.

Thus, overall, there is robust evidence that fixed exchange rates affect trade. This effect is economically meaningful, as well as statistically significant. The estimated effect from our preferred specification, the one presented in column 2 that uses CFE, is that fixed exchange rates result in an increase in bilateral trade by about 38 percent (calculated from $e^{0.324} - 1$), ceteris paribus. This effect is similar in magnitude to other important factors, such as sharing a border, having a common language, or entering a regional free trade agreement.

There is less evidence that indirect pegs significantly affect bilateral trade. The coefficient on this variable is significant only in the case of the estimates with year fixed effects, and is not significant when CFE or CPFE are used. Currency unions have a highly significant effect on trade. The estimated percentage increase in trade due to a currency union is also large, almost 250 percent ($e^{1.231} - 1 = 2.42$). This estimated currency union effect is largely based on trade between developing countries, and it is much lower than the trade between countries with fixed exchange rates, since the latter is mostly between an industrial and a developing country.[26] With CPFE, the currency union effect is reduced to the same order of magnitude as a direct peg. There are far fewer currency union switches in the modern era than direct peg switches, so time-series evidence is a less appropriate way to estimate the currency union effect.[27]

The estimated impact of exchange rate volatility is negative and statistically significant in the various specifications in table 9.1. This is a little surprising, given the general tenor of the results discussed in section 9.1. But the economic relevance of this effect is relatively small. The mean of volatility in this sample is 0.059, and therefore reducing exchange rate volatility from this value to zero suggests only a 1 to 2 percent impact on trade. As mentioned above, this suggests that measured exchange rate volatility may not fully capture the increased certainty afforded by fixed exchange rates, even when controlling for country-pair fixed effects that may be correlated with both the level of trade and the choice of exchange rate regime.

We conclude this section by investigating the estimated effect of fixed exchange rates on trade when using two of the other classification systems presented in chapter 3; the IMF *de jure* classification based on countries' declared exchange rate status and the *de facto* classification of Reinhart and Rogoff (2004). We collapse the multiple categories in these classification schemes into either pegged or floating, as we did in chapter 3. We might expect that coefficients on direct peg dummy variables based on the IMF *de jure* scheme would be less significant than coefficients presented in table 9.1, since, as discussed in chapter 3, the *de jure* classification is misleading at times. It is not as clear *a priori* what we might expect for the direct peg variable from the Reinhart–Rogoff classification scheme as compared to what is presented in table 9.1. One might expect a less significant coefficient on the Reinhart–Rogoff direct peg dummy than on the Shambaugh direct peg dummy, since the latter captures the possible effect on trade of year-to-year instability while this instability may not alter the pegged status of a country in the Reinhart–Rogoff classification. On the other hand, we might expect a more significant coefficient on the direct peg dummy based on the Reinhart–Rogoff classification if their market-based exchange rates better capture the relevant exchange rate used in international transactions than the official rate used by Shambaugh.

Table 9.2 shows the results using these two alternative classifications with country year fixed effects included (i.e., it is comparable to the results in column 3 of table 9.1). For purposes of comparison this table also reports results using the Shambaugh classification but with the smaller sample that is available when using the Reinhart–Rogoff classification. The results in this table show a strong similarity when using either the Shambaugh or the Reinhart–Rogoff classification schemes. The smaller data set has led to a slightly increased standard error for the Shambaugh codes, pushing it past standard confidence intervals. There is a bit more of a difference in the value of the coefficient on the

Table 9.2
Results across different classifications

Code	1 RR	2 JS	3 IMF *de jure*
Direct peg	0.319*	0.264	0.146
	(0.157)	(0.163)	(0.176)
Indirect peg	0.112+	−0.070	−0.046
	(0.064)	(0.055)	(0.057)
Currency union	1.331**	1.298**	1.295**
	(0.178)	(0.177)	(0.178)
Exchange rate volatility	−0.086	−0.091+	−0.091
	(0.055)	(0.055)	(0.055)
(exchange rate volatility)^2	0.002	0.002	0.002
	(0.001)	(0.001)	(0.001)
Ln(distance)	−1.308**	−1.311**	−1.311**
	(0.029)	(0.029)	(0.029)
Common language	0.340**	0.344**	0.345**
	(0.056)	(0.056)	(0.056)
Border	0.517**	0.512**	0.513**
	(0.135)	(0.135)	(0.135)
Regional Trade Agreement	0.068	0.081	0.080
	(0.185)	(0.185)	(0.185)
Common colony	0.625**	0.625**	0.624**
	(0.083)	(0.083)	(0.083)
Current colony	−0.183	−0.172	−0.183
	(0.413)	(0.424)	(0.426)
Former Colony	1.244**	1.246**	1.266**
	(0.124)	(0.124)	(0.127)
Observations	123,393	123,393	123,276
R^2	0.76	0.76	0.76

Note: + significant at 10% *significant at 5%; **significant at 1%.
All columns include country year fixed effects. Constant not reported.
Standard errors are clustered at the country–pair level and reported below coefficients.

indirect pegs, but the confidence intervals overlap at the 95 percent level of significance. Thus, overall, the results are robust to using either of these two *de facto* exchange rate classification schemes. In contrast, results are weaker when using the IMF *de jure* classification. The estimated effects of a *de jure* direct peg, reported in column 3 of table 9.2, are both smaller than the respective results for either of the *de facto* pegs, and the coefficients on the *de jure* direct pegs are not significant.

In many other chapters we have been concerned that omitted variables correlated with pegging could drive the results. As noted, our fixed effect specifications were pursued with this in mind. In this case one may be even more concerned that these results reflect some reverse causality; pegs might have begun in anticipation of an increase in trade. While sound excludable instruments are difficult to find, Klein and Shambaugh (2006) explore an instrumental variable estimation using the exchange rate regime of neighboring countries as an instrument. Results obtained with this method are very similar to those that do not instrument for the peg variable.[28]

9.3 Conclusion

One of the presumed benefits of a fixed exchange rate is that it should expand trade, at least with the base country. This has motivated calls for fixed exchange rates in various parts of the world, and is a cornerstone of OCA analysis as well (see chapter 2). Empirical backing for this presumption, however, has proved elusive. This chapter shows that when one focuses on bilateral exchange rate regimes as coded from *de facto* performance, rather than using bilateral exchange rate volatility as a proxy for regimes, there are statistically and economically significant impacts on trade from a fixed exchange rate. Thus, while the previous chapter showed pegs contribute to a loss of monetary autonomy for countries with open capital markets, this chapter demonstrates that pegging promotes an expansion of bilateral trade with the base country. Which of these effects is more important likely depends on how important trade with the base country is to the economy, and how appropriate the base country's monetary policy is for the pegging country. Thus the general lessons from the trilemma and OCA analysis discussed in chapter 2 have empirical support as a basis for choosing an exchange rate regime. The next two chapters examine more general aspects of macroeconomic performance across exchange rate regimes, the behavior of inflation and economic growth across different regimes.

10   Exchange Rate Regimes and Inflation

Inflation is always and everywhere a monetary phenomenon.

—Milton Friedman and Anna Schwartz, *A Monetary History of the United States, 1867–1960*, 1963

Exchange rate regimes are monetary constructs. This is evident from the policy trilemma, since monetary policy becomes subject to exchange rate management when a country has open capital markets. Thus the famous dictum of Friedman and Schwartz that serves as the epigraph of this chapter suggests that inflation would likely differ systematically between countries that peg and countries that do not peg during the modern era.

The stark assertion by Friedman and Schwartz, of a monocausal source of inflation, has another implication for the role of the pegged exchange rates in determining inflation; there should be no effect of a peg on inflation over and above the direct discipline it imposes on monetary policy. Theoretical research on the credibility of monetary policy, however, provides an additional channel by which the choice of the exchange rate regime may affect inflation performance. This theory suggests that the perception of the central bank's policy preferences affects inflation performance. This credibility effect operates separately from actual monetary policy, although eventually there must be a consistency between perceptions and reality.[1] Empirical analysis supports this theory, showing that central bank credibility affects inflation.[2] Thus we may expect a peg to contribute to lower inflation beyond its effect on disciplining monetary policy to the extent that it bolsters the anti-inflation reputation of a central bank.

The credibility effects of the exchange rate regime on inflation are likely to differ across time horizons. We might expect to find a stronger credibility effect of a peg, over and above its discipline effect, at shorter time horizons as compared to longer time horizons. Over a long horizon, perceptions reflect actions. A central bank can sustain a "hawkish" reputation over time only if it persistently conducts policy in an anti-inflationary manner. Thus, when looking at data representing average values over a decade or two, actual monetary growth will fully capture both the disciplinary and credibility effects of an exchange rate peg. In this case inflation will appear as solely a monetary phenomenon, and there will be no additional effect of a long-lived pegged exchange rate regime on inflation other than its effect on money growth rates.[3] An analysis of annual data, however, may uncover a role for a pegged exchange rate to temper inflation beyond its direct effect on monetary policy. Over this shorter horizon, expectations of future inflation may respond to an exchange rate peg, and not just monetary growth that year, since the peg is a highly visible and easily monitored monetary commitment mechanism.[4]

In this chapter we investigate the links between the exchange rate regime and inflation performance. We begin with a discussion that frames the analysis. We then review the empirical literature on this topic. This literature generally finds that the exchange rate regime significantly affects inflation, even controlling for the influence of other factors. In the third section we present our own estimates. These are based on a data set representing the experience of 80 countries (22 industrial, and 58 nonindustrial) over the period 1980 to 1999. Using annual data, we find evidence that a peg affects inflation through both a disciplinary role and a credibility role. We also find that the peg affects average inflation rates over this entire period by disciplining monetary policy of nonindustrial countries, but it does not have a similarly significant role for industrial countries. There is also no evidence of a distinct credibility role for average inflation over these two decades.

10.1 Exchange Rate Regimes and Inflation: A Basic Framework

The view of inflation as a monetary phenomenon suggests a model of inflation based on money demand and money supply. We present a heuristic approach to this problem in this section. We discuss the manner in which an empirical specification can reflect both the disciplinary and the credibility effects of an exchange rate peg. The appendix to this chapter supports these specifications with a more formal approach based on an explicit model.

A very general specification of money demand for a time-series cross-sectional data set takes the form

$$M_{i,t}^d = P_{i,t} \times L(\underset{(-)}{i_{i,t}}, \underset{(+)}{Y_{i,t}}),$$ (10.1)

where $M_{i,t}^d$ is the demand for money, $P_{i,t}$ is the price level, $Y_{i,t}$ is real income, and $i_{i,t}$ is the nominal interest rate, all for country i at time t. The price level is included because the demand for money is a demand for real balances, that is, $(M_{i,t}/P_{i,t})$. The liquidity demand function is $L(\underset{(-)}{i_{i,t}}, \underset{(+)}{Y_{i,t}})$, where the signs under the arguments represent their respective effects on the demand for money. Money demand increases with real income because this variable serves as a proxy for the volume of the desired transactions that require money. Money demand decreases with an increase in the nominal interest rate, since this raises the opportunity cost of holding money rather than interest-bearing assets. The nominal interest rate incorporates people's views on expected inflation. This is shown by the Fisher equation,

$$i_{i,t} = r_{i,t} + \pi_{i,t}^e$$ (10.2)

where $r_{i,t}$ is the real interest rate and $\pi_{i,t}^e$ is the expected inflation rate.

The central bank supplies money to an economy. Equilibrium in the money market requires that money demand equals money supply, $M_{i,t}^S$. Since money demand and money supply are the equal in equilibrium, and since the money market, like other asset markets, clears virtually moment-by-moment, we will denote both money demand and money supply by $M_{i,t}$. Thus in equilibrium we have

$$M_{i,t} = P_{i,t} \times L(\underset{(-)}{r_{i,t} + \pi_{i,t}^e}, \underset{(+)}{Y_{i,t}})$$ (10.3)

which can be rewritten as

$$P_{i,t} = M_{i,t}/L(\underset{(-)}{r_{i,t} + \pi_{i,t}^e}, \underset{(+)}{Y_{i,t}}).$$ (10.4)

As shown in the appendix, this relationship can be expressed in percentage change terms. In this case inflation (the percentage change in prices), $\pi_{i,t}$, is a function of the percentage change in money supply, the percentage change in income, and the expected inflation rate. Thus a regression equation based on this relationship is

$$\pi_{i,t} = \beta_E \pi_{i,t}^e + \beta_M \%\Delta M_{i,t} - \beta_Y \%\Delta Y_{i,t} + \varepsilon_{i,t},$$ (10.5)

where $\%\Delta M_{i,t}$ is the percentage change in the money supply, $\%\Delta Y_{i,t}$ is the growth of real national income, and $\varepsilon_{i,t}$ is a regression error term.[5]

This specification can be modified to consider the effect of a pegged exchange rate on inflation. A peg potentially affects two of the variables in (10.5): the contemporaneous growth of money $\%\Delta M_{i,t}$ through its discipline effect; and expected future inflation rate $\pi^e_{i,t}$ through its credibility effect. We can jointly test for the discipline and credibility roles of a peg by estimating

$$\pi_{i,t} = \beta_P PEG_{i,t} - \beta_Y\%\Delta Y_{i,t} + \varepsilon_{i,t}. \tag{10.6}$$

We expect that the estimate of $\beta_P < 0$ because money growth is systematically lower in years in which a country pegs than in years in which it does not, and for countries that persistently peg than for countries that do not.[6] In addition to this discipline effect, the PEG dummy variable in this specification also captures the credibility effect of fixing the exchange rate on expectations of future inflation. This would bolster the estimated negative value of β_P since, with a persistent peg, expected inflation will be lower in the future. As shown in (10.5), this tempers inflation in the present.

An empirical specification that focuses only on a peg's credibility effect is

$$\pi_{i,t} = \beta_P^C PEG_{i,t} + \beta_M\%\Delta M_{i,t} - \beta_Y\%\Delta Y_{i,t} + \varepsilon_{i,t}. \tag{10.7}$$

We expect $\beta_P < \beta_P^C < 0$ because (10.7), unlike (10.6), controls for the discipline effect of the peg through the inclusion of money growth as a separate explanatory variable. The credibility effect of the peg operates through its effect on expected future inflation, and therefore depends on the likelihood of the persistence of the peg as well as the effect of the peg on inflation. In the data we use in section 10.3, the probability that a country maintains a peg from one year to the next is 90 percent, a figure in line with the statistics presented in chapter 4. The credibility effect also depends on the recognition that inflation is lower under a peg than under a float. Table 10.1 (in section 10.3) demonstrates that the average inflation rate when there is a peg is 56 percent of the average inflation rate when a currency floats in the sample used in this chapter.

An alternative to estimating cross-sectional time-series regressions with annual data is to estimate the effects of the exchange rate regime on inflation for a long-horizon cross section. In section 10.3, along with regressions that use annual data for a cross section of countries, we also present estimates of equations (10.6) and (10.7) where we use the average value of the variables for countries over the period 1980 to 1999. A significant discipline effect of a peg that distinguishes it from a float would lead to a negative coefficient on the peg variable in (10.6). But, as discussed above, one would not expect a credibility effect of a peg over and above its effect on monetary discipline in these cross-sectional regressions, since expectations over twenty years should be broadly consistent with actual behavior. Therefore we can reasonably expect the long-run marginal credibility effect to be zero, even if we find a significant credibility effect in the annual data.

The specifications presented in this section generally correspond to ones used in empirical analyses of this topic. This discussion provides a framework for interpreting results from the literature discussed in the next section, as well as our own estimates that are presented in section 10.3.

10.2   Empirical Studies of Exchange Rate Regimes on Inflation

There are two types of country-level empirical studies of the effects of the exchange rate regime on inflation. One type considers particular events in which the exchange rate serves a central role as a nominal anchor in a disinflationary strategy. These studies typically consider the chronology of particular episodes, or the experience of a small set of countries suffering from high inflation. For example, Collins (1988) shows that the establishment of the European Monetary System in 1979 was not a significant contributing factor to the subsequent fall in inflation rates among its members, despite claims made at that time, and Végh (1992) studies the role of exchange rate targets in efforts to tame hyperinflations.[7] A second type of empirical analysis focuses on the systematic effects of the exchange rate regime on inflation across a wider cross section of countries, which is the focus of the analysis in this chapter. In this section we review existing research on this topic.[8]

Ghosh et al. (1997) conducted one of the first studies of the effects of the exchange rate regime on inflation in a wide cross section of countries. Their analysis uses a tripartite classification system ("pegs," "intermediate," and "float") and includes the experience of 140 countries over the time period 1960 to 1990, using annual data. They document differences in inflation under the three exchange rate arrangements. They find that the average inflation rates were 8.4 percent in pegs, 11.6

percent in intermediate regimes, and 15.2 percent in floating regimes, although the pegs were predominantly in the 1960s when worldwide inflation was lower.

Ghosh et al. also estimate the conditional effect of the exchange rate regime on inflation.[9] Their regressions include peg and intermediate exchange rate dummy variables, the growth in real income, the change in the nominal interest rate, an indicator of central bank turnover, and an indicator of trade openness.[10] Thus this specification is an augmented version of equation (10.6), and the coefficients on the peg dummy variables (analogous to β_P) represent both credibility and discipline effects. Their estimates suggest that a peg lowers inflation by 5 percentage points as compared to a float (an estimate significant at better than the 99 percent level of confidence), and an intermediate exchange rate regime lowers inflation by 1.5 percentage points as compared to a float (significant at better than the 90 percent level of confidence). They also present regressions that include money growth rates as well as the other regressors (so the coefficients on the peg dummy variables are analogous to β_P^C in equation 10.7). The coefficients on the pegs are smaller (in absolute value) in these regressions than in regressions that do not include money growth. The estimated effect of a peg is the statistically significant reduction of inflation by 1.8 percentage points as compared to a float, while inflation performance under an intermediate exchange rate regime is not statistically distinguishable from that under a float. Money growth is highly significant in this regression. Thus these results suggest that a pegged exchange rate affects annual inflation through both a disciplinary and a credibility role while an intermediate regime only affects inflation through the direct discipline it imposes on monetary policy. The significant effect of a peg on inflation is robust to other specifications, including a simultaneous equation model in which the decision by a country as to whether or not to peg is jointly determined with the inflation rate.

Ghosh, Gulde, and Wolf followed up this working paper with a chapter on the effects of the exchange rate regime on inflation in their 2002 book. They report similar results with respect to the effect of pegged exchange rates and intermediate regimes on inflation. An important extension in this book is that they estimate the effect of exchange rate regimes on inflation for subsamples of the data. The effects reported in their earlier working paper, that pegged exchange rates lower inflation as compared to floats while intermediate regimes do not, holds for upper middle-income countries. Both pegs and intermediate regimes are associated with lower inflation than what occurs with floating exchange rates for lower middle-income countries, while neither have a significant effect for upper income countries.

Differences in the effects of the exchange rate regime on inflation across income groups are also found by Levy-Yeyati and Sturzenegger (2001). Their results are based on annual data, from 1974 to 1999, for 154 countries. Like the research by Ghosh et al., they also use a tripartite exchange rate regime classification, although one drawn from their own classification scheme (which is discussed in chapter 3). Their regression estimates show a significant reduction in inflation if a country pegs, conditional on a number of other factors including money growth. Interestingly, the reported estimate is that pegs lower inflation by 1.8 percentage points as compared to floats, the same point estimate found by Ghosh et al. (1997). Also, as in Ghosh, Gulde, and Wolf (2002), Levy-Yeyati and Sturzenegger find an effect of pegs on inflation for low-volatility and nonindustrial countries but not for industrial countries. Furthermore, by splitting the sample, Levy-Yeyati and Sturzenegger distinguish between pegs in place for five or more consecutive years ("long pegs") and those in place for less than this amount of time ("short pegs"). They find that long pegs, but not short pegs, contribute to lower inflation for nonindustrial countries.

Husain, Mody, and Rogoff (2005) also find differences in the effect of the exchange rate regime on inflation across income groups. They use yet another exchange rate classification, the Reinhart–Rogoff classification (see chapter 3), in a data set with annual data for 158 countries covering the period 1970 to 1999 (the data, but for the classification scheme, is from Ghosh, Gulde, and Wolf 2002). In regressions that include money growth rates, as well as other regressors mentioned above, they find a significant negative effect of pegging, as compared to freely floating, only for emerging market and developing countries. In addition, pegs delivered lower inflation than limited flexibility or managed floating for developing (but not emerging market) countries. Similarly Bleaney and Francisco (2007) report a significant negative effect of pegs on inflation in a time-series cross-section analysis that does not include money growth as a regressor.

Alfaro (2005) uses annual data for 130 industrial and developing countries over the period 1973 to 1998 to investigate whether inflation is negatively related to openness, as proposed by Romer (1993). Romer argued that the advantages of surprise inflation decrease with the openness of an economy and, for that reason, inflation expectations, and inflation itself, are lower in open economies, all else equal.[11] His empirical tests using cross-country averages of inflation and openness confirm this prediction. Alfaro also shows a negative relationship between inflation and openness in a cross-section of countries. But she finds no relationship between openness and inflation in a time-series cross section when she includes year and country dummy variables. More to the point for this chapter, she finds that the exchange rate regime is a statistically significant and economically relevant determinant of inflation in the time-series cross-sectional data set. She uses the IMF *de jure* classification scheme as well as a coding based on the Reinhart–Rogoff *de facto* classification scheme. Estimates using either scheme show a statistically significant reduction in inflation from about 25 to 40 percent when a country has a peg as compared to when it has a floating exchange rate, while controlling for other factors (but not controlling for money growth).

The papers discussed in this section are relatively consistent in their findings of a negative relationship in annual data between pegged exchange rates and inflation through the discipline effect, that is, when monetary growth is not included as a regressor. There is less evidence of an effect conditional on money growth, one that would reflect a credibility channel over and above that provided by actual monetary growth. In the next section we present our own results on this topic.

10.3   Evidence on Inflation and the Exchange Rate Regime

The discussion to this point suggests that the empirical link between the exchange rate regime and inflation depends on the way the analysis is framed. Inflation is likely to be lower when countries peg than at other times, something that can be determined by estimating a simple bivariate relationship using a peg dummy variable. Augmenting this regression with other variables that affect inflation, other than the growth of the money supply, offers estimates of the role of a peg on inflation through the discipline it imposes on monetary policy as well as the credibility it confers concerning future policy. Adding the money growth rate shows the role played by the peg through its effects on credibility alone. In this section we present our own findings on the role of the exchange rate regime on inflation for a cross section of countries using each of these approaches.

The main data set we use covers the experience of 80 countries over the twenty-year period 1980 to 1999. Results are presented for the full set of 80 countries, as well as for the subset of the 22 richest countries (labeled "Industrial countries" in the tables) and the 58 emerging-market and developing countries (labeled "Developing countries").[12]

Most results for the set of developing countries exclude eleven countries that had an inflation rate above 100 percent for any year of the sample (of course, none of the industrial countries had an inflation rate this high during the sample period). This exclusion is an effort to limit influence of outliers that would tilt estimates toward a significant tempering of inflation by pegs. In one instance the significance of a peg differs depending on whether the results are based on the group of 58 developing countries that had no experience with very high inflation or the wider set of 69 countries. In this case the table includes results for both sets of developing countries. In all other cases, however, the results concerning the significance of a peg on inflation are the same across the 58-country and 69-country samples.[13]

The top panel of table 10.1 presents some basic statistics on inflation in the 80-country data set and its subsets. The distribution of inflation rates is skewed, as shown by the fact that the average inflation rate (10.34 percent) is almost 45 percent bigger than the median rate (7.15 percent). Also, as might be expected, the average annual inflation rate among developing countries is more than 80 percent larger than that

Table 10.1
Inflation statistics, 1980 to 1999

	Inflation: average	Inflation: median	Obser-vations	Peg obser-vations (%)	Countries
All countries	10.34%	7.15%	1,473	549 (37%)	80
Industrial countries	6.47%	4.02%	418	111 (27%)	22
Developing countries	11.87%	8.58%	1,055	438 (42%)	58

Pegs and inflation
$\text{Inflation}_{i,t} = \beta_0 + \beta_{PEG}\text{PEG}_{i,t} + \varepsilon_{i,t}$

	All countries	Industrial countries	Developing countries
β_0	11.90*	7.59*	14.05*
	(1.13)	(1.32)	(1.44)
β_{PEG}	−4.20*	−4.20*	−5.25*
	(1.19)	(1.35)	(1.49)
Adjusted R^2	0.032	0.055	0.045

Note: *significant at better than the 95% level of confidence.
Standard errors are clustered at the country level and reported below coefficients.

of industrial countries, while the median inflation rate for developing countries is more than twice as big as that of industrial countries.

The lower panel of table 10.1 presents estimates of bivariate regressions that use a dummy variable that equals 1 in years in which a country pegs (the peg dummy is based on the Shambaugh classification scheme described in chapter 3).[14] Inflation is significantly lower in years in which there is a peg as compared to other years. The average inflation rate for all countries for years in which there is not a peg is 11.90 percent, while it is 7.70 percent when there is a peg. The effect of a peg on reducing inflation is highly significant for both developing and industrial countries.

These estimates, however, do not show the direct effects of a peg on inflation since other factors may systematically differ with the presence of a peg. Rather, we want a model-based analysis, like the specifications (10.6) and (10.7), to show how pegs contribute to tempering inflation. Table 10.2 offers an analysis of this type. The first three columns of table 10.2 present estimates that do not include money growth while the other four columns include the current and lagged money growth rates. The regressions also include other variables that potentially affect inflation. The growth in real GDP is expected to have a negative effect on inflation, as shown in section 10.1. Also, as discussed in the literature review section, other variables have also been used in panel regressions. Greater trade openness is expected to be associated with lower inflation since the adverse consequences of inflation are bigger for a more open economy, as pointed out by Romer (1993). More openness with respect to capital flows, as well as trade flows, is also theoretically associated with lower inflation, so the expected effect of capital controls is to contribute to higher inflation. Research has shown that leadership turnover at a country's central bank is associated with higher inflation. Finally adverse terms of trade shocks can also contribute to inflation.

The results reported in the first three columns of table 10.2 show a highly significant effect of pegs on inflation for the full set of countries, as well as for the subsets of industrial countries and developing countries. Controlling for other factors, inflation is estimated to be lower by 4.35 percentage points in industrial countries and 4.16 percentage points in developing countries (that had no experience with very high inflation) in years in which there is a peg than in other years. This could reflect both the discipline and credibility effects. The results in columns 4 through 7 of table 10.2 reflect only the credibility effects

Table 10.2
Inflation regressions, annual data, 1980 to 1999

	Country group						
	I All	II Industrial	III Developing[a]	IV All	V Industrial	VI Developing	VII Developing[a]
Peg dummy	-3.70*	-4.35*	-4.16*	-1.29*	-2.27*	-1.26	-1.81*
	(1.13)	(1.57)	(1.46)	(0.63)	(0.55)	(0.79)	(0.83)
%Δ money				0.35*	0.24*	0.39*	0.56*
				(0.05)	(0.10)	(0.05)	(0.05)
Lag %Δ money				0.26*	0.22*	0.26*	0.07*
				(0.03)	(0.07)	(0.04)	(0.02)
%Δ real GDP	-0.36*	-0.65*	-0.39*	-0.62*	-0.62*	-0.64*	-0.67*
	(0.09)	(0.16)	(0.10)	(0.09)	(0.12)	(0.10)	(0.08)
Trade openness	-1.20	4.09+	-3.24+	0.68	1.06	-0.70	-0.95
	(1.30)	(2.30)	(1.70)	(0.86)	(1.22)	(1.06)	(1.03)
Capital controls	5.19*	7.44*	0.60	2.93*	4.21*	2.59	2.67+
	(1.50)	(1.93)	(2.69)	(0.91)	(1.17)	(1.44)	(1.39)
CB turnover	8.58*	-2.71	8.24*	2.90+	-3.63	3.57*	3.69*
	(3.45)	(6.88)	(3.20)	(1.64)	(4.53)	(1.52)	(1.58)
%Δ total	-0.11	0.67	0.36	-2.22	-6.38	-1.88	-3.43
	(2.37)	(7.91)	(2.41)	(1.95)	(8.43)	(2.01)	(2.25)
Adjusted R^2	0.14	0.30	0.13	0.48	0.62	0.44	0.56
Observations	1,473	418	1,055	1,472	418	1,054	1,211

Note: *significant at better than the 95% level of confidence; + significant at between 90% and 95% levels of confidence.
a. Includes countries that experienced high (>100%) inflation, though years with high inflation are omitted.
Standard errors are clustered at the country level and reported below coefficients.

since money growth is included in these regressions. As predicted in section 10.1, the coefficients on the peg dummy variable are smaller (in absolute value) when the money growth variables are included in the regression. The credibility effect is significant among industrial countries and, for these countries, about half of the effect of the peg on inflation is through the credibility effect and half through the discipline effect. There is no evidence of a significant credibility effect for the subset of 58 developing countries. This differs from results from previous research, as discussed in section 10.2, which tended to find significant effects for a peg, while controlling for monetary growth, for developing and emerging market countries but not for industrial countries. Part of the reason for this is differences in the samples. To illustrate this point, we present, in column 7, estimates that include the experience of the eleven countries with experience of high inflation as well as the other 58 developing countries, although we omit observations for years in which inflation exceeded 100 percent. Comparing the results in columns 6 and 7 shows that these additional 157 observations cause the coefficient on the peg variable to increase by over 40 percent. Also this coefficient is significant at better than the 95 percent level of confidence.[15]

The results in table 10.2, and indeed all estimates in this chapter, are consistent with the basic model presented in section 10.1, since the coefficients on the money growth variables and the growth of real GDP are always significant at better than the 95 percent level of confidence. The results for the full set of countries in table 10.2 show that an increase in the rate of money growth by 10 percentage points, all else equal, raises inflation by 3.5 percentage points that year and by 2.6 percentage points in the subsequent year. A one percentage point increase in national income, all else equal, lowers inflation by 0.62 percentage points. Capital controls are associated with significantly higher inflation in industrial countries. There is also evidence that central bank turnover is associated with higher inflation in developing countries.

One possible concern with these results is that the choice of whether to peg could itself be a function of the inflation rate. If a country is more likely to peg in years in which it has low inflation, then the coefficient on the peg dummy variable will overstate the effect of the peg on inflation. But, in chapter 5, we showed that a country's choice to peg its currency tends to be associated with variables that, if they change at all, tend to do so slowly. This would suggest that endogeneity might not be a major concern. Nevertheless, to check for this possibility, we present instrumental variable (*IV*) estimates in the first three columns of table 10.3. The top panel presents estimates that do not include money growth while the bottom panel includes current and lagged money growth. In each case, the two excluded instruments are dummy variables showing whether a country pegged its currency continually for the prior three years, and continually for the prior five years. The coefficient on the three-year prior peg dummy variable is positive and very significant in the first-stage of the instrumental variable estimation and, as reported in the table, the adjusted R^2 statistics on the first stage are good. The pattern of the significance of results of the *IV* estimates are the same as those of the OLS estimates presented in table 10.2; the peg dummy is significant at better than the 95 percent level of confidence for the full sample, and both subsamples, when money growth is excluded from the regression but is only significant at this level of confidence for the industrial country sample when money growth is included.[16] Concerns about biased OLS results due to endogeneity are also allayed by the fact that the coefficients on the peg dummy variable estimated with instrumental variables are uniformly larger than those estimated with OLS.

Another potential concern is that countries that tend to peg also have lower inflation for reasons unassociated with the peg that are not fully captured through the inclusion of other variables in the regression. One way to address this is to estimate the regressions using country fixed effects (CFE). The coefficients in these estimates show the effect on inflation that occurs when a country switches to a peg. These estimates are presented in the columns 4 through 6 of table 10.3, with estimated excluding money growth presented in the top panel and estimates including money growth included in the bottom panel. In this case, inflation is significantly lower only in the case of industrial countries that switch to a peg, not for developing countries.[17] This result for industrial countries is found for both the estimates that exclude money growth and those that include money growth, so there is evidence of significant credibility and discipline effects.[18]

The final sets of results, presented in table 10.4, correspond to the specifications where we use a data set in which the dependent variable is the average rate of inflation over the years 1980 to 1999, and the independent variables are the average rates of money growth, real GDP growth, trade openness, capital controls, and central bank turnover over this period. The peg indicator is a dummy variable that equals 1 if, during the twenty-year period, there was a continuous peg spell

Table 10.3
Inflation regressions, annual data, 1980 to 1999: Alternative estimation methods

	Discipline and credibility effects					
	Country group			Country group		
	All	Industrial	Developing	All	Industrial	Developing
	IV Estimates			Estimates with CFE		
Peg dummy	−4.83*	−5.37*	−5.88*	−3.08+	−2.47*	−3.08
	(1.49)	(2.04)	(1.88)	(1.70)	(0.79)	(2.22)
%Δ real GDP	−0.36*	−0.65*	−0.38*	−0.32*	−0.90*	−0.28*
	(0.09)	(0.16)	(0.10)	(0.10)	(0.22)	(0.10)
Trade openness	−0.86	4.85+	−2.80	12.65*	18.85*	12.42*
	(1.42)	(2.67)	(1.82)	(3.29)	(8.99)	(3.45)
Capital controls	5.18*	7.36*	0.61	4.42*	6.05*	2.86
	(1.51)	(1.90)	(2.69)	(0.95)	(1.20)	(1.90)
Central bank turnover	8.68*	−3.03	8.46*	2.19	−10.55	5.42*
	(3.41)	(6.98)	(3.10)	(3.78)	(13.27)	(2.47)
Adjusted R^2	0.14	0.30	0.13	0.45	0.46	0.43
IV: first-stage adjusted R^2	0.57	0.48	0.60			

Only credibility effects

	IV Estimates			Estimates with CFE		
Peg dummy	−1.74+	−4.09*	−1.52	−1.89	−1.81*	−1.93
	(0.97)	(1.16)	(1.12)	(1.23)	(0.53)	(1.57)
%Δ money	0.35*	0.23*	0.38*	0.26*	0.21*	0.28*
	(0.05)	(0.10)	(0.05)	(0.05)	(0.10)	(0.05)
Lag %Δ money	0.26*	0.21*	0.27*	0.19*	0.20*	0.19*
	(0.03)	(0.07)	(0.04)	(0.04)	(0.07)	(0.04)
%Δ real GDP	−0.61*	−0.63*	−0.64*	−0.46*	−0.75*	−0.45*
	(0.09)	(0.12)	(0.10)	(0.09)	(0.12)	(0.09)
Trade openness	−0.54	2.48+	−0.64	6.99*	14.06	6.60*
	(0.92)	(1.37)	(1.10)	(2.35)	(8.25)	(2.36)
Capital controls	2.95*	4.17*	2.60+	3.06*	3.66*	3.03+
	(0.92)	(1.15)	(1.44)	(0.92)	(1.60)	(1.68)
Central bank turnover	3.00+	−4.20	3.65*	1.35	−7.26	3.41+
	(1.64)	(4.80)	(1.49)	(2.38)	(7.17)	(1.75)
Adjusted R^2	0.48	0.61	0.60	0.57	0.66	0.54
IV: first-stage adjusted R^2	0.58	0.50	0.44			
Observations	1,472	418	1,054	1,472	418	1,054

Note: *Significant at better than the 95% level of confidence; + significant at between 90% and 95% levels of confidence. Standard errors are clustered at the country level and reported below coefficients.

that lasted for at least ten years or two continuous peg spells that each
lasted for at least six years.[19] As discussed in section 10.1, we expect a
significant and negative coefficient on the peg dummy variable when
average money growth is excluded from the specification if the peg
has an important discipline effect on monetary policy, and a coefficient
statistically indistinguishable from zero when average money growth
is included since any credibility effects should be captured in the monetary growth variable.

Results in the first three columns of table 10.4 show that the coefficient on the peg variable is negative and significant in the regressions
that exclude money growth for the sample of 58 developing countries,
and for the full sample, but not for the sample of 22 industrial countries. Thus a peg seems to have a significant role in disciplining monetary policy for developing countries, but not for industrial countries,
over this time horizon. This could be a reflection of the fact that, over
this period, there was a starker distinction between the monetary policy of developing countries that tended to peg and the monetary policy
of developing countries that did not tend to peg than that between in-

Table 10.4
Cross-country regressions, 1980 to 1999 average inflation rates

| | Country group | | | | | |
	All	Industrial	Devel- oping	All	Industrial	Devel- oping
Peg's average	−3.50*	−1.53	−3.65*	0.25	−0.70	0.80
value	(1.44)	(2.16)	(1.75)	(0.72)	(0.94)	(0.84)
%Δ money				0.88*	0.56*	1.00*
				(0.06)	(0.10)	(0.07)
%Δ real GDP	−0.47	−0.49	−0.73	−1.38*	−1.15*	−1.43*
	(0.37)	(0.82)	(0.50)	(0.28)	(0.51)	(0.26)
Trade openness	−1.49	0.17	−4.12+	−0.06	−1.06	1.25
	(1.72)	(2.68)	(2.13)	(0.87)	(1.94)	(0.91)
Capital controls	4.77*	5.89*	−0.59	2.48*	3.84*	3.94*
	(2.05)	(2.07)	(3.25)	(0.89)	(1.17)	(1.17)
Central bank	16.24*	26.13*	10.45	1.16	4.35	1.77
turnover	(7.10)	(10.10)	(6.43)	(2.45)	(6.51)	(2.86)
Adjusted R^2	0.32	0.73	0.33	0.86	0.90	0.87
Observations	80	22	58	80	22	58

Note: *significant at better than the 95% level of confidence; + significant at between
90% and 95% levels of confidence.
Standard errors are robust to heteroskedasticity and reported below coefficients.

dustrial countries that tended to peg and the other industrial countries. Pegging may have been an effective disciplinary device for developing countries, but industrial countries did not need to peg in order to conduct monetary policy in a disciplined fashion.

The importance of monetary growth for inflation is shown in columns 4, 5, and 6 of table 10.4. In each of these columns the coefficients on the average money growth and average GDP growth are of the expected signs and highly significant (note the change in the significance of the coefficient on average GDP growth when money growth is included as a regressor). The R^2 statistics in these columns indicate that these models do a very good job of explaining the cross-country variation in inflation. But, as predicted in section 10.1, whether a country pegs is not a significant part of this explanation, once money growth is included in the regression. The point estimates of the coefficients on the peg indicator are small and insignificant when average money growth is included. These results seem to suggest that average inflation over two decades is, in fact, a monetary phenomenon.

10.4 Conclusion

The discussion of the policy trilemma in chapters 2 and 9, along with a framework in which prices reflect monetary developments, suggests an important role for the exchange rate regime in influencing inflation. In this chapter we have shown that inflation is significantly lower when countries peg than when they float. There are at least two possible reasons for this, one linked to the discipline a peg imposes on monetary policy and another corresponding to the manner in which a peg affects expectations over and above its direct influence on monetary policy. There is evidence for both of these channels being important, at least in annual data. There is also evidence of the role of a peg in disciplining monetary policy of developing countries over longer horizons, but it is less clear that a peg offers a discipline to central banks of industrial countries that they would not otherwise exhibit.

These results suggest that pegged exchange rates can help discipline policy in a way that can temper inflation. Previous chapters have shown that pegged exchange rates can help foster bilateral trade but generate a loss of monetary autonomy. Are there more consequences for other economic outcomes, like economic growth, that add to the cost–benefit calculus of exchange rate regime choice? We turn to that topic in the next chapter.

Appendix

The ideas presented in section 10.1 can be motivated through an analysis based on the classic Cagan (1956) money demand function. This function takes the form

$$\frac{M_t^d}{P_t} = Y_t^\alpha e^{-\lambda i_t}, \tag{10A.1}$$

where M_t^d is the demand for money, P_t is the price level, Y_t is real income, and i_t is the nominal interest rate, all at time t. Equilibrium in the money market requires that money demand equals money supply. We assume that the effective money supply at time t, M_t^S, is a function of a broad monetary aggregate, M_t, and a random element, V_t, such that[20]

$$M_t^S = M_t e^{V_t}.$$

Another important component in this analysis, one discussed in section 10.1, is the Fisher equation:

$$i_t = r_t + \pi_t^e,$$

where r_t is the real interest rate and π_t^e is the expected inflation rate, which we defined as

$$\pi_t^e = \ln(P_{t+1}^e) - \ln(P_t).$$

Setting money supply equal to money demand, taking the natural logarithm of this equilibrium equation, using the Fisher equation, and representing the logarithm all variables other than interest rates by lowercase letters (so $\ln(X_t) = x_t$), we have

$$m_t + v_t - p_t = \alpha y_t - \lambda(p_{t+1}^e - p_t).$$

Subtracting this equation from its one-period lead, and defining $\Delta x_t = x_{t+1} - x_t$, we obtain, after some rearranging,

$$\pi_t = \frac{\lambda}{1+\lambda}\pi_{t+1}^e + \frac{1}{1+\lambda}\Delta m - \frac{\alpha}{1+\lambda}\Delta y_t + \varepsilon_t, \tag{10A.2}$$

where we have defined the regression error term as the sum of the unobservable change in the real interest rate and the change in the money supply shock, that is,

$$\varepsilon_t = \frac{\lambda}{1+\lambda}\Delta r_t + \frac{1}{1+\lambda}\Delta v_t.$$

This equation serves as the basic framework for an analysis of the effect of the exchange rate regime on inflation, once we also specify a link between the exchange rate regime and inflation expectations.

Under the assumption of long-run monetary neutrality, the long-run proportional change in the price level equals the long-run proportional change in the money supply, that is,

$$\bar{\pi} = \overline{\Delta m}.$$

Furthermore, with purchasing power parity (PPP), the proportional change in the exchange rate is the difference in the rates of money growth between the home country and the foreign country, that is,

$$\overline{\Delta e} = \overline{\Delta m} - \overline{\Delta m^*}.$$

An implication of this equation is that the expected long-run inflation rate of a country with a credible peg is the expected long-run inflation rate of its base country. If this inflation is less than the expected long-run inflation rate that the country would otherwise have, then expected adherence to the peg tempers inflation expectations, which, as shown by (10A.2), lowers current inflation. This effect may be present even when controlling for money growth over a short time horizon. Over a longer horizon, however, a peg only operates through its effect on actual monetary growth if expectations of monetary policy are, on average, consistent with actual monetary policy.

11 Exchange Rate Regimes and Economic Growth

Everything reminds Milton Friedman of the money supply. Well, everything reminds me of sex, but I keep it out of the paper.

—Robert Solow

Long-run monetary neutrality is one of the oldest, and most widely accepted, propositions in macroeconomics. One implication of this proposition is that the long-run real value of an economy's output cannot be altered simply by printing money. More broadly, long-run monetary neutrality implies that no nominal variable has an effect on real outcomes over an extended period of time (though there is debate on the time frame over which this proposition holds).[1]

A corollary of long-run monetary neutrality, one of interest for the topic of this book, is of the long-run neutrality of the choice of the exchange rate regime. In particular, monetary neutrality implies that the choice of an exchange rate regime has no impact on long-run economic growth. Given the widespread acceptance of monetary neutrality, one can take this as the baseline view on the topic of the effect of exchange rate regime on long-run economic growth.

Arguments are made, however, that the exchange rate is a particularly important price, and efforts to manage it might have long-run consequences.[2] The channels by which this operates could be through effects discussed in earlier chapters of this book. Those chapters demonstrate aggregate and macroeconomic consequences of the choice of the exchange rate regime, albeit at shorter time horizons than those usually considered in discussions of long-run growth: a link between real exchange rate volatility and the nominal exchange rate regime is discussed in chapters 6 and 7; the implication of the exchange rate regime for the conduct of monetary policy is the central theme of chapter

8; evidence presented in chapter 9 shows that fixed exchange rates promote bilateral trade; and the previous chapter discusses the role of the
exchange rate regime in long-run inflation performance. Real exchange
rate volatility, macroeconomic stability, trade, and inflation are potential determinants of long-run economic performance. Therefore there
are potential roles for the exchange rate regime to influence long-run
economic growth through its effect on these variables. In addition there
may be other channels as well, such as the effect of the exchange rate
regime on the volatility of the terms of trade, on the persistence of the
overvaluation or the undervaluation of the exchange rate, on financial
development, and on the frequency and severity of financial crises.

Ultimately, the question of the effect of the exchange rate regime on
long-run economic growth is judged by empirics rather than theory. In
this chapter we address this question. We begin, in section 11.1, with a
discussion of the potential roles that the exchange rate regime can have
on growth. This section also includes a survey of the literature on this
topic. In section 11.2 we present an empirical analysis of the effects of
the exchange rate regime on long-run economic growth using a standard cross-country growth regression framework. This framework is
informed by one of the central themes of this book, the impermanence
of the exchange rate regime for many countries. The results presented
in chapter 4 show that while some countries maintain a peg or a floating regime for an extended period of time, others flip from one type of
regime to another. Therefore, to capture this behavior, in our empirical
analysis we distinguish between countries that tend to peg their currency, countries that tend to allow their currency to float, and countries
that tend to flip from one type of regime to another over the relevant
period.

The basic result, of both the majority of papers surveyed and our
own empirical analysis presented in this chapter, is that there is little
evidence of the exchange rate regime *per se* on long-run economic
growth once one controls for other variables that typically are included
in growth regressions. This conclusion depends, to some extent, by
what is meant by the long run. Analysis of long-run economic growth
typically considers experience over a minimum of a decade, and, more
often, over the course of two or more decades. We find little evidence
of a role for the exchange rate regime on growth over twenty years,
but some evidence for its effects over the course of a decade, or a five-
year horizon. We also find the effect of the exchange rate regime on
growth depends on whether one is considering the richest industrial

countries or a set of developing and emerging market countries. There is stronger evidence of an effect in the latter group than in the former. Thus our basic conclusion concerning the effect of the exchange rate on twenty-year growth agrees with Ghosh, Gulde, and Wolf (2002) who write "Overall, and in line with the theoretical literature, the results do not suggest a strong link between the exchange rate regime and real GDP growth" (p. 98). We find more support for the contention that pegged exchange rates are associated with slower growth in developing and emerging market countries over shorter horizons.

11.1   Theories and Evidence on the Exchange Rate Regime and Growth

At the outset of the modern era, certain economic implications of exchange rate regimes were quickly evident; for example, it was soon clear that flexible rates were more volatile than what was predicted by simple monetary models. At that early stage, however, it was difficult to attribute differences in economic performance to a change in the prevailing exchange rate regime. The decade of the 1970s was marked by a number of factors, such as high energy and food prices and monetary instability, which distinguished it from earlier postwar decades. It was not until the end of the 1980s that the first empirical efforts to consider the differences of long-run economic performance across a wide cross section of countries that were attributable to exchange rate regimes were published. In an influential work, Baxter and Stockman (1989) showed that real exchange rate volatility differed in fixed and flexible exchange rate regimes, but growth of GDP and consumption were statistically similar in both regimes.

A few years after the publication of Baxter and Stockman's work, Summers and Heston published *The Penn World Table*, a data set providing data on income, growth, investment, and other macroeconomic variables for a wide set of countries (Summers and Heston 1991). These data enabled researchers to run cross-country growth regressions, and many quickly took advantage of this opportunity. A focus of the first papers in this area was to test for convergence, that poor countries grow faster than rich ones, and for conditional convergence, that convergence occurred once one controlled for other factors suggested by the Solow (1956) growth model, such as population growth and initial investment (which was taken as a proxy for the savings rate). Influential papers that presented some of the first evidence for conditional convergence include Barro (1991) and Mankiw, Romer, and Weil (1992).

The cross-country empirical growth framework then became very popular for analyzing the effects of a wide range of political, economic, and social variables on the long-run performance of economies. The Solow model suggests that any factor that affects the long-run steady state level of income per capita of an economy can be used as a regressor in a properly specified growth equation. A positive and significant coefficient on one of these variables suggests that it contributes to higher levels of long-run growth, conditional on the other variables included in the regression.[3]

Analyses of the effect of the exchange rate regime on growth typically take this tack, and go beyond simple correlations between the exchange rate regime and growth performance to the augmentation of a standard growth regression with an indicator of the exchange rate regime. An important contribution along these lines is by Levy-Yeyati and Sturzenegger (2003). They use the exchange rate classification system they developed (see chapter 3) to generate regressors representing fixed exchange rate regimes, intermediate regimes, and floating exchange rate regimes. Their main regressions include annual data from 1974 to 2000 for 183 countries (though not all countries have observations for all years). Thus these regressions are not testing long-run growth performance *per se*, rather annual growth over 26 years for a panel of countries. They present evidence that countries that have a floating exchange rate in a particular year grow significantly faster than countries with less flexible regimes, with an estimated difference of 0.78 percent per year (their table 5, column ii). They point out that this is due to the performance on nonindustrial countries. In this subset, the estimated significant difference in economic growth between countries that have a floating exchange rate in a particular year and countries that do not is over 1 percent (their table 5, column iv). They also present cross-sectional analyses for the 1974 to 1999 period in which the dependent variable for a single observation represents the average rate of growth of a country over these twenty-five-years. The independent variable representing the exchange rate regime is either the percentage of years that a country had a fixed exchange rate during this period, or the average of the LYS classification index for a country during this period. As with the regressions utilizing annual data, they find that greater exchange rate flexibility is associated with significantly higher growth rates, especially for nonindustrial countries.

While they conclude with some suggestions for reasons behind these results, they also write: "As it stands, the paper opens more questions than it answers. If we accept the results reported here, one can only wonder why countries have opted so pervasively for unilateral pegs" (p. 1188).

There are reasons that policy makers, especially in nonindustrial countries, may opt for pegged exchange rates, notwithstanding the Levy-Yeyati and Sturzenegger results.[4] Fixed exchange rates are associated with higher bilateral trade (as shown in chapter 10). Increased trade is associated with faster economic growth (Frankel and Romer 1999; Feyrer 2008). However, the growth effect concerns multilateral trade while the exchange rate peg only affects bilateral trade flows with the base country, and with other countries that peg to the same base. There is also the Baxter and Stockman (1989) evidence that real exchange rates are more stable when a country operates with a peg than when it allows its currency to float, as well as more recent evidence that shows a similar result for the terms of trade (Broda 2001). A fixed exchange rate may also be one way in which a country obtains a persistently undervalued real exchange rate which can be a vehicle for promoting export-led growth (Mundell 2000; Rodrik 2008). Macroeconomic stability, especially low inflation that accompanies a strongly pegged exchange rate, can also contribute to growth by promoting the development of a country's financial sector (Dornbusch 2001).

Alternatively, the Levy-Yeyati and Sturzenegger (2003) result, that for nonindustrial countries flexible exchange rates are associated with better growth performance, is consistent with analyses that focus on the potential instability associated with pegged exchange rates. Calvo (1999) argues that investment can be diminished, and therefore long-run growth adversely affected, in a country with a pegged exchange rate because interest rates rise due to both the uncertainty associated with potential collapse of a peg and the defense of a peg under attack. The evidence of a link between exchange rate crises and banking crises (Kaminsky and Reinhart 1999), and the large adverse consequences of banking crises on growth, also points to a potential reason why Levy-Yeyati and Sturzenegger found greater exchange rate flexibility associated with better growth performance in nonindustrial countries.

But just as theory does not point unambiguously toward the role of exchange rate regimes on growth, empirical work also offers mixed results. Miles (2006) augments the Levy-Yeyati and Sturzenegger regressions for nonindustrial countries with an additional regressor, the black market premium, which represents distortions in the economy. He finds that a fixed exchange rate regime has no independent effect on growth but may exacerbate existing distortions and, in so doing, adversely affect growth. Ghosh, Gulde, and Wolf (2002) find some evidence that basket pegs and various intermediate regimes are associated with higher growth rates than either flexible exchange rate regimes or pegged exchange rate regimes, when controlling for other factors that are typically considered determinants of economic growth. Nevertheless, their overall conclusion, cited in the introduction of this chapter, is one where they eschew a "strong link" between the exchange rate regime and economic growth.

The Levy-Yeyati and Sturzenegger result is somewhat supported by two papers written by Bailliu, Lafrance, and Perrault, although in each case there is a caveat. In their 2000 paper, employing a panel of twenty-five emerging-market countries over the 1973 to 1998 period, they find that flexible exchange rates are associated with higher economic growth for emerging market countries if those countries are open to international capital flows. In their 2003 paper, they use a larger panel of sixty countries over a shorter time period of 1973 to 1988 and presents evidence that more flexible exchange rate regimes are associated with faster growth if the country also has a monetary anchor, but slower growth if the country does not.

Husain, Mody, and Rogoff (2005) also find that floating exchange rates are associated with faster growth, but only for richer economies. Using the Reinhart–Rogoff classification scheme, they find that the category of floating exchange rates is not significantly associated with faster growth for emerging market and developing countries, and the category of "freely falling" is associated with lower growth. This contrasts with the Levy-Yeyati and Sturzenegger result as regards the effect of exchange rate volatility on growth for nonindustrial economies. Husain, Mody, and Rogoff attribute the difference in their results to those of Levy-Yeyati and Sturzenegger to the fact that "Several missing and inconclusive observations in the Levy-Yeyati and Sturzenegger (2003) classification raise concern about their conclusions" (p. 60, n.21). But Bleaney and Francisco (2007) find that results using the Reinhart–Rogoff classification scheme differ from those using four other classifications (three discussed in chapter 3, IMF *de jure*, LYS, Shambaugh, and additionally one developed by Bubula and Ötker-Robe 2002). They present evidence that the Reinhart–Rogoff classification scheme yields much worse outcomes for floating than any other classification.

They attribute this result to "some unanticipated biases in the RR's float classification, which may be exacerbated by its relative rarity" (p. 12), which "raise some questions about its reliability" (p. 14). Bleaney and Francisco conclude that hard pegs are associated with slower growth, floating is not linked to faster growth (in contrast to LYS), and that four of the five classification schemes show that growth rates in developing countries are similar under soft pegs and floats. Their estimates that use the Reinhart–Rogoff classification differ markedly from the ones they present that use other classification schemes.

We summarize the research discussed here in table 11.1. As shown in this table, and as discussed above, the contrasting results in this line of research do not point toward a single interpretation of the evidence. Therefore we offer our own empirical analysis in the next section.

11.2 Exchange Rate Regimes and Growth: An Empirical Analysis

In this section we present our empirical analysis of the effects of exchange rate regimes on economic growth. The sample includes 92 countries over the period 1980 to 1999. The analysis addresses a number of issues raised in our discussion above. We present results both for the full sample of countries and for the two subsamples (22 industrial countries and 70 nonindustrial countries), since previous research shows cases of important differences between industrial and nonindustrial countries. To address the issue of the relevant time frame for the analysis, we present three sets of regressions: a twenty-year panel with one observation per country; a panel with two decade-long nonoverlapping observations per country; and a panel with four observations for each country, each one representing a nonoverlapping five-year period.

The central variables of interest in these regressions are the indicators of exchange rate regime. For each time frame we have three categories of exchange rate regime: peggers, floaters, and flippers. We do not simply look at average time pegging because consistently pegging differs from flipping. The general rule we employ is that a country is classified as a pegger if it was in either one peg spell, or cumulatively in two peg spells, for at least 75 percent of the sample period. For example, in the twenty-year panel, a country is categorized as a pegger if it has a peg spell of at least fifteen years, or if its two longest continuous peg spells combined are at least fifteen years (this is based on the Shambaugh exchange rate classification discussed in chapter 3).

Table 11.1
Survey of literature

Publication	Countries	Sample and observation horizon	Exchange rate classification	Results
Levy–Yeyati and Sturzenegger, *AER*, 2003	183 (annual) or 88 (x-section) (with 73 nonindustrial)	1974–2000 for annual analysis; 1974–1999 for x-section; 1976–2000 for 5-year average	LYS, 3 categories (annual) or % years fixed or LYS average (x-section)	No effect for industrial countries; float significant (+) for nonindustrial; peg significant (−) x-section
Miles, *JED*, 2006	72 developing countries (including Luxembourg, South Africa)	1976–2000 for annual analysis; 1975–2000 for 5-year average; 1975–2000 for x-section	LYS average, 3 categories (float, intermediate, peg)	Fix has (−) sig. effect in 5-year (include black market premium); not independently significant in annual or in x-section
Bailliu, Lafrance, and Perrault 2000	25 emerging market countries	1973–1998 for 5-year average	IMF *de jure* and HMR 2-step system (3 categories)	Change in ERR significance (−); flexible has faster growth in countries with more open capital markets
Bailliu, Lafrance, and Perrault, *International Finance*, 2003	60 developing and industrial countries	1973–1998 for 5-year average	IMF *de jure* and HMR 2-step system (3 categories)	Intermediate and flex faster, but only if with monetary anchor
Ghosh, Gulde, and Wolfe 2002	158 countries	1970–1995	IMF *de jure* and "consensus"	Peg, intermediate significance (+), more so for lower and lower middle income countries
Husain, Mody, and Rogoff, *JME*, 2005	158 countries: 32 advanced, 25 emerging, 103 developing	1970–1999 annual data	IMF *de jure* and Reinhart–Rogoff	More flexible weakly + in advanced countries

Likewise a country is categorized as a floater if it has a float spell of at least fifteen years, or if the sum of its two longest continuous float spells is at least fifteen years. A country that is neither a floater not a pegger is categorized as a flipper. There are comparable rules for the ten-year panel and the five-year panel. The peg and float dummy variables equals 1 in the ten-year panel if a country had a peg or a float, respectively, of at least eight years, or its two longest continuous pegs or floats, respectively, are at least eight years. In the five-year panel, an observation requires four years of a peg or a float, either in one or two continuous spells, in order to be categorized as a peg or a float, respectively.[5]

Table 11.2 presents the number of observations counted as pegged or floating in the twenty-year panel, the ten-year panel, and the five-year panel. There are proportionately fewer flippers as we move from the twenty-year panel (in which there are 33 of the 92 countries) to the ten-year panel (in which there are 41 out of the 184 observations) to the five-year panel (with 51 flippers out of the 368 observations). The lower panels of table 11.2 include results based on the subsets of industrial countries and nonindustrial (i.e., developing and emerging market) countries. These lower panels show that the proportion of flippers drops off dramatically for the nonindustrial countries, from 28 of 70 in the twenty-year panel, to 30 of 140 in the ten-year panel, and to 36 of 280 in the five-year panel. This proportionate change is smaller for the industrial countries, with the number of flippers changing from 5 of 22 in the twenty-year panel, to 11 of 44 in the ten-year panel, and to 15 of 88 in the five-year panel. Thus, as we move to longer horizons, the countries counted as peggers or flippers will change. Also the difference in results at twenty-year and five-year horizons may not simply be the different effects of an exchange rate regime at different horizons, but may also come from the fact that pegging for twenty straight years is very different from pegging for five straight years.

Table 11.2 also includes results for the simple regressions

$$Growth_{i,t} = \beta_0 + \beta_{PEG}PEG + \beta_{FLIP}FLIP + \varepsilon_{i,t} \qquad (11.1)$$

where $Growth_{i,t}$ is the average annual rate of real per capita income growth for country i over time period t, with $t = 1980$–1999 for the twenty-year panel, $t = 1980$–1989 and 1990–1999 for the ten-year panel, and $t = 1980$–1984, 1985–1989, 1990–1994, and 1995–1999 for the five-year panel. The results in the table include values of the coefficients β_{PEG} and β_{FLIP}, which tests for the difference between pegs and floats and

Table 11.2
Regressions with only exchange rate regime dummy variables

Sample and its characteristics	Coefficient	20 year	10 year	5 year
Full sample: 92 countries, average annual growth of 1.19%	PEG (vs. FLOAT)	−0.010+ (0.0056)	−0.012* (0.004)	−0.011* (0.004)
	FLIP (vs. FLOAT)	−0.000 (0.004)	0.012* (0.004)	0.009* (0.005)
	PEG − FLIP	−0.010+ (0.006)	−0.024* (0.004)	−0.020* (0.005)
	Adjusted R^2	0.05	0.14	0.05
Observations with	PEG = 1 / Total	18 / 92	49 / 184	112 / 368
	FLOAT = 1 / Total	41 / 92	94 / 184	205 / 368
	FLIP = 1 / Total	33 / 92	41 / 184	51 / 368
Industrial country sample: 22 countries, average annual growth of 2.11%	PEG (vs. FLOAT)	0.008 (0.007)	0.007 (0.004)	0.008* (0.004)
	FLIP (vs. FLOAT)	0.004 (0.005)	0.004 (0.004)	0.008 (0.006)
	PEG − FLIP	0.004 (0.008)	0.003 (0.006)	0.000 (0.006)
	Adjusted R^2	0.14	0.07	0.06
Observations with	PEG = 1 / Total	3 / 22	7 / 44	20 / 88
	FLOAT = 1 / Total	14 / 22	26 / 44	53 / 88
	FLIP = 1 / Total	5 / 22	11 / 44	15 / 88
Nonindustrial country sample: 70 countries, average annual growth of 0.90%	PEG (vs. FLOAT)	−0.012* (0.006)	−0.014* (0.004)	−0.015* (0.004)
	FLIP (vs. FLOAT)	0.001 (0.005)	0.015* (0.005)	0.009 (0.006)
	PEG − FLIP	−0.013* (0.006)	−0.029* (0.005)	−0.024* (0.007)
	Adjusted R^2	0.07	0.18	0.07
Observations with	PEG = 1 / Total	15 / 70	42 / 140	92 / 280
	FLOAT = 1 / Total	27 / 70	68 / 140	152 / 280
	FLIP = 1 / Total	28 / 70	30 / 140	36 / 280

Note: *represents significant at 95% level of confidence or better; + represent significant at 90% to 95% levels of confidence. Standard errors are corrected for heteroskedasticity (robust standard errors) and reported below coefficients. Sample: 1980–2000.

flips and floats respectively, as well as results from performing the test $\beta_{PEG} - \beta_{FLIP}$, which tests for the difference between pegs and flips.

Results for the pooled sample of industrial and nonindustrial countries, presented in the top panel of table 11.2, show that growth is lower during periods that countries tend to peg than during periods that countries tend to float or during periods that countries flip exchange rate regimes. These differences are only significant at between the 90 percent and 95 percent level of confidence for the twenty-year panel, but at better than the 95 percent level of confidence for both the ten-year and five-year panels. The results in the lower two panels of this table, however, caution us that we should consider the experiences of the 22 industrial countries separately from that of the 70 nonindustrial countries. The only significant result for the industrial countries is faster growth for countries during five-year periods when they peg as compared to when they float. Nonindustrial countries, however, show significantly slower growth when pegging as compared to both floating or flipping across all three time horizons. These results are economically meaningful as well as statistically significant. For example, the average growth rate for nonindustrial countries was 0.9 percent per year over the sample period. Coefficients in the twenty-year panel of -0.012 and -0.013 show that there was an economically meaningful difference, not just a statistically significant difference, in the experience of peggers versus floaters, and peggers versus flippers respectively.

This basic correlation of peg status and growth does not represent a properly specified growth regression. A significant coefficient on *PEG* in these regressions implies permanently different growth rates, and hence indefinitely diverging levels of output. Including the initial income level in the regression, however, means that a significant coefficient on the peg variable signals a difference in the long-run level of output rather than indefinitely diverging levels of output.[6]

In addition, there is a concern that the *PEG* variable may simply be correlated with a set of omitted variables that affect growth and does not itself directly affect growth. Thus a question that is more interesting than the one answered by the results in table 11.2 concerns the effects of the exchange rate regime over and above other variables that are typically considered as determinants of economic growth. Table 11.3 addresses this question by presenting results for regressions that include variables other than the exchange rate regime dummy variables. These regressions include three economic variables that are typically found in growth regressions; the logarithm of initial income

Table 11.3
Regressions with exchange rate regime dummy and additional controls

Industrial country sample: 22 countries	PEG (vs. FLOAT)	0.011 (0.008)	0.009+ (0.005)	0.007+ (0.004)
	FLIP (vs. FLOAT)	0.005 (0.005)	0.006 (0.005)	0.006 (0.006)
	PEG − FLIP	0.005 (0.008)	0.003 (0.006)	0.000 (0.006)
Other significant coefficients of expected sign[a]	Adjusted R^2	0.27	0.14	0.18
Nonindustrial country sample: 70 countries	PEG (vs. FLOAT)	−0.002 (0.005)	−0.006 (0.004)	−0.005 (0.004)
	FLIP (vs. FLOAT)	−0.003 (0.004)	0.0093* (0.0047)	0.005 (0.006)
	PEG − FLIP	0.001 (0.006)	−0.015* (0.006)	−0.010 (0.007)
Other significant coefficients of expected sign[b]		**Y, P, I, E**	**Y, P, E**	**Y, P, I, E**
	Adjusted R^2	0.47	0.36	0.24

Note: *represents significant at 95% level of confidence or better; + represents significant at 90% to 95% levels of confidence. Standard errors are corrected for heteroskedasticity (robust standard errors) and are reported below coefficients. Initial income, population growth, and initial investment/GDP added to regressions from table 11.2.
a. Coefficients on initial income, population growth, initial Inv/GDP, and African and East Asian dummy variables are not shown.
b. Coefficients on these variables of the expected sign and significant and at the 95% level of confidence or better (**bold**) or 90% to 95% levels of confidence (*italic*) are denoted by Y (initial income, negative coefficient), P (population growth, negative coefficient), I (initial investment, positive coefficient), A (Africa), E (East Asia) Q (institutional quality), and π (standard deviation of inflation).
Years: 1980–2000.

($\ln Y_0$), population growth (P), and initial investment rates (I_0/Y_0). They also include two regional dummy variables often employed in these regressions, one that identifies sub-Saharan African countries (A) and another that identifies nonindustrial countries in East Asia (E). These regressions take the form

$$Growth_{i,t} = \beta_0 + \beta_1 \ln(Y_0) + \beta_2 P + \beta_3 \frac{I_0}{Y_0} + \beta_4 A + \beta_5 E$$

$$+ \beta_{PEG} PEG + \beta_{FLIP} FLIP + \varepsilon_{i,t}. \tag{11.2}$$

Growth theory predicts that β_1 and β_2 are negative, and that β_3 is positive. In addition there is the expectation that β_4 is negative and β_5 is positive. The literature reviewed in the previous section, as well as the results presented in table 11.2, suggest that β_{PEG} is negative (i.e., growth is slower under pegs than under floats). The effect of flips versus floats is less clear, but given the results in table 11.2, the question is whether the positive value of β_{FLIP}, which shows the effects of flips compared to floats, is preserved with the inclusion of other variables. Likewise there may be an expectation, given the results in table 11.2, that the difference in the two coefficients $\beta_{PEG} - \beta_{FLIP}$ is negative. A significantly negative result would show that countries that peg grow more slowly than countries that flip their exchange rate regime, conditional on the other variables included in the regression.

The results presented in table 11.3 show that the inclusion of these additional variables in the regression eliminates the significance of the exchange rate regime dummy variables (at the 95 percent level of confidence) for nonindustrial countries in the twenty-year panel and the five-year panel. There is still a positive and significant effect of flipping exchange rate regimes in the ten-year panel, both as compared to floating and as compared to pegging. These significant coefficients are smaller than those reported in table 11.2. The coefficients on initial income, population growth, and the East Asian dummy variable are all of the expected sign and significant at better than the 95 percent level of confidence for the nonindustrial country sample. The coefficient on the initial investment share is also significant and of the expected sign in the five-year panel, and significant at the 90 percent level in the twenty-year panel. Thus the results reported in this table indicate a more limited role for the exchange rate regime for nonindustrial countries, but they still show a benefit of changing regimes (in the form of flipping) as compared to pegging or floating, in the ten-year panel.

Before taking these results of the effects of exchange rate regimes on growth as conclusive, however, we may be concerned with the role of factors other than those typically incorporated in standard growth regressions. This concern comes from the discussion in the previous section, as well as the discussion in chapters 5, 9, and 11. The discussion in chapter 5 shows that exchange rate regimes are typically linked to institutional quality, and there is a literature that links institutional quality to growth. The discussion in chapters 8 and 10 links the exchange rate regime to short-run macroeconomic performance, and the short-run performance of the economy may spill over and affect its long-run growth. We therefore run a set of regressions augmented with two other variables, an indicator of institutional quality, Q, and

Table 11.4
Regressions with exchange rate regime dummy and additional controls

Sample	Coefficient	20 year	10 year	5 year
Industrial	PEG (vs. FLOAT)	0.009	0.008	0.005
country sample:		(0.009)	(0.005)	(0.004)
22 countries	FLIP (vs. FLOAT)	0.006	0.005	0.005
		(0.004)	(0.005)	(0.005)
	PEG – FLIP	0.003	0.003	0.000
		(0.008)	(0.006)	(0.006)
Other significant coefficients of expected sign[a]		Y, π		
	Adjusted R^2	0.34	0.16	0.22
Nonindustrial	PEG (vs. FLOAT)	−0.002	−0.004	−0.004
country sample:		(0.005)	(0.004)	(0.004)
70 countries	FLIP (vs. FLOAT)	0.001	0.008+	0.005
		(0.004)	(0.004)	(0.006)
	PEG – FLIP	−0.003	−0.013*	−0.009
		(0.005)	(0.005)	(0.006)
Other significant coefficients of expected sign[b]		**Y, P, π, Q, A, E**	**Y, P, π, I, A, E**	**Y, P, π, Q, A, E**
	Adjusted R^2	0.60	0.45	0.29

Note: *represents significant at 95% level of confidence or better; + represent significant at 90% to 95% levels of confidence. Standard errors are corrected for heteroskedasticity (robust standard errors) reported below coefficients. Initial income, population growth, initial investment/GDP, institutional quality and standard deviation of inflation added to regressions reported in table 11.2.
a. Coefficients on initial income, population growth, initial Inv/GDP, and African and East Asian dummy variables not shown (reported in the appendix to chapter).
b. Coefficients on these variables of the expected sign and significant and at the 95% level of confidence (**bold**) or 90% level (*italic*) are denoted by Y (initial income, negative coefficient), P (population growth, negative coefficient), I (initial investment, positive coefficient), A (Africa), E (East Asia) Q (institutional quality), and π (standard deviation of inflation).
Years: 1980–2000.

the standard deviation of inflation, $sd(\pi)$, to attempt to ensure that the exchange rate regime is not serving as a proxy for institutional quality or macroeconomic stability. Table 11.4 presents results for cross-country growth regressions

$$Growth_{i,t} = \beta_0 + \beta_1 \ln(Y_0) + \beta_2 P + \beta_3 \frac{I_0}{Y_0} + \beta_4 A + \beta_5 E + \beta_6 Q$$

$$+ \beta_7 sd(\pi) + \beta_{PEG} PEG + \beta_{FLIP} FLIP + \varepsilon_{i,t} \qquad (11.3)$$

where we expect that β_6 is positive and β_7 is negative.

The results presented in table 11.4 show that both institutional quality and the standard deviation of inflation are significant determinants of growth in the twenty-year panel, while the former is significant in the five-year panel and the latter is significant in the ten-year panel (and significant at better than the 90 percent level of confidence in the five-year panel). More to the point, the estimated effect of the exchange rate regime on growth for the nonindustrial sample that was reported in table 11.3 is very similar to that reported in table 11.4. The significant difference between flips and floats in the ten-year sample drops from better than 95 percent significance to significant at between the 90 percent and 95 percent levels. In the industrial country, sample the positive and (somewhat) significant effects of pegs versus floats in the ten- and five-year panels does not survive the inclusion of these two additional regressors.

The overall results from the regressions presented in this section suggest that there are important differences in the effect of exchange rate regimes on growth between industrial and nonindustrial countries. There is some evidence that flipping—as opposed to staying in one regime—is associated with faster growth in nonindustrial countries, even when controlling for other factors that may be associated with the exchange rate regime. But this is a somewhat limited result, and only found in ten-year panel regressions. There is little evidence that the exchange rate regime is a significant determinant of growth among industrial countries, even when one does not control for other variables.

11.3 Conclusion

In standard models, long-run economic growth depends on real variables like the savings rate, the rate of population growth, and initial income. These models have been augmented along several dimensions. One line of research has explored whether nominal factors have an effect long-run growth. One branch of that research has looked at the potential impact of the exchange rate regime on long-run growth. As discussed in section 11.2, this literature has come up with mixed results, although there is some evidence that greater exchange rate flexibility is associated with faster economic growth in nonindustrial countries.

Our own results, presented in section 11.3, support the view that there is little impact of the exchange rate regime on long-run growth.

The literature has some well-known results that challenge the theoretical inconsequence of exchange rate regimes for long run growth. Levy-Yeyati and Sturzenegger (2003) have argued that floats grow faster for nonindustrial countries, and Husain, Mody, and Rogoff (2005) have argued that industrial countries that float grow faster than industrial countries that peg. We find support for neither hypothesis. In regressions without proper controls we see pegs growing slower for nonindustrial countries, but the result disappears with proper controls. The only result that stands after proper controls are included is a weak result that countries that flip may grow faster than either long-term pegs or long-term floats in nonindustrial countries (but only at the ten-year horizon, not the five or twenty). This result, that neither pegging nor floating but changing regimes is weakly beneficial in nonindustrial countries, may be seen as consistent with the results of Ghosh, Gulde, and Wolf (2002) in their finding of a positive growth effect for intermediate regimes. As noted above, they also argue exchange rate regimes are generally not important for growth.

Thus, we do not see any compelling evidence that the exchange rate regime affects the long-run level of output. This lack of a finding is consistent with the general theory of long-run monetary neutrality. This is not to say, however, that the exchange rate regime has no effect on the behavior of real national income at shorter time horizons. By restricting monetary autonomy, pegging may lead to more real income volatility at the business cycle frequency because the central bank cannot respond to shocks. As mentioned in chapter 8, the work of di Giovanni and Shambaugh (2008) shows that real GDP growth rates of countries that peg are reduced when the base country raises interest rates. This is an important real consequence of the exchange rate regime, but it is one that is distinct from long-run economic growth.

Appendix

Countries in analysis (92):

Industrial (22): Australia, Austria, Belgium, Canada, Denmark, Finland, France, Greece, Iceland, Ireland, Italy, Japan, Luxembourg, Netherlands, New Zealand, Norway, Portugal, Spain, Sweden, Switzerland, United Kingdom, United States

Nonindustrial (70): Algeria, Argentina, Bahamas, Bahrain, Bolivia, Botswana, Brazil, Burkina Faso, Cameroon, Chile, Colombia, Costa Rica,

Cote d'Ivoire, Cyprus, Dominican Republic, Ecuador, Egypt, El Salvador, Ethiopia, Gabon, The Gambia, Ghana, Guatemala, Haiti, Honduras, Hong Kong, Hungary, India, Indonesia, Iran, Israel, Jamaica, Jordan, Kenya, Korea, Madagascar, Malawi, Malaysia, Malta, Mexico, Morocco, Nicaragua, Niger, Nigeria, Pakistan, Panama, Papua New Guinea, Paraguay, Peru, Philippines, Poland, Qatar, Saudi Arabia, Senegal, Sierra Leone, Singapore, South Africa, Sri Lanka, Sudan, Suriname, Syria, Tanzania, Thailand, Togo, Trinidad and Tobago, Turkey, Uganda, Uruguay, Venezuela, Zimbabwe

Countries with twenty-year peg (18): Austria, Luxembourg, Netherlands, Bahamas, Bahrain, Burkina Faso, Cameroon, Cote d'Ivoire, Egypt, Gabon, Hong Kong, Niger, Panama, Qatar, Saudi Arabia, Senegal, Syria, Togo

Countries with twenty-year float (41): Australia, Canada, Finland, Greece, Iceland, Japan, New Zealand, Norway, Portugal, Spain, Sweden, Switzerland, United Kingdom, United States, Algeria, Bolivia, Brazil, Chile, Colombia, Costa Rica, Ecuador, Ghana, Hungary, India, Israel, Kenya, Madagascar, Malawi, Malaysia, Malta, Morocco, Pakistan, Peru, Poland, Sierra Leone, South Africa, Sri Lanka, Tanzania, Turkey, Uruguay, Zimbabwe

V   Conclusion

12 Exchange Rate Regimes in an Interdependent World

Perhaps no single price attracts as much attention as the exchange rate, the price of one currency in terms of another. Certainly no other price has an entire branch of economics dedicated to its study. In some ways the exchange rate is simply an asset price like any other, responding to fundamentals and expectations. At the same time it serves as the translator of the value of goods, services, and assets in one country compared to another. Consequently no other price has as much government intervention as the exchange rate and the decision of how to treat it—whether to fix its price or let it float and be determined by the market—is considered a crucial economic policy decision for many countries.

In this book we have characterized this decision—the choice of the exchange rate regime—and its impacts over the last thirty-five years. The modern era, as we have dubbed it, differs crucially from previous eras in that countries have a legitimate choice as to whether to peg or float. Countries making different choices exist side by side at the same time, and individual countries have changed policies frequently within the era. A floating exchange rate, in the modern era, is not simply a failure to peg and, thereby, to not participate in the international system as in previous eras. Rather, floating is now a viable policy option pursued by many countries, in some cases for long spells and in others for brief episodes between pegging. Pegging is likewise a country's choice that is typically not linked to the decision of whether to join an overarching system. We have documented the dynamics of this choice as some countries have stayed in a particular exchange rate regime for extended periods and many others have flipped back and forth across regimes.

We have also shown the choices countries make with respect to the exchange rate regime matter. First and foremost the exchange rate regime has a substantial direct effect on the behavior of the exchange rate itself, with floats exhibiting considerably more volatility than pegs. Despite the fact that countries can only peg to one other currency, even multilateral volatility, the average against other exchange rates, shows significant differences across regimes. Unlike bilateral volatility where floats and pegs are truly distinct, however, many floats have low multilateral volatility. Also some pegged countries that peg to a base that is moving against the rest of the world have some multi-lateral volatility. But still, on average, pegs and floats are different on both measures. Given these exchange rate effects, it is plausible the exchange rate regime will affect other economic outcomes, and we find that it does.

As predicted by economic theory, monetary autonomy is severely limited by pegging such that countries that peg and have an open financial market are limited in their ability to set interest rates with regards to local economic circumstances; instead, they must follow the interest rate policy of the country to which they are pegged. At the same time a pegged country does trade more with its base country since nominal exchange rate volatility has been eliminated between the two countries, and more importantly, there is more long-run certainty of the future exchange rate.

The constraint that pegging places on monetary autonomy means that a fixed exchange rate disciplines the central bank and prevents extensive monetary easing. This leads to significantly lower inflation rate in pegged countries. At shorter horizons, this effect operates even over and above the direct effect that pegs have on limiting increases in the money supply since pegs can establish low inflation credibility by providing a visible nominal anchor. In the long run, however, monetary policy must match reputation, and the only impact of the exchange rate regime is to discipline developing countries' monetary policy (advanced countries seem to be able to limit money growth with or without a fixed exchange rate in the long run).

Finally, as important as exchange rate regimes can be, we would not expect them to determine the long-run productive capacity of an economy, even though they can affect real variables at shorter time horizons. Long-run levels of national income are determined by endowments, labor, capital, technology, and institutions. Over this horizon, it does not appear that fixing the currency, allowing it to float, or flipping back and forth across these choices has an independent effect on a nation's standard of living.

This book represents both new work and a synthesis of the recent wave of research that show the exchange rate regime to be quite important to many economic outcomes in this modern era. As the modern era progresses and the choices and experiences of many countries change and evolve, we are sure to learn more about exchange rate regime choice and outcomes. We hope this book informs economists, practitioners, and students about some of the important lessons learned about this fundamental policy choice thus far in the modern era.

Notes

Chapter 1

1. There were a variety of exchange rate regime choices during the two-decade interwar period, but this was a time of great economic instability. For an authoritative account of this period, see Eichengreen (1992).

2. See Bordo, Edelstein, and Rockoff (2002).

3. See Meissner (2005) for a discussion of the development of the gold standard.

4. International economists often refer to the period studied in this book as the "Post–Bretton Woods" era. But, since this period has, by now, lasted longer than the preceding Bretton Woods era, it deserves its own name. We have chosen "modern era" because it has a parallel in art history. The "modern period" of art is marked by a great heterogeneity in styles and approaches existing side by side in the same time period.

5. Original contributions to the monetary approach to exchange rates include Frenkel (1976) and Bilson (1978). Boughton (1988) discusses the empirical failure of this model, although DeJong and Husted (1993) suggest this might be due to the low power of the tests used.

6. See Rogoff (2002) for a review of the influence of the Dornbusch overshooting model.

7. Theoretical research by Krugman (1979), Flood and Garber (1984), and Obstfeld (1994) offered frameworks for understanding these events. Empirical research on the antecedents to these crises (Berg and Pattillo 1999) and their effects, added importantly to our understanding of some of the implications of the choice of a fixed exchange rate regime.

8. See Obstfeld and Rogoff (1995).

9. See Calvo and Reinhart (2002).

Chapter 2

1. For example, see Corden (2004) for a discussion of some of the current issues in exchange rate regime debates.

2. Dollarization is simply dispensing with using a national currency and using the currency of another country. A currency union involves creating a new common currency

across member countries and having supranational institutions (such as a central bank) to manage the currency.

3. See Krugman and Obstfeld (2008) for an explanation of the policy trilemma in the context of a simple macroeconomic model of an open economy. For a more advanced treatment, see Obstfeld and Rogoff (1996).

4. It is theoretically possible to break the policy trilemma if fiscal policy could be directed toward exchange rate management while monetary policy was used separately to set interest rates. This is not a realistic situation, however, since fiscal policy is not nimble enough to respond in a timely way such that it serves to peg the exchange rate. Alternatively, sterilized intervention, whereby the monetary authority alters the outstanding stock of assets denominated in domestic currency while maintaining separate control over the money supply and interest rates, also breaks the policy trilemma. In this case, however, there is little empirical evidence that sterilized intervention has consistent and long-lived effects on exchange rates except possibly as signaling future monetary policy. Since these signals need to be backed up by actual policy, sterilized intervention provides little promise of breaking the trilemma.

5. Even in a broad system where many countries peg together, most fixed exchange rate systems have been asymmetric in that a "center" country has a free hand in setting policy while all other participating countries direct their policies to the maintenance of the peg. In this case, the center country has both a fixed exchange rate (through the actions of other countries) and a free hand to set its own monetary policy.

6. See Frankel (2003).

7. The argument about the way in which the relative merits of exchange rate regimes depends on the source of shocks to an economy is an open-economy version of the well known analysis of Poole (1970).

8. The formal abandonment of the system of fixed but adjustable parities was made by an Interim Committee of the IMF at a meeting in Kingston, Jamaica in January 1976.

9. The Nobel Memorial Prize in Economics was awarded in 2004 to Finn Kydland and Edward Prescott for their contribution on policy credibility. See Kydland and Prescott (1977), as well as Calvo (1978) and Barro and Gordon (1983) for some early and influential contributions.

10. For a review of these experiences, see Végh (1992).

11. Klein and Marion (1997) show that a loss of competitiveness due to inflation in excess of that of the base country is an important predictor of the end of a fixed exchange rate.

12. For example, Klein, Schuh, and Triest (2003) show that real exchange rates are an important determinant of job destruction in US manufacturing industries.

13. See Frankel (1999).

14. OCA theory was originally concerned with the adoption of a single currency, but its ideas translate to issues of a fixed exchange rate as well.

15. It is important to recall, however, that the United States has not always had a single currency. Up until the Civil War there were a variety of monies circulating. For a discussion of this see Sheridan (1996) and Shambaugh (2006).

16. For example, Bayoumi and Eichengreen (1998) compared the correlation of economic disturbances across the countries of Europe to that across regions in the United States, and Blanchard and Katz (1992) considered labor mobility and fiscal transfers across states in the United States, which serves as a benchmark for these features in Europe. Bean (1992) also offered a prospective view of monetary union in Europe.

17. A dominant international exchange rate system, such as the gold standard, can influence national decisions about the choice of an exchange rate regime. See Broz (1997) and Frieden (1993).

18. We provide evidence in chapter 10 that fixed exchange rates between two countries promotes trade between them.

19. Exporting and importing firms also serve the domestic market, so their desire for exchange rate certainty versus policy flexibility when dealing with business cycles is not straightforward.

20. Another issue that potentially limits the interest group influence on exchange rate policy can be understood by contrasting it with the interest group effect on trade policy. Legislation for specific tariffs or quotas can be very firm-specific, and, with these concentrated benefits, there may be extensive lobbying. The benefits of exchange rate policies are more diffuse and give rise to free riding and, therefore, a smaller interest group effect.

21. In his Nobel Prize acceptance speech, Robert Mundell suggested that these changes in the international monetary system were a crucial cause of many of the major economic and political events of the 20th century, ranging from the Depression, to the rise of fascism and World War II, to the inflation of the 1970s, to the subsequent rise of conservative political forces. See Mundell (2000)

22. See Eichengreen (1996) and Obstfeld and Taylor (2004) for clear descriptions of this era.

23. A handful of countries broke their peg to gold and re-pegged, but by and large, once commitments were made, they were locked in and, by 1905, nearly all countries with independent economies were on the gold standard. We date the gold standard from 1880. In some countries, notably the United Kingdom, it began earlier, and between 1870 and 1880 a number of countries joined. See Meissner (2005) for a description of the rise of the gold standard system.

24. See Obstfeld, Shambaugh, and Taylor (2004) for a discussion of the interwar years in the context of the trilemma.

25. See Eichengreen (1992) and Eichengreen and Sachs (1985).

Chapter 3

1. Frankel (2004).

2. These reports were initially titled *Annual Report on Exchange Restrictions*, which reflected the lack of variety of exchange arrangements during the Bretton Woods period. The title changed to *Annual Report on Exchange Arrangements and Exchange Restrictions* with its 1979 volume.

3. Fischer (2001), using the classification scheme in the last column of table 3.1, places the category "conventional peg arrangements" into an intermediate regime, but one could

easily imagine this category combined with "no separate legal currency" and "currency boards" into an aggregate peg category distinct from an intermediate regime that represents limited flexibility.

4. Frankel et al. (2001) discuss the length of time it can take to discern the true weights in a basket. Given that if the weights are not declared, and that they may be changing over time, it is very difficult, as a practical matter, to use a *de facto* method classify such countries on an annual basis.

5. The Reinhart–Rogoff classification will code countries as following a *de facto* SDR pegs if it is a true *de facto* SDR peg, but this is a rare occurrence. More commonly, they code declared SDR pegs as nonpegs or as direct pegs to a particular base since few declared SDR pegs are in fact SDR pegs.

6. Other classifications include Moreno (2001) and Dubas et al. (2005), among others, but these three have been used most frequently in the literature and the choices they make span many of the options allowing for a rich discussion of the issues involved. Ghosh et al. (1997) made an early contribution in adjusting *de jure* codes for clear errors and Ghosh et al. (2002) also make a *de facto* classification for the purpose of looking for a "consensus" where *de facto* and *de jure* agree.

7. The least flexible arrangements are assigned the value 1 in the coarse grid, and the most flexible are assigned the value 5. The fifteen fine grid categories (and their assignments to the coarser grid) are: "no separate legal tender," "preannounced peg or currency board arrangement," "preannounced horizontal band that is narrower than or equal to ±2 percent," and "de facto peg" (coarse grid 1); "preannounced crawling peg," "preannounced crawling band that is narrower than or equal to ±2 percent," "de facto crawling peg," "de facto crawling band that is narrower than or equal to ±2 percent," and "preannounced crawling band that is wider than ±2 percent (coarse grid 2); "de facto crawling band that is narrower than or equal to ±5 percent" "noncrawling band that is that is narrower than or equal to ±2 percent," and "managed floating" (coarse grid 3); "freely floating" (coarse grid 4); "freely falling (includes hyperfloat)" (coarse grid 5).

8. To determine the base country, this system tests the exchange rate against the dollar, all major currencies, and major regional currencies to find any potential fixed exchange rate relationship. When a country pegs or occasionally pegs, determining the relevant base currency is straightforward. It becomes more difficult to assign a relevant base for nonpegged observations of countries that generally float, do not peg for a substantial amount of time, or switch base currencies. In these cases, judgment was used, and the base is the currency with historical importance for the local country, the nearby dominant economy to which other currencies were pegged, or, if no other currencies seem a good candidate for the base, the US dollar as a default.

9. Again, most basket pegs either stay stable to one particular currency (in which case they are coded as a peg) or appear to float either by changing weights frequently or simply ignoring the basket index.

10. The use of ±1 percent bands rather than ±2 percent bands, and the decision to include single peg breaks, has little effect on the results in the paper. Only 5 percent of observations coded as pegs are realignments. 38 percent never have the exchange rate change, 45 percent have changes but stay within 1 percent bands and the remaining 12 percent move outside 1 percent bands but stay within 2 percent bands.

11. See note 7.

12. See also Klein and Shambaugh (2008), Shambaugh (2004) or Frankel (2003) for comparisons of different *de facto* classification schemes. The statistics shown do not include countries that have no legal tender or are part of a currency union with the base as these somewhat trivially generate agreement amongst all three classifications.

13. It should be noted that these statistics include Reinhart–Rogoff managed floats (fine classification 12) as floats, not intermediate. If they are considered intermediate, 52 percent of Reinhart–Rogoff spells are coded as intermediate. This also drives down their rate of agreement with other classifications since most others code the bulk of these observations as floats. If the managed floats are considered intermediate, the rate of agreement with Reinhart–Rogoff drops to 62 percent for the Shambaugh classification, 52 percent for the LYS classification, and 53 percent for the *de jure* classification.

14. See for example Ghosh, Gulde, and Wolf (2002).

15. It is worth noting that even different *de jure* codings, all of which rely on the same IMF yearbooks, disagree because researchers differ in how they aggregate declared regimes. For example, a "cooperative system," which is how the EMS was listed, could be considered a peg or an intermediate regime. Likewise managed floats can be called intermediates or floats. Thus, using *de jure* classifications does not change the fact that a researcher must decide what behavior is considered a peg and what is not.

Chapter 4

1. The significance of exchange rate regimes for economic performance also depends on a significant *de facto* difference of exchange rate behavior across exchange rate regimes. The influence of the exchange rate regime would be limited if pegs did not really bind exchange rates because they were frequently broken, or if governments actually limited exchange rate movements during times when countries were purportedly floating. We turn to this topic in chapter 6.

2. Obstfeld and Rogoff (1995).

3. See Mussa (1989) and Flood and Rose (1995).

4. Frankel and Wei (1994) is an example of this literature, which focused on the effect of exchange rate volatility, rather than exchange rate regimes, on bilateral trade. We return to the issue of exchange rate regimes and trade in chapter 10.

5. There is reasonable evidence that nearly all single year pegs are in fact legitimate pegs and do not simply represent a random lack of volatility of shocks across two countries. There are 39 country–year observations that are single year pegs that are not also declared pegs and are not classified as pegs by Levy-Yeyati and Sturzenegger or Reinhart and Rogoff. Within this set, the exchange rate of 12 single year pegs remained within a ±1 percent band, a situation that is highly unlikely to have arisen accidentally. Thus we focus on the 27 "questionable peg" observations that are within 2 percent bands and are neither declared nor identified as a peg by Reinhart and Rogoff nor by Levy-Yeyati and Sturzenegger. This set of observations represents 20 countries and 16 different years, and, therefore, is not evidence of a lack of world volatility in a particular year or country. It also includes many country–year observations that are widely considered to be *de facto* pegs, such as Malaysia and Indonesia in 1996, as well as countries whose currency was clearly shadowing that of another country, such as Portugal in 1975, which was linked to the DM unofficially in the snake. Other countries, such as India, Pakistan, Tunisia, and Jamaica, all of which have two "questionable" single year pegs, have many other

unquestionable pegs in the sample, making it unlikely that the "questionable" peg is just an accident of coding. Thus, while the official Shambaugh classification does not include single year pegs, if it is important to include them for the question studied (as we feel it is in this case), it is probably accurate to consider them pegs.

6. Below we compare the results in table 4.1 to those obtained through the use of the other exchange rate regime classification schemes discussed in chapter 3.

7. We limit the sample to countries with populations of at least 400,000, in part to match the data set in Obstfeld and Rogoff (1995). The United States is not included in the sample of 125 countries, nor do we include spells that represent currency unions.

8. There are 3,924 observations, rather than $125 \times 32 = 4000$, because 76 observations represent currency unions.

9. See Klein and Marion (1997) and Obstfeld and Rogoff (1995).

10. In a second panel in their table 2, Obstfeld and Rogoff list 17 small countries that had pegged to the US dollar for at least five years. They write "The striking conclusion from table 2 is that aside from some small tourism economies, oil sheikdoms, and highly dependent principalities, literally only a handful of countries in the world today have maintained tightly fixed exchange rates *against any currency* for five years or more" (p. 87, italics in original).

11. The panel is roughly balanced with between 122 and 125 countries in the sample. The slight variation comes from the fact that currency unions are eliminated from sample with the exception of spells that began as pegs and converted to currency unions (e.g., some EMU observations).

12. Pegs lasting at least 5 years in 2000 includes some oil countries and the CFA countries, but also many EU nations as well as Argentina, China, and El Salvador. The full list is: Argentina, Austria, Bahrain, Belgium, Benin, Burkina Faso, Cameroon, Central African Republic, Chad, China, Comoros, Republic of Congo, Cote D'Ivoire, Denmark, Djibouti, El Salvador, Equatorial Guinea, Gabon, Hong Kong, Jordan, Lebanon, Lesotho, Luxembourg, Mali, Namibia, Nepal, Netherlands, Niger, Oman, Qatar, Saudi Arabia, Senegal, Swaziland, Syria, Togo, and the United Arab Republic.

13. The presence of "inconclusive" observations, and the lack of complete coverage, prevents the inclusion of exchange rate spells based on the Levi-Yeyati and Sturzenegger exchange rate classification scheme.

14. The Reinhart–Rogoff and IMF classification schemes could be used to generate a spell-based analysis in which there were more than two types of spells, but we continue to focus on a bivariate scheme for purposes of comparison and also because it offers a cleaner and less ambiguous classification system than one that includes a category of "limited flexibility," or some other type (or types) of intermediate regimes.

15. See Kiefer (1988) for a good introduction to duration analysis and hazard functions.

16. Research by Masson (2001), Masson and Ruge-Murcia (2005) and Eichengreen and Razo-Garcia (2006) is related to this analysis, although these papers focus on whether the international monetary system is moving toward an "empty middle" consisting of mainly currency unions, on the one hand, and free floats, on the other, or, alternatively, whether transitions are slow and countries shift back to the middle, not exclusively away from it. These papers look at switching propensities across hard pegs, intermediate regimes (including pegs) and floats. Their results are related to our observations that nei-

ther pegging nor floating is an absorbing state, and flipping back and forth is common. The focus in these papers on extreme polar cases, and the inclusion in the broad middle band of what we define as both pegs and nonpegs, however, distinguishes this work from those papers.

17. Hazard functions may or may not be monotonic. Some hazard functions have derivatives that change sign for different values of t.

18. The covariates are not intended to be exhaustive, but rather illustrative. Klein and Marion (1997) provide an example of a detailed analysis of the end of a peg. We keep the list of covariates limited for comparability across the peg and float spells.

19. The estimated λ is less than one and significant even if no covariates are included. For peg spells the estimate of λ is 0.798 with a standard error of 0.032, and for float spells the estimate of λ is 0.845 with a standard error of 0.034.

20. The United States is the base country for 51 percent of the pegs in this sample. The other base countries include France (the base for 27 percent of the pegs), South Africa (6 percent), the United Kingdom (2 percent), Belgium (1.5 percent), India (1 percent), Portugal (less than 1 percent), Malaysia (less than 1 percent), and Australia (less than 1 percent).

21. Thirty-three pegs that broke re-formed within a six- to ten-year gap, leaving 91 (27 percent) that do not re-form for at least ten years (or did not re-form by the end of the sample period). Eighteen of the breaks that did not re-form involve switches in the base country and, in these cases, countries may not have floated, but the original peg is not reconstituted if there is a peg to another base (most of these involved switches from the British pound sterling as the base to the US dollar during the 1970s).

22. Because they so distort the average, we calculate the average without including three extreme outliers: Nicaragua in 1988, Surname in 1994, and Zimbabwe in 2003. In addition, when these breaks re-form (Nicaragua after 4 years and Suriname after 2 years) they are again excluded from the average.

23. The Shambaugh and Reinhart–Rogoff classifications in fact refer to these as pegs, allowing for a break in the rate as long as the overarching regime has not changed.

24. This is not to argue that no countries manage their exchange rates if they are not literally pegged, nor that no countries mis-declare their regimes. Rather, our point is that some countries actually do float and their exchange rates are notably more volatile than those that peg.

25. The implications of these distinct effects between bilateral and multilateral outcomes relate to differences in trade and macroeconomic outcomes since bilateral volatility affects bilateral trade and macroeconomic stability while economic growth, for example, may require a broader effect across many sectors that is more closely associated with multilateral stability.

Chapter 5

1. Currency union countries will not be included in the empirical analysis in this chapter.

2. The question of the determinants of exchange rate regime choice is different from that of the factors that contribute to the end of a pegged exchange rate spell. The distinction between these two questions is discussed further in the next section.

3. In this context, the difference between a currency union and a fixed exchange rate is the greater perceived permanence of the former relative to the latter. As shown in chapter 9, both fixed exchange rates and currency unions promote bilateral trade. Also, as shown in chapter 8, the macroeconomic constraints imposed by pegging a currency for a country whose government allows capital mobility hold for fixed exchange rates as well. Therefore Mundell's OCA analysis is relevant for fixed exchange rates, and not just currency unions.

4. Recall that if there are n countries in a currency union, $n - 1$ countries must follow the monetary policy of the central country unless the currency union is truly symmetric, in which case no country has a free hand in setting its own monetary policy.

5. As shown in chapter 9, a fixed exchange rate positively affects trade between two countries, so there is some potential for endogeneity by which the dependent variable, regime choice, affects the regressor, the level of trade.

6. This would not hold, of course, for countries that have high levels of income per capita because of an abundance of a natural resource like oil. One could easily control for this in a regression by including a variable to capture a country's dependence on oil exports, or by including a dummy variable that identifies major oil exporters.

7. This is a distinct reason from the issue of the natural level of trade of an economy that is dominated by the production of a single good, although both of these affect the preference for a peg relative to a float in the same direction.

8. Distance could change with the change in the base country, but this is a rare occurrence. More important, Feyrer (2008) has shown that there has been a shift in international trade from shipping by sea to shipping by air. This has implications for the costs of transport and the effective distance between trading partners.

9. Important theoretical contributions include Krugman (1979), Flood and Garber (1984), and Obstfeld (1994). Various empirical approaches to this topic are evaluated by Berg and Pattillo (2002) in the context of the Asian financial crisis of the late 1990s.

10. Although there is some research on exchange rate regime choice in the interwar period. See, for example, Eichengreen (1992). There has also been interesting work recently on the spread of the gold standard. See Meissner (2005) and citations therein.

11. Other variables studied by Rizzo that are not associated with OCA theory, such as terms of trade, government revenue, the current account balance, the level of external debt, and the government budget deficit, are less consistently associated with exchange rate regime choice.

12. Alesina and Warner (2006) also consider sources of differences in the *de facto* and *de jure* exchange rate regimes. They find that the *de facto* pegs of countries with poor institutions tend to break. Countries with good institutions are more likely to have *de facto* pegs than *de jure* pegs, that is, they actually peg more often than they announce that they peg, which is consistent with the Calvo and Reinhart (2002) "fear of floating" result.

13. In contrast, time-varying dummy variables that indicate the year just before an election and the year just after an election (when, respectively, a float is more likely and a peg is more likely, extending the political business cycle logic from the cross section to the time series) are not statistically significant.

14. A similar result is presented by Méon and Rizzo (2002).

15. Carmignani, Colombo, and Tirelli (2008) report a significant effect of political frag-mentation on increasing the likelihood of a *de facto* floating exchange rate in their sample of 96 industrial and developing countries.

16. A linear probability model might be inappropriate if the impact on the choice is non-linear and a logit or probit model might be preferable if the functional form imposed by those techniques better fit the data. A linear model can impose an unrealistic shape on the predicted values (predicting results below zero or above one) but that is not a prob-lem in this case. Our predicted values rarely stray above one or below zero. Further, there is no evidence that the specific nonlinear model of a probit fits better and the linear model offers much more straightforward interpretation.

17. A discrete choice analysis would not allow a pure cross section of the full panel as the dependent variable would not be binary, but the percentage of time a country was pegged.

18. Geographical variables (distance, contiguous, colonial status, landlocked status) come from the CEPII database of geographical data. Macroeconomic data such as GDP, population, government share of the economy, and trade share, come from the WDI. Fi-nancial openness is from Edwards (2005) and democracy and corruption data are from the *International Country Risk Guide* published by the PRS group.

19. We use the Klein-Shambaugh *de facto* classification in which devaluations count as a break in a peg. Results are very similar using the Shambaugh or Reinhart–Rogoff classifi-cations. One exception is that using the Reinhart-Rogoff classification leads to a result where open financial markets are significantly associated with pegging (even more often than the results presented here). This is because countries that peg the official rate but have capital controls and have a diverging black market rate will not be considered pegs in the Reinhart–Rogoff classification.

20. It is important to note that studies that do not appropriately control for serial correla-tion will have incorrectly low standard errors and present a disproportionate number of significant coefficients. In the regression in column 1 of table 5.1, 5 of 11 variables have coefficients statistically different from zero at the 95 percent confidence level. Had the standard errors been estimated in a standard manner, or only robust to heteroskedastic-ity, 8 of the 11 would have appeared significant.

21. Half the 35 countries eliminated have populations less than 800,000 in 2000, while only 5 percent of the remaining sample is as small. Of these 35 countries, 66 percent are pegged as opposed to 40 percent of the remaining countries, and average GDP per capita is less than $2000 (in 1995 US dollars) as opposed to over $6000 for the remaining countries.

22. While most countries that peg do not, in fact, border their base, it is the converse that drives this result; a majority of countries that border their base country peg. Examples in-clude European countries like France and Austria, countries on the subcontinent that peg to India, and countries in southern Africa that peg to South Africa.

23. There is little difference in any of these results if we restricted ourselves to a later (post-1989) sample.

24. As noted, once a peg has commenced, some variables (e.g., real exchange rate appre-ciation) can tell us about the likelihood of the peg collapsing, but these are not necessarily correlated with floating in general as much as with a peg breaking. Further, these

variables are of no help in informing us as to when a peg will re-form; thus they are of limited information regarding the flipping nature of pegs.

25. Our data set stops in 2002 (in part due to the political variables) but this is convenient because it means that we can tell if a peg that began in 2000, or even 2002, did in fact last for a full five years.

26. Here a point raised in Klein and Shambaugh (2008) is relevant. While a majority of pegs break quickly—and hence a majority of peg spells are classified as short peg spells—long pegs are observed far more frequently in annual data (because each year that they last represents an observation) and hence the panel estimation in table 1 is largely based on longer pegs.

27. Seventy-five percent of the countries coded as flippers spent at least half of their time in short spells. The remaining 25 percent did spend a fair amount of time in both long pegs and long floats, but also flipped a number of times.

Chapter 6

1. Calvo and Reinhart focus on *de jure*, not *de facto*, pegs, and show that many countries that say they float do not really do so. But this paper has had a strong influence and its message has sometimes been extrapolated more broadly to mean that floats do not really float at all.

2. Grilli and Kaminsky (1991) worried that the results could be driven by differences in eras rather than regimes since so much of the regime differences were Bretton Woods versus non Bretton Woods. Mussa, though, uses Canada's float during Bretton Woods and Ireland's switch of base country from United Kingdom to Germany as counterpoints and, in response to Grilli and Kaminsky's argument, Liang uses exchange rate regimes from the modern era for his tests.

3. The bilateral exchange rate used to calculate volatility is the month end official exchange rate, converted to be the bilateral exchange rate against the relevant base country, reported in line *ae* in the International Monetary Fund's IFS database. This measure of volatility does not line up exactly with the rule for coding an exchange rate experience as a peg regime in the Shambaugh or Klein–Shambaugh classification schemes since the exchange rate regime coding requires staying within a tight range over the course of a year. For example, a country with a steady crawling peg may exhibit low exchange rate volatility from one month to another but it would not be classified as having a peg if it violates the condition of staying within a 2 percent band over the course of a year.

4. As in chapter 4, the sample used does not include very small countries or countries that maintain a currency union with their base country.

5. A similar analysis using the peg and float spells discussed in chapter 4 produces very similar results. See section 6.4 and Klein and Shambaugh (2008) for more results.

6. Including the "soft peg" marker shows that all the nonpegged observations in the second and third quintiles are soft pegs, meaning the gap between true pegs and true floats is even larger.

7. The end of the chapter examines these results across different exchange rate regime classifications discussed in chapter 3.

8. A significant difference between this discussion and research that studies bilateral volatility overall is our focus on volatility against the base country. Lane and Devereux (2003) is a leading example of tests of bilateral volatility across many country pairs. In their work, the goal is to explain why countries may try to lower exchange rate volatility, rather than the impact of exchange rate regimes as we study here. Many of their variables (e.g., distance or debt burden) are time invariant across countries or close to being so. As such, our use of country fixed effects eliminates most comparisons between the works. They find that bilateral external debt is a significant explanatory variable in explaining volatility for developing countries, and that general optimal currency variables (trade, correlation of shocks, country size) are more important for industrial countries.

9. Standard errors are clustered at the country level. This allows for an unstructured autocovariance matrix that can correct for heteroskedasticity and autocorrelation. The dependent variable $EVOL$ is persistent, but nowhere near unit root levels (autocorrelation coefficients range near .3) suggesting this correction is sufficient to handle time series issues relating to the use of panel data. See Bertrand et al. (2004) for discussion.

10. That is, if one takes the standard deviation of a year in which the change in the exchange rate for six of the months is 16 percent each month and the change in each of the other six months is −16 percent, the resulting standard deviation is roughly 0.16. On the other hand, if not all the observations are at the boundaries, the range could be larger. That is, .16 is also the standard deviation if the change in the exchange rate in 3 of the months is 21 percent, in another 3 of the months is −21 percent, in a third set of 3 months is 7 percent, and in each of the remaining 3 months is −7 percent. Thus the volatility measure does not directly translate into a specific range, but gives us a sense for the size of the range. The average annual range of a float in this sample is ±14 percent (the median is ±6 percent).

11. See Klein and Shambaugh (2008) for further robustness checks on these results. The exclusion of country fixed effects makes little difference. Dropping the first year of a float spell, so that a potential crisis year is not included in the overall subsequent float spell, has some effect (with the absolute value of the coefficient falling to 0.045), but the difference between pegs and floats is still highly significant.

12. Results across classifications are shown in section 6.4. Of particular interest is the fact that consistent with Calvo and Reinhart (2002), de jure pegs have a statistically insignificant effect on volatility.

13. As in the spells estimates, including such observations just makes the gap between pegs and floats bigger, but including them leaves a false impression of the typical experience of floats.

14. The top 1 percentile of volatility observations are excluded, as in column 1 of table 6.2. We do not include the first-year float variable. By controlling for these separately, when we look at lagged pegs, we would eliminate some of the largest volatility outcomes for previous pegs and thus artificially increase the difference between lagged pegs and floats.

15. The sample does not include countries that floated at time zero but begin to peg in the next 1, 2, 3, 4, or 5 years. The result is a comparison of countries that had pegged at time zero (regardless of what they are doing now) with countries that floated at time zero and are also floating at time 1, 2, 3, 4, or 5, depending on the lag used in the bivariate regression. We want to examine whether pegs at time zero have lower volatility in the future, not whether pegs at time zero have lower volatility in the future than floats at

time zero. Pegs that continue will have lower volatility, but many of the broken pegs will re-form.

16. Ghosh et al. (2002) also examined volatility over time and also found lower volatility for pegs, but they restricted their sample to regimes that stayed pegged or stayed floating, eliminating the important role of pegs breaking or re-pegging.

17. We note that the *de jure* result is not simply due to declared floats not floating but, more important, is due to the highly volatile observations, which are labeled as pegs in the *de jure* coding.

18. Friedman (1953) argued that given underlying instability in an economy, "freezing of exchange rates cures none of the underlying difficulties and only makes adjustment to them more painful," while floating allows "continuous sensitivity" to changes in real conditions and hence smoothes adjustment.

19. The results in section 6.4 also hint at this result. Both the JS and RR classifications show lower volatility for pegs than floats despite the fact that both count discrete devaluations (or adjustments in the adjustable pegs) as part of a pegged regime.

20. Asici, Ivanova, and Wyplosz (2005), in their study of the consequences of ending a peg, show that the likelihood of a disorderly exit from a peg spell increases as the duration of that spell increases.

Chapter 7

1. Countries sometimes peg to a basket of currencies, a topic we examine later in this chapter. The weights assigned to currencies in the basket typically are not declared (although an alternative way to peg to a basket of currencies is to peg to some known composite, like the SDR).

2. Dubas, Lee, and Mark (2005) take an alternate tack by using the multilateral rates to determine exchange rate regime status. They argue that a peg is ineffective, and not really a peg at all, unless it truly stabilizes the multilateral rate.

3. This is not true for all countries. Some developing countries that peg to bases other than the US dollar still have considerable US dollar liabilities in part due to their debts to multilateral organizations such as the World Bank or the IMF.

4. The real exchange rate data (line *rec*) is available for fewer countries, roughly 93. In most of our tables, there will be 120 countries in the nominal volatility regressions and roughly 70 in the real volatility regressions.

5. As discussed in chapter 6, country fixed effects control for differences in the characteristics of countries that tend to peg rather than float, and lessen concerns of omitted variable bias. Not including the country fixed effects has a relatively small impact on the results. In a few cases the coefficients are smaller, but never significantly so.

6. As in chapter 6, the standard errors are clustered at the country level.

7. We also report the results after dropping the top 1 percent of volatility outliers. In this case, it makes little difference.

8. We use the most data that are available, therefore the sample for real and nominal are different. As it turns out, there is no difference if we limit the estimates for nominal volatility to a sample where real exchange rate data is available.

9. There is little difference in the results across industrial and developing countries. The overall volatility levels for rich countries are lower, and hence the coefficients on the peg variable are lower, but the share of variation in volatility that pegging can explain is consistent across the two samples.

10. Controlling for inflation does cut the size of the peg coefficient, but it is still statistically significant. Controlling for inflation may not be appropriate. If we think the channel that allows pegs to generate lower volatility is by providing a nominal anchor and thus having less inflation, it is possible that we should view the inflation impact on volatility as being related to the peg decision. See chapter 11 for more on this topic.

11. Empirically it can be quite difficult to verify the weights used in a basket, and hence difficult to distinguish a basket peg from a managed float, as discussed by Frankel et al. (2001).

12. We can also include controls for the share of trade with the base country, and that has no impact on the results. Thus it is not simply that pegs have lower volatility because they have stabilized trade with the base country. There is in fact no difference in trade share with the base country across the five quintiles of real or nominal volatility for either pegs or floats.

Chapter 8

1. This section is derived from Shambaugh (2004). See the full paper for more details.

2. The argument here is similar to that of uncovered interest parity (UIP), but it is less strict and does not require that UIP hold for all countries. Rather, this argument simply says if you take away the uncertainty and the exchange rate is pegged, then the results described must hold. In contrast, UIP can (and does) tend to fail for countries where there is large uncertainty in the exchange rate market and the currencies float.

3. There have been other recent studies that focused on subsets of countries. Abraham (1999) examines the relationship of Saudi Arabia's interest rate to the US rate; Cheung, Tam, and Yiu (2008) examine China's relationship with the United States; Kim and Lee (2008) look at a number of Asian countries; and Hakura (2005) examines shifts in autonomy as some emerging market countries begin to float.

4. Since the data will be differenced, the first year of a peg cannot be used as that observation will difference from a peg to a nonpeg observation. Thus the single-year pegs included in the Klein–Shambaugh data set will all be dropped, making the difference between the two classifications fairly small.

5. While we might prefer a *de facto* measure of capital controls, a number of them either have very limited availability or require the use of interest rate movements (exactly what we want to test) to determine financial openness.

6. Obstfeld, Shambaugh, and Taylor (2004) also examine results for the interwar years between World War I and World War II. Those results are consistent with the findings described in the text.

7. As in previous chapters, a country is assigned a base even when it does not peg. The base is the country to which a country would peg if it is pegged. The base is revealed since most countries peg at some point. In the rare instances it is not, we rely on currency history, a dominant regional economy, or the US dollar. See Shambaugh (2004) for details.

8. We use the changes in annual interest rates. Differencing the data removes any constant risk premium or expected depreciation from the data (as well as other details such as differential tax treatments that might make the assets imperfect substitutes). In addition, levels of nominal interest rates often behave very close to unit root series. This would raise the possibility of spurious regressions, making differencing the data preferable. Technically the interest rates are expressed as $\ln(1 + R)$. This both reduces the impact of outliers and matches the theoretical derivation of the equation. See Shambaugh (2004) for details of both issues.

9. The sample involves all three eras in the pooled era. The results are drawn from the sample of countries that have interest rates that show some changes over a two to three year horizon. The papers eliminate countries that set interest rates administratively and never change them. See Obstfeld, Shambaugh, and Taylor (2005, tab. 2) and Shambaugh (2004, tab. 5) for details.

10. Both papers experiment with the additional interaction of (peg × open financial markets). In theory, the trilemma would say only open financial market pegs show any response to the base. In fact, the results consistently show the effects of pegging and capital controls are additive, not multiplicative. That is, either opening the financial markets or pegging generates a loss of some autonomy and doing both generates a loss of even more.

11. Shambaugh (2004) shows that adding other variables interacted with the base interest rate, such as trade with the base country, controls for level of economic development, or external debt do not significantly move the coefficient on the peg variable. In related work on a different topic, di Giovanni and Shambaugh (2008) also show that the coefficient on the peg variable remains significant in estimates based on a different sample, with controls for local inflation or base country GDP growth.

12. See Shambaugh (2004, tab. 8). In this case the results show that as expected by theory, the interaction term of (peg × open financial markets) is positive and significant and when it is included, peg and financial openness on their own are not significant. This would suggest open capital market pegs face the strongest monetary autonomy constraint.

13. This technique, developed by Pesaran, Shin, and Smith (2001) allows for different critical values for series that are unit roots and non-unit roots. Thus, if a result is above or below both sets of critical values, we can ascertain if there is a relationship without having to take a stand on the order of integration of the data. See Shambaugh (2004) for details on the technique and Obstfeld et al. (2005) for more detailed results.

14. There is a long literature on this topic, exemplified by the work of Giavazzi and Pagano (1988).

Chapter 9

1. Nurkse (1944). Quoted in Kenen (1984).

2. Committee for the Study of Economic and Monetary Union, Report on Economic and Monetary Union in the European Community (Delors Report), 1989. Quote is from point 26, p. 21.

3. The 1989 Delors Report called for a move to a single currency to support the single market, and the phrase "One market, one money" served as the title of a 1992 report by the European Commission (Emerson et al. 1992).

4. Those countries are: Austria, Belgium, Cyprus, Finland, France, Germany, Greece, Ireland, Italy, Luxembourg, Malta, The Netherlands, Portugal, Slovakia, Slovenia, and Spain. Kosovo and Montenegro also use the euro as a de facto currency and special monetary agreements have been made with Monaco, the Vatican City, San Marino, and Andorra where the euro is used as the currency in these small countries as well.

5. More recently Bergin and Lin (2008) have expanded this analysis to examine in what way trade is altered by exchange rate regimes. They suggest that currency unions may have more of an effect on the extensive margin of trade (new firms exporting or new products traded) while fixed exchange rates may have more of an effect on the intensive margin (trading more of the same goods by the same firms).

6. Theory also suggested, however, that the greater volatility of profits associated with greater exchange rate volatility could increase profits, due to Jensen's inequality. This suggests the possibility of an increase in trade with higher levels of exchange rate volatility. For example, see Franke (1991).

7. The indicators of exchange rate risk vary across papers. Some of these include the absolute percentage change in the nominal bilateral exchange rate, the average absolute difference between the forward rate and the realized spot rate, the variance of the exchange rate around a trend, a moving average of the standard deviation of the exchange rate, and exchange rate variances calculated from an ARCH or a GARCH model.

8. This short synopsis cannot cover the large literature on the relationship between exchange rate volatility and trade. For a survey, see McKenzie (1999).

9. See Gagnon (1993) for more discussion.

10. Of course, exchange rate regimes refer to nominal exchange rates, not real exchange rates, and much of the work on volatility and trade focused on real exchange rate volatility. But there is a very high correlation between real and nominal exchange rate volatility in the modern era for the industrial countries that made up the samples in the majority of these studies.

11. Subsequent work on the role of currency unions on trade co-authored by Rose includes Frankel and Rose (2002), Glick and Rose (2002), and Rose and van Wincoop (2001). Other work that revisits the effect on trade of membership in a currency union includes Barro and Tenreyro (2003), Edwards (2001), Nitsch (2002a, 2002b, 2004), Persson (2001), Pakko and Wall (2001), and Thom and Walsh (2002).

12. We discuss gravity models in detail in the next section.

13. For example, Frankel and Rose (2002) present an estimated coefficient on the currency union dummy variable of 1.38 in their table 1, with an associated standard error of 0.19. This suggests that membership in a currency union triples bilateral trade, *ceteris paribus* (since $e^{1.38} - 1 = 2.97$).

14. Quah (2000), in his comment on the original Rose (2000) paper, notes that the absence of a significant effect of exchange rate volatility on trade, combined with the strong, significant effect of currency unions, implies a large discontinuity in the effects on trade of restricting exchange rate volatility.

15. There is evidence that the pre–World War I gold standard had an important role in promoting trade, and its demise contributed in an important way to the reduction in world trade in the interwar period. See Eichengreen and Irwin (1995), Estevadeordal et al. (2003), Lopez-Cordova and Meissner (2003), and Rischl and Wolf (2003).

16. Rose (2000) distinguishes between currency unions and fixed exchange rates, writing "Sharing a common currency is a much more durable and serious commitment than a fixed rate" (pp. 10–11). Tenreyro (2007) writes, "the findings from currency unions do not generalize to other regimes with lower variability."

17. This section draws from Klein and Shambaugh (2006).

18. Anderson (1979) and Bergstrand (1985) provide early theoretical justifications for the gravity model.

19. We discuss the implications of the multilateral resistance terms for estimation of the gravity model below.

20. There is a more explicit theoretical backing for the fixed effects as well. Anderson and van Wincoop (2003) discuss the importance of taking into account multilateral trade resistance terms, when estimating the gravity model and when interpreting its results. One way to take into account multilateral resistance is by including CFE. In a subsequent paper (Anderson and van Wincoop 2004), they also mention that multilateral resistance may change over time, and, for this reason separate country fixed effects should be included for each year in a panel setting (CYFE). In our data set, there are about 100 observations for every country in every year (one for each trade partner). Country year fixed effects will control for whether trade is differentially higher with a pegged trade partner in years that a country pegs than with any other trade partner that year.

21. The results in this section draw on Klein and Shambaugh (2006).

22. The actual set of variables that constitute $X_{i,j,t}$ used in the regressions include the product of the natural logarithm of income of countries i and j in period t, the product of the natural logarithm of income per capita of countries i and j in period t, a dummy variable indicating whether the two countries had a free trade agreement at time t, and another a dummy variable indicating whether one country was a colony of the other country at time t. The variables used in the regressions that do not vary over time, represented by $Z_{i,j}$, include the natural logarithm of the distance between countries i and j, the product of the natural logarithm of the land areas of countries i and j, dummy variables representing whether or not countries i and j share a common border or share a common language, and other dummy variables indicating whether one country had been a colony of the other, whether either country is landlocked, whether either country is an island, whether both countries had a common colonizer, and whether one of the countries was, at one time, a dependency, territory, or colony of the other.

23. The partial derivative of trade with respect to either a fixed exchange rate or a currency union could include both the direct effect and the separately estimated effect of a reduction in exchange rate volatility. In practice, however, the estimated effect of exchange rate volatility on trade is small and we only refer to the estimated direct effects.

24. The currency unions observations represent a small portion of world trade since they overwhelmingly represent trade between two developing countries.

25. These results are from Klein and Shambaugh (2006). The standard errors reported in the regressions are clustered at the country pair level. This both allows for different variance across the pairs and, more importantly, for an unstructured covariance within the clusters allowing for correlation across time. See Klein and Shambaugh (2006, n. 25) for more discussion.

26. Klein and Shambaugh (2006) provide results based only on trade among developing countries, only among industrial countries, and only between industrial and developing

countries. They show that the significant role that currency unions play in promoting trade is a result of bilateral trade among developing countries since there are very few observations from which to draw information about currency unions impact on industrial/developing dyads.

27. Glick and Rose use CPFE on a larger sample with more switches and find that while the effect is substantially lower than when estimated with CFE, there is still an economically large effect on trade from a currency union. Klein and Shambaugh (2006) present some evidence on a sample that includes the Bretton Woods era in addition to the modern era as well.

28. Klein and Shambaugh (2006) also present a range of other results that include consideration of effects within subsamples, the dynamics of pegs, and other estimation methods. Results presented in this chapter are robust to these alternatives.

Chapter 10

1. Seminal theoretical works in this area include Kydland and Prescott (1977), Calvo (1978), Barro and Gordon (1983), and Rogoff (1985).

2. For example, see Alesina and Summers (1993) or Cukierman (1992).

3. In fact, there is more agreement that Friedman and Schwartz's dictum holds at long horizons than at shorter time horizons.

4. The exchange rate has been used as the centerpiece of disinflationary policies in many countries, although these policies have met with mixed success. Végh (1992) discusses the role of the exchange rate as a nominal anchor in a number of efforts to stop high inflation.

5. Other theories, and previous empirical research, suggest some additional explanatory variables that we will include in the empirical analysis in section 10.3.

6. This would be consistent with the results presented in chapter 6 that show an absence of the "fear of floating" since those results demonstrated a significant and economically meaningful difference in exchange rate volatility under pegged and floating exchange rates.

7. For more on this topic, see the survey by Calvo and Végh (1999).

8. A third type of study considers the prevailing exchange rate regime on worldwide inflation. See, for example, the analysis of the effects of the move from the Bretton Woods system to generalized floating on worldwide inflation by Crockett and Goldstein (1976) in the *IMF Staff Papers*. At the outset of the modern era, when inflation was endemic across the world and the heterogeneity of exchange rate regimes in the post-Bretton Woods era was not foreseen, this issue was a source of special concern. The topic became less pressing with the subsequent fall in inflation rates, first among industrial countries in the early 1980s and, after this, among a very wide set of other countries. This general decline in inflation has been called "The Great Moderation."

9. An important consideration in this study, and the others cited here, is the potential role played by outliers that had very high rates of inflation. Ghosh, Gulde, Ostry, and Wolf use $\pi = \dfrac{d \ln(P)}{1 + d \ln(P)}$ as a measure of inflation, which mitigates the effects of outliers. Other studies drop observations representing extremely high rates of inflation.

10. The inclusion of openness is meant to capture the higher costs of monetary expansions in open economies, as discussed in Romer (1993). We return to this point below.

11. Lane (1997) also presents an alternative theory for why inflation and openness are inversely related.

12. The set of industrial countries includes the United States, the United Kingdom, Austria, Belgium, Denmark, France, Germany, Italy, the Netherlands, Norway, Sweden, Switzerland, Canada, Japan, Finland, Greece, Iceland, Ireland, Portugal, Spain, Australia, and New Zealand.

13. The developing countries with high-inflation experience include Argentina, Bolivia, Brazil, Ghana, Israel, Mexico, Peru, Suriname, Turkey, Uganda, and Uruguay.

14. These regressions, and all the others reported in this chapter, adjust standard errors for heteroskedasticity and serial correlation by clustering at the country level.

15. Thus it seems that if there is a credibility effect in the developing sample, it is limited to those countries with high inflation history. For these countries, pegging seems to not only alter the behavior of the monetary authority, but also alter peoples' expectations regarding inflation. It is sensible that a visible nominal anchor may be more important in those countries where absent the anchor people expect high monetary growth.

16. When the eleven countries that experienced high inflation are also included in the developing country sample, the coefficient on the peg dummy variable remains significant when money growth and lagged money growth are excluded, and insignificant when money growth and lagged money growth are included in the regression.

17. The coefficient on the peg dummy variable becomes significant at the 93 percent level of confidence when the 11 countries with experience with high inflation are included in the sample for the regressions that exclude money growth variables, but remains insignificant, even with these additional observations, when the money growth variables are included in the regression.

18. Like the results presented by Alfaro (2005), these estimates show a positive and significant effect of trade openness on inflation, rather than the negative effect predicted by Romer (1993).

19. There are 24 countries for which this peg indicator equals 1, 4 industrial countries and 20 developing countries. The other 56 countries have a value of the peg indicator equal to 0.

20. The random element in the money supply relationship can represent changes in the money multiplier that break the strict link between the broad monetary aggregate and the effective money supply. Alternatively, we could have also included a random element in money demand that represents, for example, innovations in the ways consumers and firms make payments.

Chapter 11

1. As mentioned in chapter 8, di Giovanni and Shambaugh (2008) show that the exchange rate regime does affect economic performance at business cycle frequencies. The focus of this chapter, however, is on the effect of the exchange rate regime on longer run economic growth.

2. Recall the epigraph to chapter 1, which states "the dollar's exchange rate against the euro is surely the world's single most important price, with potentially much bigger economic consequences than the prices of oil and computer chips, for example" (The not-so-mighty dollar, *The Economist*, December 4, 2003).

3. There are some important cases where endogeneity is a potential problem for regressors in a growth equation (e.g., the quality of institutions) and researchers have searched for instrumental variables that enable the estimation of unbiased estimates (e.g., using settler mortality rates as an instrument for institutional quality, as in Acemoglu, Robinson, and Johnson 2001).

4. Of course, there is an important political dimension to the choice of exchange rate regime, one that depends on overall growth but, more important, focuses on distributional issues, as we discuss in chapter 5.

5. We also used two different definitions for the peg, float, and flip dummies. A stricter definition for pegs and floats required that the country have a peg or a float, respectively, for all years in the period. A looser definition required that the longest peg or float spell, or sum of the two longest peg or float spells, be greater at least half the length of the period. The results across these three definitions do not vary much. The stricter definition tends not to show the same distinction between flips and floats for the nonindustrial country sample in the ten-year sample as the categorization used here. The looser definition tends to find more significant and positive effects of flips in the five-year panel for nonindustrial countries than the results presented here.

6. See Manikew, Romer, and Weil (1992) for discussion of the proper specification of a growth regression.

References

Abraham, A. 1999. Interest rate dynamics and speculative trading in a fixed exchange rate system. *International Review of Economics and Finance* 8: 213–222.

Acemoglu, D., S. Johnson, and J. A. Robinson. 2001. The colonial origins of comparative development: An empirical investigation. *American Economic Review* 91 (December): 1369–1401.

Alesina, A., and L. H. Summers. 1993. Central bank independence and macroeconomic performance: Some comparative evidence. *Journal of Money, Credit, and Banking* 25 (2): 151–162.

Alesina, A., and R. J. Barro. 2002. Currency Unions. *Quarterly Journal of Economics* 117 (2): 409–436.

Alesina, A., and R. J. Barro. 2001. Dollarization. *American Economic Review Papers and Proceedings* 91 (2): 381–385.

Alesina, A., R. J Barro, and S. Tenreyro. 2002. Optimal currency areas. NBER working paper 9072.

Alfaro, L. 2005. Inflation, openness, and exchange rate regimes: The quest for short-term commitment. *Journal of Development Economics* 77: 229–249.

Anderson, J. E., and E. van Wincoop. 2003. Gravity with gravitas: A solution to the border puzzle. *American Economic Review* 93 (1): 170–192.

Anderson, J. E., and E. van Wincoop. 2004. Trade costs. *Journal of Economic Literature* 42 (3): 691–741.

Anderson, J. E. 1979. A theoretical foundation for the gravity equation. *American Economic Review* 69 (1): 106–116.

Arize, A. C., T. Osang, and D. J. Slottje. 2000. Exchange rate volatility and foreign trade: Evidence from thirteen LDC's. *Journal of Business and Economic Statistics* 18 (1): 10–17.

Bailey, M. J., G. S. Tavlas, and M. Ulan. 1987. The impact of exchange rate volatility on export growth: Some theoretical considerations and empirical results. *Journal of Policy Modeling* 9 (1): 225–243.

Bailliu, J., R. Lafrance, and J.-F. Perrault. 2003. Does exchange rate policy matter for growth? *International Finance* 6 (3): 381–414.

Bailliu, J., R. Lafrance, and J.-F. Perrault. 2000. Exchange rate regimes and economic growth in emerging markets. In *Revisiting the Case for Flexible Exchange Rates*. Proceedings of a conference held by the Bank of Canada, November, pp. 317–350.

Barro, R. J., and D. B. Gordon. 1983. A positive theory of monetary policy in a natural rate model. *Journal of Political Economy* 91 (4): 589–610.

Barro, R. 1991. Economic growth in a cross-section of countries. *Quarterly Journal of Economics* 106 (2): 407–433.

Baxter, M., and A. C. Stockman. 1989. Business cycles and the exchange-rate regime: some international evidence. *Journal of Monetary Economics* 23 (3): 377–400.

Bayoumi, T., and B. Eichengreen. 1998. Exchange rate volatility and intervention: Implications of the theory of optimum currency areas. *Journal of International Economics* 45: 191–209.

Bean, C. 1992. Economic and monetary union in Europe. *Journal of Economic Perspectives* 6 (4): 31–52.

Berg, A., and C. Pattillo. 1999. Are currency crises predictable? A test. *IMF Staff Papers* 46 (2): 107–138.

Bergstrand, J. H. 1985. The gravity equation in international trade: Some microeconomic foundations and empirical evidence. *Review of Economics and Statistics* 67 (3): 474–481.

Bernard, A., J. B. Jensen, S. J. Redding, and Peter K. Schott. 2007. Firms in international trade. *Journal of Economic Perspectives* 21 (3): 105–130.

Bernhard, W., and D. Leblang. 1999. Democratic institutions and exchange-rate commitments. *International Organization* 53 (1): 71–97.

Bertrand, M., E. Duflo, and S. Mullainathan. 2004. How much should we trust differences-in-differences estimates? *Quarterly Journal of Economics* 119 (1): 249–275.

Bilson, J. 1978. Rational expectations and exchange rates. In J. Frenkel and H. G. Johnson, eds., *The Economics of Exchange Rates: Selected Studies*. Reading, MA: Addison-Wesley, pp. 75–96.

Blanchard, O. J., and L. F. Katz. 1992. Regional evolutions. *Brookings Papers on Economic Activity* 1.

Bleaney, M., and M. Francisco. 2007. Exchange rate regimes, inflation and growth in developing countries—An assessment. *B.E. Journal of Macroeconomics* 7 (1), article 18.

Bluedorn, J., and C. Bowdler. 2008. The empirics of international monetary transmission: Exchange rate regimes and interest rate pass-through. Working paper.

Bordo, M., M. Edelstein, and H. Rockoff. 2002. Was adherence to the gold standard a Good Housekeeping Seal of Approval during the inter-war period? In S. L. Engerman, P. T. Hoffman, J. L. Rosenthal, and K. L. Sokoloff, eds., *Finance, Intermediaries, and Economic Development*. Cambridge: Cambridge University Press, pp. 288–318.

Bordo, M., and F. Kydland. 1996. The gold standard as a commitment mechanism. In T. Bayoumi, B. Eichengreen, and M. Taylor, eds., *Economic Perspectives on the Gold Standard*. New York: Cambridge University Press.

Bordo, M. D., and R. MacDonald. 1997. Violations of the rules of the game and the credibility of the classical gold standard 1880–1914. NBER working paper 6115.

Borenzstein, E., J. Zettelmeyer, and T. Philippon. 2001. Monetary independence in emerging markets: Does the exchange rate regime make a difference? IMF working paper 01/1.

Boughton, J. 1988. The monetary approach to exchange rates: What now remains? *Princeton Essays in International Finance*, vol. 171, International Finance Section, Princeton University.

Brada, J., and J. Mendez. 1988. Exchange rate risk, exchange rate regime and the volume of international trade. *Kyklos* 41: 263–280.

Broz, J. L. 1997. The domestic politics of international monetary order: The gold standard. In D. Skidmore, ed., *Contested Social Orders and International Politics*. Nashville: Vanderbilt University Press, pp. 53–91.

Broz, J. L. 2002. Political system transparency and monetary commitment regimes. *International Organization* 56: 861–867.

Broz, J. L., and J. A. Frieden. 2001. The political economy of international monetary relations. *Annual Review of Political Science* 4: 317–343.

Broz, J. L., J. A. Frieden, and S. Weymouth. 2008. Exchange rate policy attitudes: Direct evidence from survey data. *IMF Staff Papers* 55 (3): 417–444.

Bubula, A., and I. Ötker-Robe. 2002. The evolution of exchange rate regimes since 1990: Evidence from *de facto* policies. IMF working paper 02/155.

Cagan, P. 1956. The monetary dynamics of hyperinflation. In M. Friedman, ed., *Studies in the Quantity Theory of Money*. Chicago: University of Chicago Press, pp. 25–117.

Calvo, G. A., and C. M. Reinhart. 2002. Fear of floating. *Quarterly Journal of Economics* 117 (May): 379–408.

Calvo, G., and C. Végh. 1999. Inflation stabilization in chronic inflation countries. In J. Taylor and M. Woodford, eds., *Handbook of Macroeconomics*. Amsterdam: North Holland.

Calvo, G. 1978. On the time consistency of optimal policy in a monetary economy. *Econometrica* 46 (6): 1411–1428.

Canales-Kriljenko, J., and K. Habermeier. 2004. Structural factors affecting exchange rate volatility: A cross-section study. IMF working paper 04/147.

Carmignani, F., E. Colombo, and P. Tirelli. 2008. Exploring different view of exchange rate regime choice. *Journal of International Money and Finance* 27 (7): 1177–1197.

Carrera, J., and G. Vuletin. 2002. The effects of exchange rate regimes on real exchange rate volatility: A dynamic panel data approach. University of Maryland working paper.

Cheung, Y.-W., D. C. Tam, and M. S. Yiu. 2008. Does the Chinese interest rate follow the US interest rate? *International Journal of Finance and Economics* 13 (1): 53–67.

Chowdhury, A. R. 1993. Does exchange rate volatility depress trade flows? Evidence from error-correction models. *Review of Economics and Statistics* 75 (4): 700–706.

Clarida, R., J. Gali, and M. Gertler. Monetary policy rules in practice: Some international evidence. *European Economic Review* 42: 1033–1067.

Clark, P. B. 1973. Uncertainty, exchange risk, and the level of international trade. *Western Economic Journal* 11: 302–313.

Collins, S. M. 1996. On becoming more flexible: Exchange rate regimes in Latin America and the Caribbean. *Journal of Development Economics* 51: 117–138.

Collins, S. 1988. Inflation and the European monetary system. In F. Giavazzi, S. Micossi, and M. Miller, eds., *The European Monetary System*. Cambridge: Cambridge University Press, pp. 112–135.

Committee for the Study of Economic and Monetary Union. 1989. *Report on Economic and Monetary Union in the European Community* (Delors Report).

Crockett, A., and M. Goldstein. 1976. Inflation under fixed and flexible exchange rates. *International Monetary Fund Staff Papers* 23 (3): 509–544.

Cukierman, A. 1992. *Central Bank Strategy, Credibility and Independence: Theory and Evidence*. Cambridge, MA: MIT Press.

Cushman, D. O. 1983. The effects of real exchange rate risk on international trade. *Journal of International Economics* 15: 45–63.

Cushman, D. O. 1986. Has exchange rate risk depressed international trade? The impact of third-country exchange risk. *Journal of International Money and Finance* 5: 361–379.

Cushman, D. O. 1988. US bilateral trade flows and exchange rate risk during the floating period. *Journal of International Economics* 24: 317–330.

DeJong, D. N., and S. Husted. 1993. Towards a reconciliation of the empirical evidence on the monetary approach to exchange rate determination. *Review of Economics and Statistics* 75 (1): 123–128.

Devereux, M. B., and P. R. Lane. 2003. Understanding bilateral exchange rate volatility. *Journal of International Economics* 60 (1): 109–132.

di Giovanni, J., and J. C. Shambaugh. 2008. The impact of foreign interest rates on the economy: The role of the exchange rate regime. *Journal of International Economics* 74: 341–361.

Dornbusch, R. 2001. Fewer monies, better monies. *American Economic Review (Papers and Proceeding 113th Annual Meeting of the American Economic Association)* 91 (2): 238–243.

Dreyer, J. S. 1978. Determinants of exchange rate regimes for currencies of developing countries: Some preliminary results. *World Development* 6: 437–445.

Dubas, J., Bynd J. Lee, and N. Mark. 2005. Effective exchange rate classifications and growth. NBER working paper 11272.

Edwards, S. 1996. The determinants of the choice between fixed and flexible exchange-rate regimes. NBER working paper 5756.

Eichengreen, B., and D. A Irwin. 1995. Trade blocs, currency blocs and the reorientation of world trade in the 1930s. *Journal of International Economics* 38 (1–2): 1–24.

Eichengreen, B. 1992, *Golden Fetters: The Gold Standard and the Great Depression. 1919–1939*. New York: Oxford University Press.

Eichengreen, B., and R. Razo-Garcia. 2006 The international monetary system in the last and next 20 years. *Economics Policy* 21 (July): 393–442.

Emerson, M., D. Gros, A. Italianer, and H. Reichenbach. 1992. *One Market, One Money: An Evaluation of Potential Benefits and Costs*. Oxford: Oxford University Press.

Estevadeordal, A., B. Frantz, and A. M. Taylor. 2003. The rise and fall of world trade, 1870–1939. *Quarterly Journal of Economics* 118 (2): 359–407.

Ethier, W. 1973. International trade and the forward exchange market. *American Economic Review* 63 (3): 494–503.

Feenstra, R. C. 2002. Border effects and the gravity equation: Consistent methods for estimation. *Scottish Journal of Political Economy* 49 (5): 491–506.

Feyrer, J. 2008. Trade and income: Exploiting time series in geography. Department of Economics, Dartmouth College.

Fischer, S. 2001 Exchange rate regimes: Is the bipolar view correct? Distinguished Lecture on Economics in Government. *Journal of Economic Perspectives* 15 (2): 3–24.

Flandreau, M. 1996. The French crime of 1873: An essay on the emergence of the international gold standard, 1870–1880. *Journal of Economic History* 56 (4): 862–897.

Flood, R., and P. Garber. 1984. Collapsing exchange rate regimes: Some linear examples. *Journal of International Economics* 17 (August): 1–13.

Flood, R., and A. Rose. 1995. Fixing exchange rates: A virtual quest for fundamentals. *Journal of Monetary Economics* 36: 3–37.

Forssbæck, J., and L. Oxelheim. 2006. On the link between exchange-rate regimes, capital controls, and monetary policy autonomy in small European countries 1979–2000. *World Economy* 29 (3): 341–368.

Fountas, S., and K. Aristotelous. 2003. Does the exchange rate regime affect export volume? Evidence from bilateral exports in US–UK trade: 1900–98. *Manchester School* 71 (1): 51–64.

Franke, G. 1991. Exchange rate volatility and international trade. *Journal of International Money and Finance* 10 (June): 251–276.

Frankel, J. A., E. Fajnzylber, S. L. Schmukler, and L. Serven. 2001. Verifying exchange rate regimes. *Journal of Development Economics* 66: 351–386.

Frankel, J., and A. K. Rose. 2002. An estimate of the effect of common currencies on trade and income. *Quarterly Journal of Economics* 117 (2): 437–466.

Frankel, J. A., S. L. Schmukler, and L. Serven. 2004. Global transmission of interest rates: Monetary independence and currency regimes. *Journal of International Money and Finance* 23 (5): 701–734.

Frankel, J., and D. Romer. 1999. Does trade cause growth? *American Economic Review* 89 (3): 379–399.

Frankel, J., and S.-J. Wei. 1993. Trade and currency blocs. NBER working paper 4335.

Frankel, J. 1999. No single currency regime is right for all countries or at all times. Princeton University, International Finance Section, *Essays in International Finance*, 215, August.

Frankel, J. 2003. A proposed commodity regime for small-commodity exporters: Peg the export price (PEP). *International Finance* 6 (1): 61–88.

Frankel, J. 2004. Experience of and lessons from exchange rate regimes in emerging economies. In Asian Development Bank, ed., *Monetary and Financial Integration in East Asia: The Way Ahead*, vol. 2. New York: Palgrave Macmillan, pp. 91–138.

Frenkel, J. A. 1976. A monetary approach to the exchange rate: Doctrinal aspects and empirical evidence. *Scandinavian Journal of Economics* 78: 200–224.

Frieden, J. 1993. The dynamics of international monetary systems: International and domestic factors in the rise, reign, and demise of the classical gold standard. In R. Jervis and J. Snyder, eds. *Coping with Complexity in the International System*. Boulder: Westview, pp. 137–162.

Friedman, M. 1953. The case for flexible exchange rates. In his *Essays in Positive Economics*. Chicago: University of Chicago Press, pp. 157–203.

Ghosh, A. R., A.-M. Gulde, J. D. Ostry, and H. C. Wolf. 1997. Does the nominal exchange rate regime matter? NBER working paper 5874.

Ghosh, A. R., A.-M. Gulde, J. D. Ostry, and H. C. Wolf. 2002. *Exchange Rate Regimes*. Cambridge, MA: MIT Press.

Giavazzi, F., and M. Pagano. 1988. The advantage of tying one's hands: EMS discipline and central bank credibility. *European Economic Review* 32: 1055–1082.

Glick, R., and A. K. Rose. 2002. Does a currency union affect trade? The time series evidence. *European Economic Review* 46 (6): 1125–1151.

Gotur, P. 1985. Effects of exchange rate volatility on trade: Some further evidence. *IMF Staff Papers* 32 (3): 475–512.

Grilli, V., and G. Kaminsky. 1991. Nominal exchange rate regimes and the real exchange rate: Evidence from the United States and Britain, 1885–86. *Journal of Monetary Economics* 27: 191–212.

Hakura, D. 2005. Are emerging market countries learning to float? IMF working paper 05/98.

Heller, H. R. 1978. Determinants of exchange rate practices. *Journal of Money, Credit and Banking* 10 (3): 308–321.

Holden, P., M. Holden, and E. Suss. 1979. The determinants of exchange rate flexibility: An empirical investigation. *Review of Economics and Statistics* 61 (August): 327–333.

Hooper, P., and S. Kohlhagen. 1978. The effect of exchange rate uncertainty on the prices and volumes of international trade. *Journal of International Economics* 8: 483–511.

Husain, A. M., A. Mody, and K. S. Rogoff. 2005. Exchange rate regime durability and performance in developing versus advanced economies. *Journal of Monetary Economics* 52: 35–64.

International Monetary Fund. 1984. Exchange rate variability and world trade. Occasional paper 28.

International Monetary Fund. Various dates. *Annual Report on Exchange Arrangements and Exchange Restrictions*. Washington, DC: IMF.

Jansen, W. J. 2008. Inside the impossible triangle: Monetary policy autonomy in a credible target zone. *Contemporary Economic Policy* 26 (2): 216–228.

Juhn, G., and P. Mauro. 2002. Long-run determinants of exchange rate regimes: A simple sensitivity analysis. IMF working paper 02/104.

Kenen, P., and D. Rodrik. 1986. Measuring and analyzing the effects of short-term volatility in real exchange rates. *Review of Economics and Statistics* 68: 311–315.

Kenen, P. 1985. Macroeconomic theory and policy: How the closed economy was opened. In R. W. Jones and P. B. Kenen, eds., *The Handbook of International Economics.* Amsterdam: North-Holland, pp. 625–678.

Kent, C., and R. Naja. 1998. Effective real exchange rates and irrelevant nominal exchange rate regimes. Reserve Bank of Australia Research discussion paper 9811.

Kezdi, G. 2002. Robust standard error estimation in fixed-effects panel models. Working paper. University of Michigan.

Kiefer, N. 1988. Economic duration data and hazard functions. *Journal of Economic Literature* 26 (2): 646–679.

Kim, C. J., and J.-W. Lee. 2008. Exchange rate regime and monetary policy independence in East Asia. *Pacific Economic Review* 13 (2): 155–170.

Klaassen, F. 2004. Why is it so difficult to find an effect of exchange rate risk on trade? *Journal of International Money and Finance* 23 (5): 817–839.

Klein, M. W. 1990. Sectoral effects of exchange rate volatility on United States exports. *Journal of International Money and Finance* 9: 299–308.

Klein, M. W. 2005. Dollarization and trade. *Journal of International Money and Finance* 24 (6): 935–943.

Klein, M. W., and N. P. Marion. 1997. Explaining the duration of exchange-rate pegs. *Journal of Development Economics* 54 (2): 387–404.

Klein, M. W., and J. C. Shambaugh. 2006. Fixed exchange rates and trade. *Journal of International Economics* 70 (2): 359–383.

Klein, M. W., and J. C. Shambaugh. 2008. The dynamics of exchange rate regimes: Fixes, floats, and flips. *Journal of International Economics* 75 (1): 70–92.

Klein, M. W., S. Schuh, and R. Triest. 2003. Job creation, job destruction and the real exchange rate. *Journal of International Economics* 59 (2): 239–265.

Kroner, K. F., and W. Lastrapes. 1993. The impact of exchange rate volatility on international trade: Reduced form estimates using the GARCH-in-mean model. *Journal of International Money and Finance* 12: 298–318.

Krugman, P. 1979. A model of balance-of-payments crises. *Journal of Money, Credit and Banking* 11 (August): 311–325.

Krugman, P., and M. Obstfeld. 2008. *International Economics: Theory and Policy*, 8th ed. Reading, MA: Addison Wesley.

Kydland, F., and E. Prescott. 1977. Rules rather than discretion: The inconsistence of optimal plans. *Journal of Political Economy* 85 (3): 473–492.

Lane, P. 1997. Inflation in open economies. *Journal of International Economics* 42: 327–347.

Lane, P., and J. C. Shambaugh. 2009. Financial exchange rates and international currency exposures. *American Economic Review*, forthcoming.

Leblang, D. 1999. Domestic political institutions and exchange rate commitments in the developing world. *International Studies Quarterly* 43 (4): 599–620.

Lee, J.-W., and K. Shin. 2004. Exchange rate regimes and economic linkages. Mimeo.

Levy-Yeyati, E. 2003. On the impact of a common currency on bilateral trade. *Economics Letters* 79 (1): 125–129.

Levy-Yeyati, E., and F. Sturzenegger. 2003. To float or fix: Evidence on the impact of exchange rate regimes on growth. *American Economic Review* 93 (4): 1173–9113.

Levy-Yeyati, E., and F. Sturzenegger. 2001. Exchange rate regime and economic performance. *IMF Staff Papers* 47 (special issue): 62–98.

Liang, H. 1998. Real exchange rate volatility: Does the nominal exchange rate regime matter? IMF working paper 98/147.

Lopez-Cordova, J. E., and C. M Meissner. 2003. Exchange-rate regimes and international trade: Evidence from the classical gold standard era. *American Economic Review* 93 (1): 344–353.

Mankiw, N. G., D. Romer, and D. Weil. 1992. A contribution to the empirics of economic growth. *Quarterly Journal of Economics* 107 (2): 407–437.

Masson, P. 2001. Exchange rate regime transitions. *Journal of Development Economics* 64: 571–586.

Masson, P., and F. J. Ruge-Muricia. 2005. Explaining the transition between exchange rate regimes. *Scandinavian Journal of Economics* 107: 261–278.

McKenzie, M. D. 1999. The impact of exchange rate volatility on international trade flows. *Journal of Economic Surveys* 13: 71–106.

Meissner, C. 2005. A new world order: Explaining the international diffusion of the gold standard, 1870–1913. *Journal of International Economics* 66 (2): 385–406.

Meissner, C., and N. Oomes. 2009. Why do countries peg the way they peg? The determinants of anchor currency choice. *Journal of International Money and Finance* 28: 522–547.

Melvin, M. 1985. The choice of an exchange rate system and macroeconomic stability. *Journal of Money, Credit and Banking* 17 (4): 467–478.

Méon, P.-G., and J.-M. Rizzo. 2002. The viability of fixed exchange rate commitments: Does politics matter? A theoretical and empirical investigation. *Open Economies Review* 13: 111–132.

Micco, A., E. Stein, and G. Ordonez. 2003. The currency union effect on trade: Early evidence from EMU. *Economic Policy* 18 (37): 315–356.

Miles, W. 2006. To float or not to float? Currency regimes and growth. *Journal of Economic Development* 31 (2): 91–105.

Miniane, J., and J. H. Rogers. 2007. Capital controls and the international transmission of US money shocks. *Journal of Money Credit and Banking* 39 (5): 1003–1035.

Moreno, R. 2001. Pegging and stabilization policy in developing countries. *Federal Reserve Bank of San Francisco Economic Review:* 17–29.

Mundell, R. A. 1961. A theory of optimum currency areas. *American Economic Review* 51 (3): 657–665.

Mundell, R. A. 2000. A reconsideration of the twentieth century. *American Economic Review* 90 (3): 327–340.

Mussa, M. 1986. Nominal exchange rate regimes and the behavior of real exchange rates: Evidence and implications. Carnegie-Rochester Conference Series on Public Policy.

Nitsch, V. 2002a. Honey, I shrunk the currency union effect on trade. *World Economy* 25 (4): 457–474.

Nitsch, V. 2002b. The non-causality of the common currency effect on trade: Evidence from the Monetary Union between Belgium and Luxembourg. Mimeo. Bankgesellschaft Berlin.

Nitsch, V. 2004. Comparing apples and oranges: The effect of multilateral currency unions on trade. In V. Alexander, J. Mélitz, and G. von Furstenberg, eds., *Monetary Unions and Hard Pegs: Effects on Trade, Financial Development, and Stability*. Oxford: Oxford University Press.

Nurkse, R. 1944. *International Currency Experience*. Geneva: League of Nations.

Obstfeld, M. 1994. The logic of currency crises. *Cahiers Economiques et Monetaires* 43: 189–213.

Obstfeld, M. 1998. The global capital market: Benefactor or menace. *Journal of Economic Perspectives* 12 (4): 9–30.

Obstfeld, M., and P. Krugman. 2008. *International Economics: Theory and Policy*, 8th ed. Reading, MA: Addison Wesley.

Obstfeld, M., and K. Rogoff. 1995. The mirage of fixed exchange rates. *Journal of Economic Perspectives* 9 (fall): 73–96.

Obstfeld, M., and K. Rogoff. 1996. *Foundations of International Macroeconomics*. Cambridge, MA: MIT Press.

Obstfeld, M., J. C. Shambaugh, and A. M. Taylor. 2004. Monetary sovereignty, exchange rates, and capital controls: The trilemma in the interwar period. *IMF Staff Papers* 51 (special issue): 75–108.

Obstfeld, M., J. C. Shambaugh, and A. M. Taylor. 2005. The trilemma in history: Trade-offs among exchange rates, monetary policies, and capital mobility. *Review of Economics and Statistics* 87 (3): 423–438.

Obstfeld, M., J. C. Shambaugh, and A. M. Taylor. 2008. Financial stability, the trilemma, and international reserves. NBER working paper 14127.

Pakko, M. R., and H. J. Wall. 2001. Reconsidering the trade-creating effects of a currency union. *Federal Reserve Bank of St. Louis Review* (September/October): 37–45.

Persson, T. 2001. Currency unions and trade: How large is the treatment effect? *Economic Policy: A European Forum* 33 (October): 435–448.

Pesaran, M., Y. Shin, and R. Smith. 2001. Bounds testing approaches to the analysis of level relationships. *Journal of Applied Econometrics* 16: 289–326.

Poirson, H. 2001. How do countries choose their exchange rate regime? IMF working paper 01/46.

Poole, W. 1970. Optimal choice of monetary policy instrument in a simple stochastic macro model. *Quarterly Journal of Economics* 84: 197–216.

Quah, D. 2000. One money, one market. The effect of common currencies on trade: Discussion. *Economic Policy: A European Forum* 30: 35–38.

Reinhart, C. M., and K. S. Rogoff. 2004. The modern history of exchange rate arrangements: A reinterpretation. *Quarterly Journal of Economics* 119 (1): 1–48.

Rischl, A., and N. Wolf. 2003. Endogeneity of currency areas and trade blocs: Evidence from the inter-war period. CEPR Discussion Paper 4112.

Rizzo, J.-M. 1998. The economic determinants of the choice of an exchange rate regime: A probit analysis. *Economic Letters* 59: 283–287.

Rodrik, D. 2008. The real exchange rate and economic growth. Mimeo, October, available at http://ksghome.harvard.edu/~drodrik/RER%20and%20growth.pdf.

Rogoff, K. S., A. M. Husain, A. Mody, R. Brooks, and N. Oomes. 2003. Evolution and performance of exchange rate regimes. IMF Working Paper, WP/03/243.

Rogoff, K. 2002. Dornbusch's overshooting model after twenty-five years. *IMF Staff Papers* 49 (special issue): 1–35.

Rogoff, K. 1985. The optimal commitment to an intermediate monetary target. *Quarterly Journal of Economics* 100 (November): 1169–1189.

Romer, D. 1993. Openness and inflation: Theory and evidence. *Quarterly Journal of Economics* 58: 869–903.

Rose, A. K., and E. van Wincoop. 2001. National money as a barrier to international trade: The real case for currency union. *American Economic Review Papers and Proceedings* 91 (2): 386–390.

Rose, A. 2000. One money, one market: The effect of common currencies on trade. *Economic Policy: A European Forum* 30: 7–33.

Rose, A. 2007. A stable international monetary system emerges: Inflation targeting is Bretton Woods, reversed. *Journal of International Money and Finance* 26 (5): 663–681.

Savvides, A. 1990. Real exchange rate variability and the choice of exchange rate regime by developing countries. *Journal of International Money and Finance* 9: 440–454.

Shambaugh, J. C. 2004. The effect of fixed exchange rates on monetary policy. *Quarterly Journal of Economics* 119 (1): 301–352.

Shambaugh, J. C. 2006. An experiment with multiple currencies: The American monetary system from 1838–60. *Explorations in Economic History* 43 (October): 609–645.

Solow, R. 1956. A contribution to the theory of economic growth. *Quarterly Journal of Economics* 70 (1): 65–94.

Stockman, A. 1983. Real exchange rates under alternative nominal exchange-rate systems. *Journal of International Money and Finance* 2 (April): 147–166.

Summers, R., and A. Heston. 1991. The Penn World Table (Mark 5): An expanded set of international comparisons. 1950–1988. *Quarterly Journal of Economics* (May): 327–368.

Tenreyro, S. 2007. On the trade impact of nominal exchange rate volatility. *Journal of Development Economics* 82 (2): 485–508.

Thom, R., and B. Walsh. 2002. The effect of a common currency on trade: Lessons from the Irish experience. *European Economic Review* 46 (6): 1111–1123.

Thursby, M. C., and J. G. Thursby. 1987. Bilateral trade flows, the Linder hypothesis, and exchange risk. *Review of Economics and Statistics* 69: 488–495.

Végh, C. 1992. Stopping high inflation. *International Monetary Fund Staff Papers* 39 (3): 626–695.

von Hagen, J., and J. Zhou. 2007. The choice of exchange rate regimes in developing countries: A multinomial panel analysis. *Journal of International Money and Finance* 26: 1071–1094.

Wells, S. 1968. *International Economics.* London: Allen and Unwin.

Index